EDUCATING AUSTRALIA

To my parents, Betty and Ray Marginson.
This is their story too.

EDUCATING AUSTRALIA

Government, Economy and Citizen Since 1960

SIMON MARGINSON

Centre for the Study of Higher Education

University of Melbourne

CAMBRIDGE
UNIVERSITY PRESS

PUBLISHED BY THE PRESS SYNDICATE OF THE UNIVERSITY OF CAMBRIDGE
The Pitt Building, Trumpington Street, Cambridge CB2 1RP, United Kingdom

CAMBRIDGE UNIVERSITY PRESS
The Edinburgh Building, Cambridge CB2 2RU, United Kingdom
40 West 20th Street, New York, NY 10011–4211, USA
10 Stamford Road, Oakleigh, Melbourne 3166, Australia

First published 1997

Printed in Australia by Print Synergy

Typeset in Baskerville 10/12 pt

National Library of Australia Cataloguing in Publication data

Marginson, Simon.
Educating Australia : government, economy and citizen since 1960.
Bibliography.
Includes index.
ISBN 0 521 59174 0.
ISBN 0 521 598303 (pbk.).
1. Education – Australia – History – 20th century. 2.
Education – Social aspects – Australia. 3. Education and
state – Australia – History – 20th Century. I. Title.
370.99409045

A catalogue record for this book is available from the British Library

Contents

Tables

Note: the symbol .. or ... in tables means data not available
nei means not elsewhere included.

Acronyms

ABC	Australian Broadcasting Corporation
ABS	Australian Bureau of Statistics
ACER	Australian Council for Educational Research
ACES	Australian Council of Educational Standards
ACTU	Australian Council of Trade Unions
AEC	Australian Education Council
AEU	Australian Education Union
AFR	Australian Financial Review
AGPS	Australian Government Publishing Service
ALP	Australian Labor Party
ANOP	Australian National Opinion Polls
ANTA	Australian National Training Authority
AVCC	Australian Vice Chancellors' Committee
BCA	Business Council of Australia
CA	Commonwealth of Australia
CAE	College of Advanced Education
CAPA	Council of Australian Postgraduate Associations
CBCS	Commonwealth Bureau of Census and Statistics
CBP	Commonwealth Budget Papers
CEDA	Committee for the Economic Development of Australia
COAG	Council of Australian Governments
CSC	Commonwealth Schools Commission
CSIRO	Commonwealth Scientific and Industrial Research Organisation
CT	Canberra Times
CTEC	Commonwealth Tertiary Education Commission
DE	Department of Education

DEET	Department of Employment, Education and Training
DEETYA	Department of Employment, Training, Education and Youth Affairs
DITC	Department of Industry, Technology and Commerce
ELICOS	English language intensive courses for overseas students
EPAC	Economic Planning Advisory Council
GDP	Gross Domestic Product
GNP	Gross National Product
JSCM	Joint Standing Committee on Migration
LNP	Liberal and National Parties
MCEETYA	Ministerial Council for Employment, Education, Training and Youth Affairs
MOVEET	Ministers of Vocational Education, Employment and Training
NCVER	National Centre for Vocational Education Research
NSW	New South Wales
OECD	Organisation for Economic Cooperation and Development
SC	Schools Commission
StC	Steering Committee
SMH	Sydney Morning Herald
TAFE	Technical and Further Education
TNC	Transnational Cooperative
UK	United Kingdom
UNESCO	United Nations Educational Scientific and Cultural Organisation
USA	United States of America
VG	Victorian Government

Preface

The first draft of chapters 2 to 9 of *Educating Australia* was finished in March 1996, one weekend after the election of the Howard Coalition Government promised another lurch in the never very stable settings of education policy. The text was revised again in late 1996 as the Liberal–National agenda in education and elsewhere – new in some respects, familiar in others – was taking shape. However, the book was much longer in the making. *Educating Australia* is the first fruits from the larger doctoral project on 'Markets in education' which preoccupied me from 1988 to 1996. *Educating Australia* was prepared as a discrete text, a history of government and education in Australia in the postwar period that was designed to situate the emergence of educational markets in the last decade. Chapter 9 provides a hint of the larger project (Marginson 1996a), to be published as *Markets in Education* (Marginson 1997d). Compared to that study, *Educating Australia* is less concerned with theory and more with history, with telling the story of education, government, economy and citizen.

The advantage of the narrative form is that it draws our attention to change and the historically relative character of all phenomena. For the narrative historian, time is like an ever-flowing river, in which nothing is fixed, and everything is always becoming. The disadvantage is that particular currents ('historical laws') are too readily seen as determining and fundamental in relation to all other developments. In narratives, with their serial events and their beginnings and ends, where beauty is measured by the smoothness of the flow, historical inevitability arises almost naturally, in the rhythm of the prose. At the outset, against the seductions of singular explanation and the inevitability of our fate, I want to emphasise the richness and complexity of reality, and the contingent and changeable nature of events. The evolution of

government, education and economic organisation that is described
here *might have been different*. It would be wrong to say that 'all things
are possible', because the ambit of our present is determined by what
we inherit from the past, and we are bound also by the limits of our
capacities and resources; but within this ambit there are many possibilities and choices; though more at some times than others.

The book is a story of more than three decades of Australian education which focuses most centrally on government and politics. It is
easy to justify a history which talks about this one social sector, for
education has been central to the projects of government, to national
identities and to the lives of almost every individual Australian in the
period since 1960, though it has yet to receive its due attention from
historians. In this story none of the terms in the title of the book –
'Australia', 'education', 'government', 'economy' and 'citizen' – are
fixed. All are subject to debate and change over time, and in relation
to a broad set of influences. In *Educating Australia* educational government and politics are placed alongside economic and social
changes, changes in knowledges and ideas especially ideas about government, and forms of individuality. It is a power/knowledge/
economy analysis, working at the fecund intersections of these sets:
part economic history, part political history, and partly an account of
power–knowledge and the effects of policy discourse in education. It
intersects with some of the themes of *Education and public policy in
Australia* (1993), but the approach is different. Whereas that book was
a critique of economic policies in education, *Educating Australia* sets
out to explore the historical roots of those policies, and their constructed character, which is one of the preconditions for moving
beyond them and the limits they impose. 'Since these things have
been made, they can be unmade, as long as we know how it was that
they were made' (Foucault 1988: 37).

Despite the hopes of some (for example Harris 1994) I found no
single Archimedean point where we might overturn this history, in a
sublime moment of destruction and renewal. Rather, *Educating
Australia* has a number of themes, recurring motifs and sub-plots: the
economisation of education, powerful but incomplete; modernisation
and the extension of citizenship *via* education, and the changing character of citizenship; the growing sophistication of liberal government;
the accumulating effects of competition; and the shift from universal
public provision to market systems, with their new meanings of 'participation' and 'equity'. One of these recurring motifs, citizenship, is used
in the structuring of the book. As the plan of the book also indicates,
the global political-economic crisis of 1975 and the transition from
Keynesian policies to market liberalism ('neo-liberalism') is seen as a

defining moment, whose consequences are still unfolding. That is one set of decisions that might have been different.

Two further points should be made about the approach taken in the book. First, the term 'government' refers to government-as-state and the domain of formal and informal politics implicated in and around the state, rather than the Foucauldian 'government' and 'governmentality', which group the practices of sovereignty and discipline with the management of the self. These meanings are less accessible to readers. Similarly, the implications of Ian Hunter's (1994) Foucauldian-Weberian reading of educational history are reviewed elsewhere (Marginson 1997a). In contrast with Hunter, for whom government is the domain of experts motivated by the order and prosperity of the state as an end in itself and is irreducible to democratic sanctions, in *Educating Australia* 'government' includes political debate and contestation, and is affected by the play of social interests. It is subject to determination from 'above' by powerful actors such as global corporations, but also subject to irruptions from 'below', and the slower accumulation of democratic pressures. Nevertheless the book rests partly on insights derived from Foucault and the post-Foucauldian work on governmentality (for example Burchell et al 1991; Miller & Rose 1990; Rose & Miller 1992; Rose 1990, 1993; Meredyth & Tyler 1993). Liberal government works through 'private' as well as 'public' institutions; and the liberal individual is shaped in education and elsewhere as a *self-managing* individual whose freedom takes the form of regulated autonomy. Thus we are governed for economic consumption and social rule. The implications are explored further elsewhere (Marginson 1997c; 1997d).

Second, this work is premised on a political economy of competition and markets in education influenced by post-Keynesianism and Marxism (Marginson 1995b; 1996a). Following Fred Hirsch (1976) education is seen as a 'positional good' subject to 'positional competition' between students and families, rather than 'cultural capital' in the manner of, say, Bourdieu. Positional goods are places in education which are seen to provide students with relative advantage in the social competition for income and social-occupational status. Some places in education have more 'positional value' than others, for example places in medicine courses. Both cultural capital and positional good refer to symbolic characteristics acquired in education. Positional good is used because it places one person's education in relation to another's and thus highlights education's role in social selection. There is another reason. Compared to Bourdieu's France Australia is less defined by stable class cultures and perhaps more open to modernised forms of competition, in which inherited cultural attributes are subordinated to position, more than vice versa.

For the most part the different themes are explored in macro rather than micro terms, in relation to education system design, financing and management and so on. There is another book to be written, and a program of empirical research to be conducted, that intersects the different practices of citizenship with the pedagogical techniques and micro-organisation of education institutions. This does not aim to be the definitive history of Australian education since 1960. It is one contribution among many to the large and never-to-be-quite-settled explanation of 'why we are what we are'. So while both Australian history and Australian educational history since 1960 need greater attention, some parts of the story have already been covered in detail elsewhere, and I have not sought to replicate this work. Bill Connell's *Reshaping Australian education* (1993) discusses the evolution of secondary curricula and assessment; see also Denise Meredyth (1993) and the earlier work of Bill Hannan (1985). There is a considerable literature in relation to gender, for example Lyn Yates (1993) and Miriam Henry and Sandra Taylor (1993). Non-government and government schooling are examined by Richard Teese (1981, 1984, 1989) and Don Anderson (for example 1992). I have looked further at education–labour market relations in other work (Marginson 1993b, 1995a). Those who believe there should be more about education markets are right. The formation of markets is examined briefly in Part III of chapter 9, but has been addressed in more depth elsewhere (Marginson 1995b, 1996a, 1996b, 1997d), and in Kenway (1993) and others.

It was a joy to prepare this book, a labour of love to match half a lifetime's work in education policy. It is a labour that makes no financial sense, one that the management textbooks could never comprehend. As the final chapters began to take shape, with the *Brandenburg concertos* and the *Goldberg variations* in the air, it was often exhilarating. I am very grateful for the opportunity to have done this work. Nevertheless, *Educating Australia* rests also on people other than its author. First of all Melba, and the warmth and happiness which she has created since our marriage in 1988, a happiness which is the condition of a certain kind of creativity. Also our daughter Ana Rosa, who joined us towards the end of the work and is even more wonderful than writing books.

Second, in addition to the people I thanked in the Preface to *Education and public policy in Australia*, several people played a direct role in this particular text. Stuart Macintyre taught me much about writing history, which I had not done before: his example and support were instrumental to the project. Roger Woock was a supportive and thoughtful PhD supervisor. Phillipa McGuinness was an exemplary, encouraging publisher: the final work owes much to her. Anne Findlay provided sensible copy editing. Peter Beilharz has the capacity to enter the spirit of a piece while thinking critically about it, and I have found his comments very valuable. Rob Pascoe read and improved most of the chapters. Terri Seddon, Richard Teese, Toby Borgeest and Grahame McCulloch also provided comments on drafts or associated materials. I would also like to thank Jenny Lee, Kwong Lee Dow, Fazal Rizvi, Davina Woods, Sharan Burrow, Roy Martin, Jim Williamson, Julie Wells, Susie Pascoe, Luke Slattery, Elizabeth Anderson and an anonymous Cambridge reviewer.

CHAPTER 1

Introduction

'It is now a widely accepted article of faith that everyone who can profit from a period of advanced education should be given the opportunity to have it, and that it is an obligation of government to ensure that the facilities are available.'

Professor P.H. Partridge, Director of the Research School of Social Sciences, Australian National University, 'Tertiary education – society and the future', keynote address to the 31st summer school of the Australian Institute of Political Science, 1965.

I. 'Additional opportunities and choice for Australian students'

The Coalition's education policies

The Liberal and National Parties entered the 1996 election with what was essentially a platform of no change to education programs, except for a promise to provide more leeway and more money for new private schools. Nevertheless, on taking office the new Government changed the forward projections on which the budget was based, 'discovering' an $8 billion deficit. This became the pretext for policy changes, and the new Minister for Employment, Education, Training and Youth Affairs, Senator Amanda Vanstone, made it clear that education and training would not be exempted from 'the national savings task'. In August 1996 Vanstone announced a package of new policies which reduced government outlays and pushed the higher education system further towards the model chosen by the previous Labor Government, that of a market of competing institutions.

Up to the mid-1980s higher education was largely publicly funded, but since then fee-based courses, commercial services and other private income have increased markedly, from 10 per cent (1983) to 40 per cent (1994) of all income. The Coalition now announced it would

1

reduce university operating funds by 4.9 per cent in 1997–1999; and by refusing to fund the normal academic salary rises as well, it effectively cut public funding by 12–15 per cent in real terms, driving a further increase in the dependence on market-generated income. As 'an unequivocal demonstration of this Government's commitment to an internationally competitive higher education sector' the funding cuts were to be phased in over three years rather than introduced in one hit. Institutions were allowed to reduce funded student load, signalling a weakened commitment to high educational participation. Institutions were expected to reduce funded student load first of all at the postgraduate level, ensuring that 'upfront' fees, which covered one quarter of postgraduate students, would quickly spread.

The Minister also announced a sharp increase in the basic cost of tuition, the Higher Education Contribution Scheme (HECS). Up till 1996 the HECS had functioned as a 'soft' cost with only a slight deterrent effect, and little additional effect on students from poorer backgrounds. The charge was deferred until students had the capacity to pay. However, in 1997 the HECS for new students was to rise from $2442 per year to $3300–5500 (35–125 per cent), depending on course. The income at which compulsory repayment of HECS debt began would drop from $28 495 per year to only $20 701. These changes were expected to reduce effective demand for higher education, especially among low income students.

Under the heading 'Additional opportunities and choice for Australian students' the Minister also stated that market-style fees would be extended to undergraduate education, for up to 25 per cent of students in any course, providing the target number of HECS-based places had been filled. The Australian higher education system had been free of tuition charges until 1987. Now it was becoming one of the most expensive in the world. Some HECS-paying students, for example those in arts or business, would personally carry over half the costs of their courses, and there would be no limit on the level of the fees charged directly by institutions.

Two weeks later the Prime Minister, John Howard, and the Minister for Schools and Vocational Training, Dr. David Kemp, announced that most labour market programs that provided training for unemployed people would be abolished. The Labor Government's 'new schools policy' was also abolished, deregulating private school commencements and extensions. The level of funding for new private schools was increased, making it easy to start a new private school at public expense, a return to the policies of 1976–1984 which had seen a rapid growth of small private schools. Ironically, the return to unrestricted 'freedom of choice' in private schooling, at public expense, was occurring at a time when small government schools were being forced to merge or close for reasons of economic cost. Further, the increased grants to private schooling were to be funded by reducing Commonwealth grants to the States for government schooling. These policies were expected to induce a rapid transfer of enrolments from government to private schools, weakening both the comprehensive character of the government schools, and their fiscal base. Again, the model was that of a market of competing institutions, powered by the struggle for individual advantage, rather than a system based on common good.

The politics of identity

At the same time the Government was moving on another front, with implications for education. The Labor government of 1983–1996, like its Coalition predecessor of 1975–1983, had supported a non-discriminatory immigration policy and presided over a significant growth in immigration from Asia to what was once seen as an exclusively European country. Since the late 1970s, governments had conceived Australia as a multicultural society. Further, the Keating Labor Goverment had embraced the principle of native title whereby indigenous people dispossessed by European settlement had a prior claim to land, established in the High Court's *Mabo* judgement in 1992. The Government had secured a consensus of sorts for a process of 'national reconciliation' with the Aboriginal and Torres Strait Islander people who had been displaced and dispossessed by colonisation.

In its campaign for office in 1996 the Coalition exploited the unease among many Anglo-Australians about migration, multiculturalism and the reconciliation process. Though it did not tackle those policies directly, the campaign slogan 'For all of us' was designed to cultivate a 'middle Australia' that it hoped to wean from Labor. This strategy unleashed a backlash against Asian people and indigenous rights, and a craving for a simpler kind of citizenship and national identity that was now out of reach. After the election, Prime Minister John Howard met' these attitudes half way. He refused to use the term 'multiculturalism'; denounced the notion of indigenous rights distinct from mainstream law; and was slow to distance himself from the extreme views of independent MP Pauline Hanson on Asian immigration. As the political Right saw it, the education system, especially government schools, was partly responsible for the 'undermining' of traditional Australian identity. Education institutions had embraced multiculturalism, were admitting growing numbers of international students (chapter 9), and by focusing on the dispossession and slaughter of indigenous people, had promoted what Howard called a 'black arm-band' view of

Australian history instead of the triumph of progress and the virtues of monoculture. Yet in recognising and administering 'difference', education institutions had in reality been responding to the programs of government, of which they were one of the chief instruments.

II. Citizen formation in education

The roles and reach of education

Once again the education 'system' was at the centre of public debate and national life. This is not surprising. Education, along with health care, is one of the largest single functions of government, and education touches the lives of every citizen. Its size alone ensures its importance. In 1995 Australia had 7122 government schools, 1693 Catholic schools, 833 other private schools, 1124 registered training locations, including Technical and Further Education (TAFE) institutions, many unregistered private training providers, 43 Commonwealth funded higher education institutions and 3 unfunded private institutions. Over five million Australians were students.

In 1991 there were 316 524 women and 171 286 men working in education, libraries and museums, a labour force of 487 910 persons. Education was a vital source of scarce employment. Between 1976 and 1991 the whole workforce grew by 22.8 per cent, while the education workforce grew by 49.9 per cent. More than *10 per cent of women workers* were in education (ABS 2710.0).

The overlapping set of institutions that comprises the education 'system' is also complex, performing a number of social roles: child management and pastoral care, the inculcation of knowledges and behavioural values, civic and political learning, research and product development, preparation for work in most occupations, and social

Table 1.1 Total education students by sector, full and part-time* Australia 1960 and 1995

	Primary schooling	Secondary schooling	Higher education	Technical TAFE	All sectors*	Proportion of population %
1960	1 477 404	553 379	53 391	239 427	2 323 601	22.6
1995	1 833 681	1 275 656	604 177	1 661 195	5 374 709	29.8

* Includes slight double-counting due to enrolments in more than one sector.
Sources: Anderson & Vervoorn 1983; ABS 4202.0; ABS 4221.0; Martin 1964: 17; DEET 1996a; NCVER 1996.

Table 1.2 Education workforce* as a proportion of total workforce, Australia, census data, 1911 to 1991

	Women %	Men %	Persons %
1911	5.19	0.72	1.59
1921	6.61	0.72	1.92
1933	5.99	0.94	2.04
1947	5.23	1.10	2.03
1954	6.13	1.39	2.47
1961	7.18	1.84	3.18
1971	7.51	2.39	4.00
1976	9.53	3.44	5.62
1981	10.11	3.79	6.15
1986	10.89	4.27	6.87
1991	10.46	4.20	6.86

* Also includes libraries, museums and art galleries.
Sources: Martin 1964: 9; ABS 2710.0.

selection (Marginson 1993a). Ian Hunter describes the school as an 'improvised assemblage' designed to meet historical contingencies, so that there can be 'no ruling "idea" of education' (Hunter 1994: xvii, 91). Recent policies have emphasised the role of education in the economy, and its functions of preparing and selecting people for employment, and have tilted the balance towards these functions, but there is always more to education than that. For the Howard Government in 1996, as for all of its predecessors, the stakes in education policy are high. Education shapes people as citizens. There are also other institutions that do this – for example the family, work, the churches and consumption – but none of these sites are as open to governmental intervention and social change.

Creating the self-managing citizen

Through education people are endowed with certain *individual* potentials created by educational techniques that define and rank them (curriculum, examination, streaming, certification, specialised training). They are also formed as *social* beings in the social systems of education: the modes of inclusion and exclusion, the relations of equality and justice, the relations of power; the mono and multi-cultures; the systems of value and its measurement. 'The human being', states Marx, 'is an of article designanimal which can individuate itself only in the midst of society.' Or as Lyotard remarks, echoing Donne, 'no self is an island; each exists in a fabric of relations now more complex and mobile than ever before . . . one is always located at a post through which various kinds of message pass' (Marx 1973: 84; Lyotard 1984: 15). Burchell quotes a masculinist Hobbes: 'man is made fit for society not by nature but by education' (Burchell 1995: 543). All governments in liberal societies set out to create self-managing citizens, and use the autonomous individuals thus created as a vehicle of order and rule. Despite those philosophers or economists who believe that human nature is fixed – the notion of a transcendental moral citizen–subject, a kind of 'civic theology' (Burchell 1995: 549) – the particular content of citizenship may vary. The attributes and capacities of citizens, including those rights which society might identify as common or universal, are deliberately formed in social institutions. Citizens are not born but made; and citizenship is not fixed in stone but an evolving agenda for governments and others to consider.

This means that what happens in education really matters. It also means that because what happens in education can change, it is possible to change the character of people's social attributes – their nature as citizens. In the short course of Australian history different models of citizen have come to the fore, each with echoes in education. The founding of the government school systems in the nineteenth century was associated with the extension of the suffrage and the universal rule of law, and the desire to create a citizenry capable of bearing expanded civic and political responsibilities (Macintyre 1995; Hunter 1994: 48). For much of the twentieth century, the formation of citizens with economic and vocational attributes has been a theme of education and economic policy. The formation of British, and later Australian, outlooks in students has also preoccupied officials and educators. At any given time there is usually more than one kind of citizen-in-formation in education. The very incidence of diversity in citizenship (diversity within, and between, the models of citizenship) also varies. Precisely because liberal education forms people as self-governing and as *self-forming* individuals, the tension between citizenship as a normalising code of behaviour tending to repress difference, and citizenship as tolerance and the free expression of difference, is never quite resolved.

The fact that liberal government in education forms people as self-governing individuals, who manage their lives as their own project (Rose 1990) means that within the limits of the attributes so created, people can also take their destiny into their own hands. Governmental programs are never absolutes, and the governed citizen might cease to be governed in the manner intended. This imparts to the government of education a special complexity, and underlines the importance of the stakes in education policy.

This book

The four-part structure of *Educating Australia* rests on two premises. First, government in education affects the formation of people as self-managing citizens, embedded in social relations. Second, these effects tend to vary over time. We can discern at least four practices of citizenship since 1960, all of which have been associated with educational practices: the modernised and modernising citizen of the postwar boom (Part I); the anti-citizen or ultra-individual of market liberalism (Part II); the economic citizen of micro-economic reform and global economic competitiveness (Part III); and the multi-citizen, the more complex identity of the 1990s (Part IV).

This is not to say one citizen neatly gave way to another at the right moment, like soldiers on parade – for example modernisation did not cease in 1975, and is still with us – but that at different times one or another practice of citizen and citizenry was added to the complex mix, and became an important part of governmental strategies and changes in education. Each chapter begins with a 'Prelude', a historical snapshot that sharpens some of the themes and issues discussed in the chapter.

PART I

THE MODERN CITIZEN 1960–1975

'The desire of bettering our condition . . . comes with
us from the womb, and never leaves us till we go into
the grave.'

Adam Smith, The wealth of nations, *Penguin,
Harmondsworth, 1776/1979, p. 441.*

In the long economic boom after World War II the growing role of
education broadened the boundaries of modern consumption and the
scope for educated labour, underwritten by Keynesian social investment. Educational competition and selection reconciled opportunity
with economy, though with growing difficulty. The great advances in
public sector provision of education climaxed with the Whitlam Labor
Government (1972–1975). It was a more generous regime than those
which followed, but its central rubric of 'equality' was more ambiguous
than it seemed.

CHAPTER 2

The expansion of education to 1975

'This is going to be an education program. We are going to eliminate poverty by education, and I don't want anybody to mention income distribution. This is not going to be a handout, this is going to be something where people are going to learn their way out of poverty.'

Lyndon B. Johnson, President of the United States, launching the Federal Government's Headstart *program in schools, 1965 (OECD 1981b, p. 2).*

Prelude: The Martin report (1964)

On 27 August 1964 the Minister-in-Charge of Commonwealth Activities in Education and Research, Senator John Gorton (later Prime Minister 1968–1971) received the report of the Committee on the Future of Tertiary Education in Australia, known as the Martin report after the chair Sir Leslie Martin. The report declared that 'public interest in, and government support for, higher education have greatly increased during the last decade. The climate of opinion favours further expansion.' Higher education should be available to all citizens according to their needs and capacities. Not only would this enable individual aspirations to be fulfilled, 'the factors which determine national survival in the modern world require the Australian community to provide talented young people with opportunities to develop their innate abilities to the maximum'. The benefits of higher education to individual students were 'only a fraction of the benefits accruing to society' (Martin 1964):

Education should be regarded as an investment which yields direct and significant economic benefits through increasing the skill of the population and through accelerating technological progress. The Committee believes that economic growth in Australia is dependent upon a high and advancing level of education . . . It is both beneficial and realistic to regard education as a form of national investment in human capital' (Martin 1964: 1–2).

11

The report quoted Phillip Coombs, the United States' Assistant Secretary of State for Educational and Cultural Affairs, who chaired the 1961 OECD conference in Washington on economic growth and investment in education. Increasingly, growth depended on education and scientific research. 'There is in consequence an absolute necessity for the economic and educational spheres of policy to be much more closely in contact than in the past.' To achieve these economic benefits, those class differences producing 'unnatural' inequalities in educational attainment, 'inequalities which do not rest on differences of endowment', would have to be overcome. The 1961 OECD seminar in Kungalv, Sweden, on equality of educational opportunity had been told that the equal and rational utilisation of 'ability' from *all* social strata was a powerful source of growth (Husen 1979: 12; Martin 1964: 2, 43). At the same time, education was important for 'non-material' as well as 'material' reasons. The education system produced 'responsible rather than anti-social citizens'.

> Men and women who are capable of benefiting from higher education are also citizens. They share with their fellows the responsibility for making judgements on issues of all kinds, including apparently humble and private matters. Yet these decisions are ultimately to be made in terms of values, values which can be discerned only in the light of a sound general education (Martin 1964: 8).

The modern state 'requires a well educated population capable of making reasoned judgements against a background of change'. Education sharpened the analytical powers of the mind, it stirred the imagination, it 'enables the individuals to make choices and decisions at personal and political level which are well informed and objectively assessed'. Again, private individuality and social need coincided. A 'growing' minority of people now recognised that 'education is something more than preparation for a job and it goes deeper than mere instruction'. It was concerned with 'the quality of personal experience'. A 'sound general education' was also justified in vocational terms; it offered 'the best guarantee of a flexible workforce whose members are capable of turning to new tasks' (Martin 1964).

The committee did not dwell on its own paradox, that the private need for education which it sought to fulfil – indeed, the very existence of a modern choice-making individual with needs to be met – was also the creature of its own policy. This was a formula for an ever-growing provision, in which private demands for education and its social supply by governments would spiral upwards after each other. The committee was sanguine about this. 'At this stage of Australia's development, there is no conflict between these two motives for the provision of education', the individual and the social. It was better to produce too many graduates than to run the risk of producing too few. 'The entry of students into the various courses of higher education' should *not* be 'restricted by forecasts of future needs. Such a policy would not only run the risk of grave error, but it would also restrict educational opportunity to an undesirable degree' (Martin 1964: 1–12).

The committee recommended that student numbers should be doubled, from 117 900 in 1963 to 248 000 in 1975, with emphasis on non-university technical courses that prepared graduates for industry. By 1975 enrolments in higher education had reached 273 137, and were running ahead of target.

I. Postwar boom and modernisation

Keynesian economic management

The policies of educational development which culminated in the Martin report had their origins in World War II (1939–1945). The war provided government with a newly universal reach, and with some of the techniques of population management used in the postwar period. Britain devised the macro-economic tools of national accounting and economic growth, and Pay As You Earn taxation which enabled the fiscal base to be expanded (Thompson 1984). Australia formulated a technical training scheme and a program of Commonwealth assistance to university students in areas of strategic importance, precursors of the postwar systems of labour and education planning in which education was central to modernisation.

After the war government was informed by the advice of John Maynard Keynes, shaped in the great depression of the 1930s, on managing a national market-polity. 'The outstanding faults of the economic society in which we live are its failure to provide for full employment and its arbitrary and inequitable distribution of wealth and incomes', stated Keynes. Everyone should be able to work and to accumulate wealth. 'The central controls necessary to ensure full employment will, of course, involve a large extension of the traditional functions of government', he stated (Keynes 1936: 372–379). Heald comments that 'Keynesian ideas facilitated the survival of a predominantly privately owned, market-oriented economy, albeit with a much enlarged non-market sector' (Heald 1983: 4, 258).

The *White Paper on Full Employment*, tabled in the Australian parliament on 30 May 1945, pledged that 'full employment is the fundamental aim of the Commonwealth Government'. In the Keynesian framework, selective deficit financing was used to increase employment and to stimulate economic activity in the private sector. Fixed international exchange rates, established under Keynes' advice in the 1944 Bretton Woods agreement, allowed each national economy to be regulated as a discrete entity and thus contained the inflationary consequences of deficit financing. Keynes argued that his system of regulation abolished the need for international economic competition: 'if nations can learn to provide themselves with full employment by their domestic policy . . . there need be no important economic forces calculated to set the interest of one country against that of its neighbours' (Keynes 1936: 382). The 'long boom' of the postwar years – the sustained regime of high economic growth from the late 1940s to the early 1970s – provided the conditions for a major increase in public spending on education and other social programs.

The public sector grew more slowly in Australia than most economies. Government outlays were 28.6 per cent of Gross Domestic Product (GDP) in 1950–51 but only 27.6 per cent in 1960–61, rising to 29.6 per cent in 1970–71 and 35.9 per cent in 1974–75 (Foster & Stewart 1991: 55). But the social programs expanded more quickly than this suggests. The governmental role in public enterprises and infrastructure projects was reduced, and after 1963–64 social programs were responsible for the entire increase, including a 6 per cent rise during the Whitlam Labor Government of 1972–1975 (Scotton 1978). Between 1965–66 and 1975–76 Commonwealth spending on social programs rose from 7.4 to 14.4 per cent of GDP.

The report of the Commonwealth's Committee of Economic Enquiry noted that 'since the war, governments have been expected to accept responsibility over a much wider area'; which they were able to exercise because of 'greater insight into the workings of the economy stemming largely from the "Keynesian revolution" in economic thought' (Vernon 1966: 3). No social problem seemed beyond solution. A tremendous confidence in government was developing, and education was becoming a primary governmental instrument for solving problems. In 1965 United States President Johnson declared 'war on poverty', using project *Headstart* to provide selective grants for schools in poorer districts. Poverty would be overcome not by income redistribution, entailing a zero-sum confrontation between the powerful classes and the state, but through the positive-sum instrument of education. When the educational standards of the poor were raised poverty would disappear, amid general economic growth. Similarly in Britain the Plowden report proposed a strategy of positive discrimination. More slowly, Australian policy was moving in a similar direction.

Citizenship and education

Contemporaries saw the power of government and the scope of citizenship as developing together (Hindess 1987). Following John Stuart Mill, the 'collectivist liberalism' of the early twentieth century had sought to combine national economic efficiency with universal political suffrage, universal citizenship and the common good (Hall 1984: 19–21). In the postwar period the range of citizenship was again extended, incorporating not only the right to work, albeit limited to the male householder, and home ownership, but the management of life. T.H. Marshall (1950) imagined citizenship as civil rights, political rights and an array of social rights. Peter Wilenski, who served as principal private secretary to the Labor Prime Minister Gough Whitlam, later argued that government was extended because for the first time the capacities necessary to the democratic citizen – secondary education, adequate income and time to organise – were almost universal. By the same token, those capacities for democratic freedom were themselves produced by government: 'the expansion of government under electoral pressure has thus greatly widened the opportunities and choices for most people by providing them with education, mass transport systems, recreational facilities, basic health support and so on – all services which the market has failed to supply' (Wilenski 1986: 19).

Liberalism, that most flexible rationality of government, was the medium for exploring citizenship, and education the pre-eminent means for forming the citizen. Drawing on Millian liberalism, Fabian socialism, academic idealism, postwar rehabilitation and adult education, with bits of Durkheim and Dewey, a new momentum for education developed. The sovereign liberal individual, on which strategies of citizenship were premised, was at the same time a product of government programs. Brown observes that 'the dominant figure in postwar social analysis was an individual who was to be governed, and to be encouraged in her or his capacity for self-government, not so much through the directives of the state but in terms of the relation between the state and its citizens and the self-regulation of their more subjective propensities' (Brown 1995: 10). The modern systems of government and economic consumption *required* a self-determining citizen, with the kinds of competences and sensibilities formed in the modern systems of education. Rose comments that the idea of education as an 'equalising enterprise', producing bearers of citizenship rights, also carried 'a hope that the educational apparatus would be the means of inculcating the *aspirations* of citizenship in children – the will, as well as the means, to organise their lives within a project of self-betterment through diligence, application and commitment to work, family and society' (Rose 1990: 187–188). Citizens banded together to extend the state provision of education for their children. At the same time, they were accomplices in a process of citizen formation in which the state was often an unwilling paymaster, but was always a willing partner. With the tasks of government shifting 'from managing a population to governing prosperity', the capacity for self-regulation became more imperative. Citizenship was defined not just through participation in public life but 'through individual attitude and personality' (Brown 1995: 10, 166, 169). Whereas in the nineteenth century the creation of the public systems of elementary education was often linked to the extension of the suffrage, in the 1960s and early 1970s there was a growing emphasis on other themes: the provision of opportunities for social mobility and individual accumulation, and individual choice in consumption, the 'quality of life' and identity ('lifestyle').

The interim report of the Whitlam-appointed Priorities Review Staff on that government's *Goals and strategies* (1973) argued that 'universal and high quality education is a basic ingredient of an egalitarian and open society'. Education was essential to 'a high degree of personal freedom in thought and action', and the 'opportunity to choose among various lifestyles'. Non-vocational education broadened personal horizons.[1] New technologies in telecommunications, television and computers were 'a new and major force in shaping future life styles in Australia' and could substantially change the way people communicated with each other, formed interest groups and were able to 'acquire and distribute knowledge' (PRS 1973: 10, 17–19). Whitlam's democratic–political citizen was also an individual choosing between the different 'lifestyles' offered by government and market. Labor's 'three great aims' were to promote equality, to involve people in political decisions, and 'to liberate the talents and uplift the horizons of the Australian people'. 'There is no greater social problem facing Australia', he stated, 'than the good use of leisure' (ALP 1972: 5, 35).

Citizenship rested on a formal equality *as citizens* that sat uneasily with relations of social class, characterised by socio-economic inequalities and relations of domination–subordination. Citizenship did not vanquish class, except in the important sense that words about class were excluded from mainstream political discourse and the normalising technologies of government rested on formal equality. Social citizenship was grounded not on equality in economic resources or powers, but on equal legal and political rights; and access to health care, social security and especially education opening the way to the dynamic growth of educational services (see below). Late in the boom period, Whitlam's Government added urban amenities, transport, cultural activities and, less certainly, housing and participation in local affairs to this list.

It was actually more trenchant in its determination to remove non-class barriers to equality. 'Girls in our society are often trained to aspire to, and accept, inferior and sometimes subordinate positions in almost all aspects of social and economic life' stated the Priorities Review Staff (1973: 6–7). Women were 'all but absent in the political sphere' and under-represented at university. Adequate child care and pre-school education were preconditions of women's full participation in the workforce. Migrants had unequal access to education and justice. The non-recognition of overseas qualifications deprived them of income earning opportunities. Aboriginal and Islander people were 'the most deprived groups in Australian society in terms of their command over goods and services'. Here there was a rare acknowledgement of the problem of difference; though the implications for citizenship, and education, were not developed.

> Many of the most important innovations may be those that sharpen the Aboriginal's sense of identity and purpose. . . . Some Aborigines do not want to be part of white Australian society and hence the term 'inequality' used in the sense of access to goods and services valued by whites may not be appropriate. However, Aboriginal policy should continue to present opportunities to Aborigines who want to raise their material standards and become part of white society, while also allowing those who want to develop a separate identity to do so. There can be no one Aboriginal policy because Aborigines have a variety of needs and experiences (PRS 1973: 7).

Social reformers hoped that equal citizen rights would eventually determine class, rather than vice versa, if not displace it altogether. It was hoped that universal education would achieve this by establishing a system of social selection in which success would be distributed on the basis of individual merit rather than social origin. This was the essence of the liberal–democratic notion of equality of opportunity. It was what Whitlam meant when he stated in the 1972 Labor policy speech that 'education is the key to equality of opportunity'; and 'education should be the great instrument for the promotion of equality' (ALP 1972: 5, 12). Aitkin notes that in the postwar period these expectations of education were widely held and 'on both sides of politics' (Aitkin 1981: 40). Education was expected to do what the universalisation of the franchise by itself had been unable to do: to provide all people with an equal prospect of social power. But citizen power was defined as the right of access to career and consumption, rather than an equal measure of economic resources and important social decisions.

The Whitlam modernisation

'I do not for a moment believe that we should set limits on what we can achieve together, for our country, our people, our future', stated Whitlam at the close of his 1972 policy speech (ALP 1972: 47). In 1973 the Priorities Review Staff defined 'the basic concerns' of the Whitlam Government as the advance of social equality, the quality of life, the expansion of civil rights, the stable growth of economic prosperity, national identity and security, and a just international order. With its sudden transformations in official programs, in foreign policy and in social values, the Whitlam Government contrived an air of perpetual, unstable change, almost a caricature of modernity, which no doubt contributed to its demise. Yet in retrospect, its policies and methods of government were less inconsistent with its predecessors than was argued at the time (Beilharz 1994: 81–115).

If modernity is characterised by the building of a democratic nation–state, the Whitlam Government was a quintessential moderniser. The Australian constitution combined a narrow legal-political notion of Australian citizenship with the richer tradition of the British subject. As the status of British subject lost its relevance, a vacuum was left behind (Macintyre 1995); Labor set out to fill that vacuum. Whitlam's policy speech declared that 'we have a new chance for our nation'. He talked about Australia's role in the Asian region (ALP 1972: 4); and used government programs to protect and promote a distinctive Australian culture and outlook. If modernity rests on mass consumer markets, the Whitlam Government strengthened national infrastructure and trade, and embraced more complex forms of cultural differentiation. If modernity means the formation of self-regulating citizens, the Whitlam regime was an aggressive moderniser. Based in the liberal intelligensia and middle-class professionals, it substituted the universal language of citizenship, of equality of access and quality of life for the sectional interests of the labour movement. Instead of celebrating the downtrodden, or tearing down their masters, it promised to use the GDP to abolish poverty, and celebrated the deferred gratifications of education.

Labor sought to provide its broader range of personal choices, to open its new 'horizons', first of all through the public sector, using the range of social policies. The Priorities Review Staff emphasised that choice depended not only on the attributes of the individual chooser, but on 'the maintenance and development of a diverse and interesting physical, social and cultural milieu'. This called up policies on cities, work, communications and the environment, as well as education (PRS 1973: 15). In broadcasting and the open university, the government might need to move ahead of the market. Whitlam argued for a 'positive' conception of equality where citizenship was conceived in terms of equal access to public services. Government should directly participate in the production of goods and service where it could do so efficiently; where it was 'the appropriate organisational base', or it was the 'prime customer of the product in question'. Poverty was defined not only as lack of income but lack of access to services, for example on the outer fringes of the larger cities (Whitlam 1975: 6, 7; Whitlam in Evans 1977: 329–330; Whitlam 1985: 355–356).

> Increasingly, a citizen's real standard of living, the health of himself and his family, his children's opportunity for education and self-improvement, his access to employment opportunities, his ability to enjoy the nation's resources for recreational and cultural activity, his legacy from the national heritage, his scope to participate in the decisions and actions of the community, are determined not so much by his income but by the availability and accessibility of the services which the community alone can provide and ensure. The quality of life depends less and less on the things which individuals obtain for themselves and can purchase for themselves from their personal incomes and depends more and more on the things which the community provides for all its members from the combined resources of the community (Whitlam 1985: 3).

The claim that 'the community alone can provide' and the market could not was the rationale for the Whitlam Government's late Keynesian program of communal lifestyles and cultures provided by government *via* taxation and financed from the fruits of the market economy. Whitlam's support for free, high quality universal government services, funded by increased taxation, contrasted with the conservative governments of 1949–1972 and 1975–1983, and the Hawke and Keating Labor governments of 1983–1996. Combined with a modest support for income redistribution and a deeper concern to eliminate poverty, it marked the Whitlam Government as a distinctly social democratic regime along European lines (Beilharz 1994). At the same time, in sectors such as education and health the growth of public institutions was also in continuity with the previous decade's policies. The Whitlam years saw the culmination of previous trends, and also the first signs of the future movement away from government provision. The 1972 ALP policy argued that 'the great weakness in Australian social welfare is that we rely almost wholly on the provision of cash benefits' to individuals rather than community services (ALP 1972: 17). But a year later the Priorities Review Staff was arguing that while 'we do not see income redistribution as a panacea', direct income transfers 'help more of the poor, more efficiently, than provision of services' (PRS 1973: 9). Later governments were to abandon both redistribution and universal provision in favour of targeting and a return to transfer payments.

Whitlam specified in 1972 that economic growth rates of 6 to 7 per cent were needed to pay for Labor's social program. At the same time, 'the program itself will be the basis of strong growth' (ALP 1972: 9–10). The postwar boom provided the conditions for Whitlamite modernisation. It generated the tax revenues and the ambit for a tax-spending redistribution of resources. 'In an increasingly prosperous community the burden of egalitarian measures is lessened since relative shares of the cake may be adjusted with smaller absolute sacrifices by the more affluent' (PRS 1973: 4). Likewise, if growth came an end, the expectations generated by government could no longer be met. Taxation revenues would fall, the cost of welfare would increase and it would become more difficult to persuade middle income groups to contribute to community provision. While it would not necessarily mean an end to modernisation programs, it would make it more difficult to supply these programs through government provision, at least on the scale envisaged by the Whitlam Government.

II. The postwar expansion of education

The growth of participation

The 1945 *White Paper* discussed full employment in terms of the provision of growing opportunities for upward individual mobility, and the number of university students, augmented by the Commonwealth Reconstruction Scheme for returned service men and women, rose from 15 586 in 1945 to 32 453 in 1948 (Anderson & Vervoorn 1983: 18–20). The 1948 level of enrolments was not to be achieved again until 1956, but it was the outrider of the greater changes to come. In the three decades after the war there was a spectacular expansion in the size and social reach of the education systems, so that universal secondary education, and mass systems of upper secondary education and tertiary education, became central factors in Australian life. Secondary students increased by four times, technical enrolments increased five times and higher education students rose from 15 585 in 1945 to 273 137 in 1975. The expansion gathered pace as it went. In the two decades after 1955, the total Australian population rose by 51 per cent but enrolments in education doubled. While the labour force grew by 62 per cent, university enrolments increased almost nine times (Table 2.1).

In the wake of the accelerated immigration program and the postwar 'baby boom' the number of people in Australia aged between 5 and 14 years rose 40 per cent between 1947 and 1954,

Table 2.1 Growth in education, population and labour force, Australia 1955, 1965, 1975, index numbers

Year	Primary schools	Secondary schools	Higher education	Technical education	All education	Population (all ages)	Labour force
1955	100.0	100.0	100.0	100.0	100.0	100.0	100.0
1965	130.8	220.2	270.6	203.7	157.3	123.3	123.7
1975	142.8	314.2	887.0	294.4	202.7	151.0	161.6

Sources: Martin 1964: 17; Anderson & Vervoorn 1983: 20–33; ABS 4221.0; ABS 4202.0; CTEC and predecessors; Foster & Stewart 1991.

and 30 per cent between 1954 and 1961, so that for governments the first task was to expand the capacity of the schooling systems. Later, the main engine of growth became increasing participation rates. By 1975 the proportion of 15-year-olds staying on at school was beginning to approach universal levels and the participation of 17-year-olds in school or higher education had reached almost 40 per cent. After the mid-sixties female retention in schooling rose faster than male retention, nearly closing the long-standing gap between them. In 1950 about 1 per cent of 17-year-old females and 2 per cent of males had commenced university studies. By 1964 the proportions had risen to more than 3 per cent and 6 per cent respectively (Connell 1993; Karmel 1966; Anderson & Vervoorn 1983). The universities were at an unprecedented size. The great period of system building had begun (as illustrated in Table 2.2 below).

Whereas in 1963 there were seven higher education institutions, all universities, by 1973 there were 17 universities and 77 advanced education institutions including the former teachers' colleges. In the five years from 1968, the number of students in advanced education rose from 28 615 to 71 509, and the number in teachers' colleges rose from 15 751 to 27 625. The number of higher degree students increased from only 151 in 1946 to 16 965 in 1975, helping to fill the growing number of academic jobs (Anderson & Vervoorn 1983: 20–21). In the 1960s the participation of 19-year-olds in full-time higher education almost doubled, although the proportion of part-timers and older students increased more slowly. By 1975 more than 15 per cent of 19-year-olds were enrolled in higher education. The proportion of females was 15.2 per cent, only slightly less than that of males at 16.1 per cent, although men dominated the older age groups (Karmel 1966; CTEC 1982: 18–20; DEET 1993). In 1975 a further 26.1 per cent of 19-year-old men were enrolled in TAFE, nearly all on a part-time basis and in courses linked to industrial apprenticeships and other vocationally

Table 2.2 Student enrolments in education by sector, Australia, 1947 to 1975

	Total student enrolments (full-time and part-time) in:			
	Primary schooling	Secondary schooling	Higher education	Technical/ TAFE**	All sectors*
1947	856 216	234 993	30 477	144 882	1 266 568
1948	883 686	238 263	32 453	150 482	1 304 884
1949	920 005	244 310	31 753	153 602	1 349 670
1950	976 360	256 674	30 630	161 564	1 425 228
1951	1 023 762	272 901	31 671	159 310	1 487 644
1952	1 092 360	390 017	29 641	169 089	1 681 107
1953	1 152 403	309 832	28 792	178 301	1 669 328
1954	1 212 937	327 969	29 374	168 923	1 739 203
1955	1 274 337	350 102	30 792	177 081	1 832 312
1956	1 330 847	382 637	34 406	...	...
1957	1 385 405	414 766	36 568	205 225	2 041 964
1958	1 429 824	458 845	41 492	220 500	2 150 661
1959	1 463 937	509 289	47 151	224 937	2 245 314
1960	1 477 404	553 379	53 391	239 427	2 323 601
1961	1 504 278	600 861	57 672	281 237	2 444 048
1962	1 612 007	641 145	63 317	299 588	2 616 057
1963	1 636 999	672 298	69 074	322 169	2 700 540
1964	1 634 694	732 085	76 188	340 080	2 783 047
1965	1 666 606	771 046	83 320	360 755	2 881 727
1966	1 703 552	800 778	91 272	375 003	2 970 605
1967	1 740 521	847 818	95 380	376 915	3 060 634
1968	1 768 744	889 855	145 903	389 309	3 193 811
1969	1 794 827	924 904	160 410	398 578	3 278 719
1970	1 812 023	956 210	175 358	387 812	3 331 403
1971	1 820 849	986 796	195 252	395 893	3 398 790
1972	1 818 345	1 020 417	211 045	...	...
1973	1 808 674	1 042 384	231 691	...	...
1974	1 811 124	1 062 885	251 633	463 363	3 589 005
1975	1 819 358	1 099 922	273 137	521 312	3 713 729

* Includes colleges of advanced education and teachers' colleges from 1968. Special education enrolments in schools not allocated to sector have been included in primary schooling.
** Number of enrolments, not number of students 1974 and 1975. TAFE/ Technical does not include Adult Education. After 1972 'technical' refers to TAFE enrolments minus the leisure and hobby stream. In 1951 and 1970 technical enrolments fell when some students were reclassified as advanced education. There are other series breaks and inconsistencies.
Sources: as for Table 2.1.

specific training. With one apprenticeship available to significant numbers of women, hairdressing, only 8.5 per cent of 19-year-old women were enrolled in TAFE. In total, by 1975 35.1 per cent of all 19-year-olds were seeking post-school credentials. Altogether, more than 44 per cent of all 15 to 19-year-olds were enrolled in full-time education and almost 60 per cent in full or part-time courses (Table 2.3). Simultaneously the number of 15 to 19-year-olds in full time employment fell from 615 000 in August 1966 to 510 000 in August 1975.

Government funding and provision

At the end of World War II the compulsory years of primary and early secondary education were dominated by state institutions, flanked by a resource-poor system of Catholic schools, while the later years of secondary education were selective and dominated by independent private schooling. Government schools educated almost four-fifths of students, nearly all in primary or junior secondary education. Catholic schools educated most of the rest, while the non-Catholic schools were a small elite sector. These shares remained fairly stable until the 1980s (Table 2.4).

Between the wars the social demography of the urban areas was transformed by first public transport and then mass ownership of cars. More spatially segregated social structures developed, in which work was separated from residence; and it was possible to separate secondary school from home as well, enabling the leading private schools to operate city-wide catchments. Affluent families clustered around the leading denominational schools. In 1948 in Victoria, 74.3 per cent of students in matriculation (the final year of secondary school) were enrolled in private schools (Table 2.5). The government schools were stronger in New South Wales. Much of Sydney's middle class used the selective

Table **2.3** Participation in full-time education, 15 to 19-year-olds* 1947, 1961, 1975

Year	Proportion of 15 to 19-year-olds in full-time education*	
	Women %	Men %
1947	10.4	12.2
1961	24.0	28.4
1975	41.4	42.9

* Schooling and higher education only. Including full-time TAFE enrolments, 1975 participation rates were women 43.7 per cent, men 44.6 per cent. Including part-time enrolments brought participation up to 52.3 per cent for women and 64.8 per cent for men.
Sources: Martin 1964: 9; DEET 1993.

Table 2.4 Proportion of students enrolled in government schools, 1891 to 1991

	%
1891	77.9
1901	78.9
1911	77.8
1921	80.3
1931	81.2
1941	76.5
1951	76.0
1961	76.0
1971	78.2
1981	77.0
1991	72.1

Sources: ABS 4221.0; Commonwealth Year Books.

Table 2.5 Matriculation classes in Victoria, 1948

	Private schools	Government schools	Total
Male students	1078	394	1472
Female students	662	207	869
Total students	1740	601	2341
Proportion of students (%)	74.3	25.7	100.0

Source: Hansen 1971: 15.

government schools, which played a much more important role than in Victoria for university entrance. It was Melbourne rather than Sydney that was the heartland of the elite Protestant establishments.

The fact that without public funding more than one-fifth of students were in the private sector, and private schools exercised a strong upper secondary role, meant Australian schooling was unable to develop along North American lines. The 'public' universities financed by all taxpayers were attended by a small handful of students and formed a circuit of privilege with the elite private schools with whom they had much in common. Participation in education was segmented; its social distinctions were regulated not only by the length of education and its institutional location, but by its cultural character.

Originally founded as laboratories for forming the colonial professions, government and business classes (Smith 1991), the private schools and the universities were always more utilitarian than their British counterparts. Their derived British curriculum was scarcely touched by criticism and reflection in the Australian context. It was used mechanically, as an instrument for assigning the cultural distinctions that regulated upward mobility and status definition in the settler states (Osborne 1991). The role of the public elementary and secondary schools was less well defined. They lay somewhere between the derived liberal cultivation of private schools, and the industrial traditions of technical education (Little 1985). Because families in the government system aspired to upward mobility they wanted cultural distinction, but they also wanted something more immediately practical. There were recurring demands for greater efficiency and relevance in the government schools that continued into the postwar period (Macintyre 1986: 109; Macintyre 1990).

Given this inheritance there were a number of ways postwar education might have developed. The task facing modernising reformers was to break down sectoral segmentation to the extent necessary to bring all children of 'ability' within reach of upper secondary and higher education. For some, who believed that the government–private school division was an obstacle to modernisation, any strategy to bring education to the whole people would necessarily be premised on a renovated government school system, and perhaps the eventual withering away of private schools (McCallum 1990: 101–124). Grounded in the strong, centralised state education departments, the great expansion of the 1960s and the early 1970s opened up first secondary and then higher and technical education as mass participation in government-owned institutions designed to service the population in common. Simultaneously, however, the private schools were renovated by public funding, and the leading universities were only partly democratised, so that the pattern of their use was broadened but not transformed. Both of these lines of development were underpinned by public financing; and the expansion of systems and financing was driven by local agitation, the mobilisation of public opinion, and electoral politics.

Governments faced a choice between modernising just the government schools, nationalising the private schools, or introducing state aid for private schools so that both parts of the dual system could be modernised. Given the political support commanded by the private schools, the last was the easiest option, though it was also expensive. The result was that the growth in government spending was even more spectacular than the growth in educational participation. Education's share of Gross National Product had risen from 0.9 to 1.4 per cent between the two world wars. In the twenty years from 1950–51 total spending on education rose in real terms from $0.96 billion to $6.55 billion, reaching 4.6 per cent of GDP. In the last five years of the postwar boom there was another near doubling of spending on education, so that it reached $10.4 billion in 1975–76, 6.2 per cent of GDP – of which government spending constituted 5.9 per cent. The growth of education funding in the late boom years was remarkable, comparable to the defence budget during wartime. In only six years from 1969–70 to 1975–76, government spending on schools rose by $2.8 billion and spending on higher education rose by $1.2 billion (Table 2.6; Butlin et al 1982: 186; ABS 5510.0; DEET 1993: 71). Even in 1975–76 the share of GDP allocated to education in Australia was only slightly above the OECD average, although it was high for a country with a tax base in the bottom third of the OECD. At the end of the 1930s governments spent 6.2 per cent of their total budgets on education (Butlin et al 1982: 185). By the end of the 1950s it was 9.4 per cent, in 1969–70 it was 12.1 per cent, and under Whitlam education reached 15.9 per cent of all government spending in Australia.

Governments financed the running costs of education, increased the level of participation using student allowances, extended and renovated infrastructure, and improved the quantity and quality of staffing. By 1975–76 governments were spending more than 10 per cent of education expenditure ($585 million) on student assistance, through Commonwealth secondary and university scholarships, teacher training scholarships and postgraduate awards. In 1951 there were 6444 merit-based university scholarships. By 1974, 54 853 full-time tertiary students

Table 2.6 Expenditure on education, Australia, 1950–51 to 1975–76*

	Expenditure on education constant 1984–85 prices			Expenditure on education as a proportion of GDP/GNP		
	Government $m	Private $m	Total $m	Government %	Private %	Total %
1950–51	790	168	958	1.34	0.28	1.62
1955–56	1363	306	1669	1.98	0.44	2.42
1960–61	2191	437	2628	2.64	0.53	3.16
1965–66	3327	698	4024	3.15	0.66	3.81
1970–71	5714	835	6548	4.04	0.59	4.62
1975–76	9847	583	10 430	5.88	0.35	6.23

* 1970–71 and 1975–76 data refer to *source* of expenditure, wherever expenditure finally took place: i.e. government grants to private institutions are recorded as public expenditure. Data before 1970–71 refer to *location* of expenditure and government grants to private institutions are recorded as private expenditure, but in those years such grants were on a small scale.
Sources: ABS 5510.0; ABS 4101.0; Karmel 1966.

received Tertiary Education Assistance Scheme (TEAS) payments, income tested rather than subject to academic competition, and 52 286 students were supported by teacher training awards, so that 64.9 per cent of eligible students were covered by one or another scheme (DEET 1988). In 1975–76 the outlay on capital works in education was $1.7 billion, two-thirds in schooling. In the fifteen years after 1960, while school enrolments expanded by 44 per cent, teachers rose from 74 289 to 152 431 (105 per cent), enabling smaller classes and more individualised pedagogies. Between 1947 and 1976 the proportion of all Australian workers who were employed in education rose from 2.0 to 5.6 per cent (ABS 2722.0).

The growing role of education placed extraordinary pressures on State budgets, which for long carried nearly all the costs of government schooling and TAFE, and part of higher education. In 1951–52 education absorbed 30.7 per cent of all State Government recurrent spending; in 1960–61 it was 38.0 per cent and in 1975–76, 43.8 per cent. Between the early 1950s and the mid-1970s, teachers as a proportion of State employees rose from 9 to 17 per cent (Davey 1978: 50; Butlin et al 1982: 207; ABS 5510.0). The resulting fiscal difficulties magnified political pressures for a greater Commonwealth role in education. The peacetime role of the Commonwealth had commenced in 1951 with the first recurrent grants to universities, following the report of the Mills committee. In the beginning, Commonwealth financing was conditional on the maintenance of a basic level of assistance from the States (Jackson 1985: 18). In 1952 the Menzies Government introduced tax deductions for private school fees (W. Connell 1993: 103, 110), and the Murray (1957) and Martin (1964) reports led to major increases in the Commonwealth funding of higher education. In 1964 state aid for science blocks in secondary schools was introduced to private and government schools. The Commonwealth began to develop a national approach to the government of education.

Public funding and public provision

In 1948–49 a fifth (20.3 per cent) of all expenditure on education came from private sources, much the same level as in 1900 (Pope 1989: 13); and between 1950–51 and 1965–66 private expenditure, mostly in the form of tuition fees in private schools and universities and contributions to education buildings and equipment, kept pace with public expenditure. Private spending hovered between 16 and 19 per cent of expenditure on education and doubled as a proportion of personal consumption expenditure (Karmel 1966: 4–6), despite the introduction of tax concessions for fees. But after the mid-1960s state aid to private schools and the post-Martin grants for tertiary education began to substitute for private spending, as well as adding to it. Private expenditure fell sharply, to 14.0 per cent in 1968–69, 10.8 per cent at the beginning of the Whitlam years and 5.6 per cent in 1975–76, a drop of $249 million in real terms in three years. Private expenditure on education was 0.66 per cent of GDP in 1965–66. By 1975–76 it was 0.35 per cent and falling (Table 2.7).

Australia was approaching the universal public financing of education. As noted, public finance was being used to fund not only government sector institutions, but education in private schools as well. In his study of the interaction between public and private outlays from 1949–50 to 1981–82, Williams noted that by the mid-1970s government grants to private schools exceeded private expenditure on all forms of education. Each $1.00 increase in government transfers to the private schools was associated with a $0.18 fall in private expenditure (Williams 1983: 2, 14). The trend away from private funding was also evident in higher education. Student fees declined as a proportion of total university income, from 31.7 per cent in 1939 to 10.4 per cent in 1971, and government funding rose. By 1973 only 20 per cent of full-time students were paying fees on a private basis (Wran 1988: 3) and fees constituted less than 5 per cent of institutional income. Even before free education was proclaimed as a right in higher education and TAFE, in 1974, tertiary fees were phasing out (Table 2.8).

Table 2.7 Proportion of total education spending provided from private sources, Australia, 1948–49 to 1975–76

	%		%
1948–49	20.3	1962–63	17.6
1949–50	18.5	1963–64	17.9
1950–51	17.5	1964–65	17.3
1951–52	16.5	1965–66	17.3
1952–53	17.1	1966–67	...
1953–54	17.9	1967–68	...
1954–55	18.3	1968–69	14.0
1955–56	18.3	1969–70	13.5
1956–57	18.7	1970–71	12.8
1957–58	19.1	1971–72	12.0
1958–59	18.3	1972–73	10.8
1959–60	17.5	1973–74	8.6
1960–61	16.6	1974–75	6.0
1961–62	16.6	1975–76	5.6

Sources: ABS 5510.0; Karmel 1966.

Table 2.8 Sources of university income, 1939, 1951, 1961, 1971

	Common-wealth Government	State Governments	Student fees, etc.	Investments, donations,	Other sources	Total
	%	%	%	%	%	%
1939	0.0	44.9	31.7	16.1	7.2	100.0
1951	20.5	43.7	16.7	8.5	10.5	100.0
1961	43.9	36.3	8.6	6.2	5.0	100.0
1971	43.0	35.7	10.4	5.5	5.3	100.0

Totals do not always equal 100.0 due to rounding.
Source: DEET 1993: 75.

The growth of enrolments and the gradual disappearance of fees were associated with a change in the character of Australian higher education. Partridge (1979) described it as a shift from a 'semi-private status' to a 'public status'. Anderson (1990) refers to the 'democratis-ation' of universities, emphasising the role of scholarships, especially teaching scholarships, in enabling participation of more women students, rural students and students from poorer backgrounds. Unlike the schools, public/private segmentation was negligible,[2] and the Commonwealth aimed to ensure all universities were of international standard. Higher education remained academically selective, in this way continuing to be the preserve of a largely middle-class minority; the traditional hierarchy within the universities also survived; and there was vertical segmentation between the universities and advanced education. Nevertheless, in the 1960s the pathway between government schools and universities was broadened. Between the wars the private schools had dominated universities. In 1939 only 24.3 per cent of the graduates of the University of Melbourne were from government schools. By 1965 the government school share of entrants to that University had reached 52 per cent, although government school leavers were much better represented in teaching and engineering than medicine and law (Anderson & Vervoorn 1983: 67–69).

Clearly, the traditional private school users of the universities faced tougher competition than before. Later the government-financed renovation of the private schools began to reverse the trend. By 1975 the proportion of University of Melbourne entrants from the government schools had fallen again to 41 per cent, with 23 per cent from the Catholic schools and 36 per cent from other private schools.

Whitlam's education programs

The centrality of education in the social vision of the Whitlam Government was matched by its education programs. 1972 to 1975 saw growth in both student numbers and government expenditure, an expansion in the role of public sector institutions (except in relation to private schooling), and growth in the role of the Commonwealth *vis-à-vis* the States. Labor greatly increased the number of post-school places, incorporated the State-based teachers' colleges into advanced education, and modernised every education sector, including TAFE which until the Kangan report (1974) was scarcely thought of as a sector in its own right. Under Whitlam education was the fastest growing area of all public expenditure. Education spending rose from 4.4 to 8.5 per cent of all Commonwealth outlays (Table 2.9).

Outlays on education rose by almost $2.7 billion (176 per cent) in the first two Whitlam budgets. Labor's assumption of full responsibility for higher education coincided with the implementation of the major increases to government and private schools recommended by the Karmel committee in 1973 (see chapter 3). By 1975-76 the Commonwealth was providing 88.3 per cent of all government funding for higher education, 37.5 per cent of government funding for TAFE, 55.6 per cent for pre-schools and other special education, and 60.8 per cent of funding for student assistance. The Commonwealth handled only 23.4 per cent of the schools budget, although providing three-quarters of student assistance in schooling, but it funded most of the government assistance to private schools. By the mid-1970s, in higher education, private schooling, and in TAFE, the policy effectuation of the Commonwealth overshadowed the States, while the States remained dominant in government schooling. The Commonwealth's share of total government funding of education rose from 2.0 per cent in 1950-51 and 9.0 per cent in 1960-61 to 41.9 per cent in 1975-76 (Table 2.10).

Table 2.9 Commonwealth spending on education by sector, 1969-70, 1972-73 and 1975-76, constant 1984-85 prices

Year	Unis	CAEs*	Sub-total higher education	TAFE	Schools & pre-schools	Student assistance	Other	Total education outlays
Outlays	$m	$m	$m	$m	$m	$m	$m	$m
1969-70	398	153	551	47	229	136	68	1031
1972-73	488	227	715	55	364	216	169	1519
1975-76	1177	862	2039	177	987	290	568	4061

* Colleges of advanced education.
Source: CBP, various years.

Table 2.10 The growing role of the Commonwealth Government in education funding, 1950–51 to 1975–76

Commonwealth spending on education as a proportion of all public spending on education					
1950–51 %	1955–56 %	1960–61 %	1965–66 %	1970–71 %	1975–76 %
2.0	4.0	9.0	13.8	21.1	41.9

Sources: Karmel 1966; ABS 5510.0; CBP.

The fast growing Commonwealth programs required an administrative machinery to develop and implement them, in the form of an Education Department and statutory education commissions. The size of the national education bureaucracy almost doubled in 1968 and it multiplied again in 1973, increasing from 397 to 2990 staff in only six years (Table 2.11).

It reached an historic high point of 3357 in 1976, the first year of coalition government, when the last Whitlam initiatives were being installed.

III. The politics of educational expansion

Explanations of the expansion

This remarkable growth in the role of education has been little discussed by general Australian historians, being mostly left to the investigations of economists and historians of education. Searching for explanations, the economists have tended to focus on isolated variables. Karmel (1966) mentioned the effects of demographically driven capital expenditures on system capacity, and an 'increase in the propensity to enrol'. For Williams (1983) government expenditure on education was primary, and 'growth in government expenditure on education can largely be explained by increases in GDP and demographic factors, although there was a once-for-all upward shift in the period 1973–1974'. The implication is that for most of the period expenditure on education was a 'natural' reflection of economic growth, but the policy interventions of the Whitlam Government modified these economic 'fundamentals'. Butlin et al (1982) cited economic and demographic growth, the demand for professional labour, and the policy emphasis on 'the need to develop and improve the stock of human capital'. Pope (1989) added rising

Table 2.11 Full-time Commonwealth staff* in education programs, 1967 to 1976

Year (June)	Number of staff	Change %
1967	397	. . .
1968	765	+92.7
1969	917	+19.9
1970	1053	+14.8
1971	1311	+24.5
1972	1548	+18.1
1973	2990	+93.2
1974	2521	- 15.7
1975	2895	+14.8
1976	3357	+16.0

*Full-time staff only, mostly employed by the Commonwealth Department of Education (92.3 per cent of 2895 full-time staff in 1975).
Source: Jackson 1985.

aspirations, the democratisation of educational opportunities, and betterments in material educational standards.

In these explanations the separated causes were insufficient, and there was little analysis of the relationship between the different elements. For example demographic pressures explain much of the growth in schooling in the 1950s but not rising participation rates. Economic growth was necessary to the expansion of education, but does not explain why the *proportion* of GDP spent on education rose; or why education assumed a greater role in the modernising strategies of government, and in popular aspirations; or took the form of public financing and largely government provision. Nor do these explanations capture the exponential nature of the expansion. The key is to make the explanation more complex. Historical accounts by Bessant and Spaull (1976), Smart (1978) and Teese (1984) draw some of the constituent elements together. The expansion of education was not a solely economic phenomenon, nor a function of policy discourses and educational technologies alone, nor the simple product of popular aspirations and politics. It combined all these elements, and all pointed in the same direction. The fiscal limits on public spending proved upwardly flexible. 'Supply' factors and 'demand' factors all tended to produce each other.

Teese (1984) notes that the expansion of education was associated with the growth and diversification of social positions for educated labour. The occupations that required education grew in relative terms.

The positional market for graduates spread across more of the work-force, and the growth of higher status work was a powerful impetus to popular participation in education. The Vernon report found that between 1947 and 1961 the proportion of the workforce in profes-sional, technical and other 'white collar' functions expanded from 32.6 per cent to 38.3 per cent (Vernon 1966: 86, 578). Above all, the times were marked by the development of government and the services sector. The sector which showed the most consistent growth this period was the 'group of industries which make the most extensive and complex play of educational credentials and which offer the richest and most important field of status distinction': the services, business and finance, retail, health, education and welfare, personal services, sport and recreation (Teese 1984: 131). In the public services, levels of edu-cation regulated merit-based selection and promotion. Governments' own needs for teachers and researchers stimulated expansion in higher education. This augmented popular aspirations for education, at the same time as these were being called up by government policies. Teese emphasises the autonomy of popular desires for education: 'the individual demand for school, however instrumental it should prove, cannot be regarded as if it were merely a translation of objective social need' (Teese 1984: 134–135).

However, a complicating factor is that this popular demand for edu-cation was not simply driven by demographic or economic demand but was also partly created by the government education programs them-selves. A major theme of postwar policy was to persuade people to act in their own interest by taking up the 'offered gift' of education (McCallum 1990: 3). It was feared that unless educational participation was largely financed by government, the rate of investment would fall short of national needs. In 1962 Karmel suggested that 'people may seriously underestimate the private benefits to be derived from education ... if the parents themselves have had relatively little edu-cation, they will tend to be ill-informed about the benefits of education and tend to demand too little' (Karmel 1962: 6–7). Not only did gov-ernments provide educational services to everyone who wanted them, a departure from earlier policy, they deliberately fostered desires for education using state provision and funding, scholarships, and talking up demand. Later, once higher demand for education was established and growing, those same governments not surprisingly found it difficult to regulate and limit.

In the 'revolution in rising expectations' which constituted the growth of education in the 1960s and early 1970s, the relationship between government and popular demand, were shaped by the two dominant policy discourses of the time: those of investment in human capital, and equality of educational opportunity (Bessant & Spaull 1976: 69–91). In the circumstances of the postwar boom, and Keynesian economic and political management, these policy discourses tended to reinforce each other, and constituted a governmental and popular *politics* of education that was the medium for expansion. The extension of education became more than the spread of skills and knowledge, or the widening of citizenship. It was the universal expectation of personal advance and a better life *via* learning, a 'promethean' culture of development and self-development (Beilharz 1993) in which the limitations of the old self would be transcended and all would be fulfilled.

Investment in human capital

Claims about the economic contribution of education were often at the heart of state intervention. The argument appealed to the rich and powerful even while holding out the prospect of prosperity for all. When Victoria's pioneering director-general of education, Frank Tate, was building support for the new secondary education system it was the economic card that he played. 'Tate continued to believe that education was of value for its own sake, but if the price of overcoming the opposition to state high schools was to link them to industrial and commercial interests he was willing to pay it' (Selleck 1982: 194). The tradition wavered in the depression of the 1930s, but by the end of the 1950s, after a decade of high economic growth and the expansion of professional employment, the circumstances were unusually favourable for the propagation of the new theory of investment in human capital developed by neoclassical economists Denison (1962), Becker (1964/ 1975), Schultz (1960; 1961) and others. The Soviet Sputnik satellite of 1957, seen as a challenge to Western science and technologies, helped provide the political basis for a major increase in national educational effort.

The human capital economists assumed a direct causal relationship between education/training and the productivity of labour, and a natural labour market relationship between labour productivity and individual earnings. Becker developed the equations which constituted the micro-economics of human capital. He assumed that education was a function of individuals' investment in their own human capital, determined by the rate of return on that investment in a competitive labour market in which labour was paid on the basis of marginal productivity. Individuals invested in education up to the point where the increased returns from the additional investment in education no longer outweighed the costs of that education (Becker 1964/1975: 7, 45). The axioms of human capital theory assumed perfect competition and no government subsidies in both the markets for labour and the markets for education. In the real world, the level of investment in education owed more to government funding than to private calculations of rates of return. But it was assumed that the economic benefits of investment would flow – however that education was funded and organised. In the most influential of all human capital studies, Denison (1962) assumed that education and research were the 'x' factor in economic growth. He found that between 1929 and 1957 education contributed 42 per cent of the increase in United States' product per worker (p. 73). Denison's argument generated tremendous excitement. It was used repeatedly to underwrite the great advance in public spending and education provision.

Among economists, only Milton Friedman questioned the wisdom of ever increasing public expenditure. He argued that vocational education should be funded entirely by the individual on the grounds that there were no social returns to the investment in human capital that were not already included in the benefits received by individuals (Friedman 1962: 100–105). This argument was to return, but in the 1960s it made little headway against Keynesian orthodoxy.

There was a close and continuing liaison between the human capital economists and the leading international bodies which championed the case for investment in education, particularly the OECD and the United Nations Educational, Scientific and Cultural Organisation, UNESCO (Husen 1979). In the foreword to a major collection of papers arguing the human capital view UNESCO acknowledged the normative character of the claims about investment in education, while assuring readers in government and economics that the optimism about education was scientifically based:

> That schooling and other forms of education are of vital economic significance has long been recognised. Nevertheless, modern theorists of development were giving it little heed even ten short years ago. Within a decade there has been a dramatic shift, and concern with potential roles of education in economic development has swept the world. In part this is no more, and no less, than the surge of a new faith, the wishful hope that schooling could unlock the gates to let loose a stream of growth. But there has been much hard thinking on this subject, too (UNESCO 1968: 15).

Human capital arguments soon appeared in Australia (Wheelwright 1962/1974: 161–171), and were endorsed at the highest level in the Martin report of 1964. Some local economists were sceptical about the calculations of rates of return and the 'residual factor' in growth (Karmel 1962; Hall 1965), and it was felt the economic externalities of education, those social benefits not captured by individuals in the form of higher incomes, might have been underestimated. There was also disquiet at the Martin report's economic instrumentalism. The report of the Robbins committee in Britain had been less sanguine about human capital theory (Robbins 1963: 204–207).

Nevertheless, educators found the funding implications of the Martin position were difficult to resist. In academic as well as policy circles it was general wisdom that 'the maintenance of a satisfactory rate of growth requires a substantially greater public investment in education (and especially in higher or advanced education) than has been maintained until now' (Partridge 1965). Human capital theory in the 1960s functioned more as a general metaphor for the benefits of education, and a blanket justification for funding, than an empirical research program. Claims about the benefits of human capital were deployed by governments and educators to achieve other and non-economic purposes. Thus the Martin committee argued for a broad general education using human capital theory; and in the Buntine Oration of 18 May 1962, Peter Karmel, a member of the Martin committee and later head of the Universities Commission, the Interim Committee for the Schools Commission and the Tertiary Education Commission, used the economic argument to justify the extension of citizenship *via* education:

> I should tonight advocate a greater educational effort in Australia, even if its sole economic consequences were to reduce national production by withholding more young people from the workforce for more years. I should do this since I believe that democracy implies making educational opportunities as equal as possible and that the working of democracy depends on increasing the number of citizens with the capacity for clear and informed thought on political and social issues. (Karmel 1962: 4–5).

But Karmel added that it would be 'foolish' to ignore the effects of education on economic growth. 'No sensible advocate discards a valid argument which may convince' (Karmel 1962: 5). Another economist stated it would not matter if the alleged economic benefits of education did not materialise, because the advocate of 'investment in man' could fall back on claims about the non-economic benefits of expenditure on education. Anyway, 'an affluent society can afford errors of judgement in the proper allocation of resources' (Hall 1965: 144, 146). There was a certain looseness, even a transparent cynicism, about these arguments. Later, the very universality of these economic claims about investment in education was to render that investment more vulnerable when the connection between education and economic growth was less self-evident, and affluence became less common and more relative.

Equality of opportunity

In the beginning, the governmental provision of equality of opportunity through education was seen as consistent with the economic argument about the benefits of education, even a subset of it. Writing in the late nineteenth century the economist Alfred Marshall, the teacher of Keynes at Cambridge, took a close interest in education's role in locating under-utilised talent, and facilitating upward social mobility:

> The laws which govern the birth of genius are inscrutable. It is probable that the percentage of children of the working classes who are endowed with natural abilities of the highest order is not so great as that of the children of people who have attained or have inherited a higher position in society. But since the manual labour classes are four or five times as numerous as all other classes put together, it is not unlikely that more than half the best natural genius that is born into the country belongs to them; and of this a great part is fruitless for want of opportunity. There is no extravagance more prejudicial to the growth of national wealth than that wasteful negligence which allows genius that happens to be born of lowly parentage to expend itself in lowly work. No change would conduce so much to a rapid increase of material wealth as an improvement in our schools, and especially those of the middle grades, provided it be combined with an extensive system of scholarships, which will enable the clever son of a working man to rise gradually from school to school till he has the best theoretical and practical education which the age can give (Marshall 1890/1920: 212).

'There is abundant room for newcomers in the upper ranks of the middle class' he stated, but 'all that is spent during many years in opening the means of higher education to the masses would be well paid for if it called out one more Newton or Darwin, Shakespeare or Beethoven' (Marshall 1890/1920: 216–217, 719). The same sentiments underpinned the developing education systems in Australia. In 1912 the Queensland Inspector-General for Education referred to education's function of 'unearthing, rearing and developing into full flower and fruit the latent seeds of genius which would otherwise perish unfulfilled or be born to blush unseen in poverty and insecurity' (Macintyre 1990: 7). Here the practices of equality of opportunity in education had discursive roots in both economics and psychology, resting primarily on the techniques for sorting the population developed by the psychologists in the early years of the twentieth century. Administratively and politically, equality of opportunity policies rested on the establishment of the state education systems of primary education, with their universal reach, and in the developing popular demand for secondary and higher education. Hunter argues that these policies required two 'interlocking and inseparable' developments:

The first of these was the apparatus of state schooling itself. Not until an institution appeared possessing the technical capacity to distribute a uniform set of cultural attributes to entire national populations would there be common forms of personhood or a common desire for access to them. The second condition – in fact the first chronologically speaking – was the bureaucratic system of political administration. It was the expert political and intellectual technologies of the bureau – specifically, those that transformed normative cultural attributes into quantifiable phenomena, measured their distribution in populations and correlated this with social problems and economic objectives – that opened the distribution of education to political rationality and political control. In other words, it was not until education had been rendered socially uniform and politically calculable, as a result of the emergence of a powerful bureaucratic school system, that the objective of equality of opportunity became politically intelligible and ethically desirable (Hunter 1993b: 273–274; see also Hunter 1993a).

But it was only in the 1960s and 1970s that equality of opportunity reached its apogee in the system organisation of government schooling. Here the formal objective of 'equality of opportunity' did not require that the gap between success and failure would be narrowed, or that the whole working class would be lifted up as some reformers hoped. It simply meant the competition for educational merit was to take in the whole population, was to be made universal. Educational merit was the individualised outcome of education. It was understood as the combination of pre-given natural talent ('ability') with work in education ('effort'). Possession of educational merit was the passport to further education, the higher echelons of the labour markets and the professions. The OECD later called equality of opportunity the doctrine of 'access to advantage' (OECD 1981b: 8). Reflecting on two decades of equality of opportunity policies, Bennett states that:

> This doctrine of equality of opportunity had enormous implications for education itself. First, it assumed that the purpose of the education system was simply personal advancement in material terms. Above all, it endorsed the principle that education, like society itself, is a competition, a process which produces winners and losers. The purpose of the policy is to ensure that the rules of this competition are fair – that is, that everyone has an equal chance (Bennett 1982: 165).

Equality of opportunity imagined a competitive selection in which ability and struggle (and chance) were combined, but it was a *simulation* of 'natural selection', in which nature was to determine the outcome, but nature was itself defined and measured by educational technologies. This owed something to Darwin and Spencer, and was also consistent with the market liberal axiom of free competition with its rejection of inherited advantage. At the same time, these equality of opportunity programs were controlled and financed by the state. The plan was nothing less than an aristocracy of merit, selected scientifically and at public expense. By this means the inequalities that resulted from social organisation would disappear, while those deriving from individual qualities, first identified in education, would remain (Tawney 1938: 39). The idea was to eliminate the effects of social origins on social destinations.

In his best-selling polemic *The myth of equality* (1970), which built much support for Whitlam's education program, National Union of Australian University Students Vice-President Tom Roper admitted 'education alone will not ensure social equality', but said 'a new social division based on educability ... may be preferable to divisions based on birth or wealth. Status would not necessarily be passed on from one generation to the next' (Roper 1970: 9). By naturalising and universalising the positional competition in education, this helped to lay the basis for the later construction of explicitly economic markets in education. But in the 1960s this positional competition and social selection were increasingly financed by the state, and in government owned institutions.

In *The social production of merit* McCallum (1990) provides an account of how the practices of educational psychology were developed in Australia between the wars, how the public school systems delivered them with the laboratory and the experimental objects that they needed, how they constituted the pedagogical and administrative systems of the postwar era, and how psychology and equality of opportunity normalised each other. The educational practices associated with equality of opportunity became embodied in state-financed teacher education, becoming general to the state teaching services in the recruiting waves of the 1950s and 1960s.

The implications of these new practices were far-reaching. It was necessary to achieve universal participation into the late secondary school years to maximise the pool of talent. The cutting edge of equality of opportunity polemics was the tragedy and injustice of wasted talent, the high ability children, usually working class, who were lost forever (Roper 1970: 15 – later, these images were to be at the heart of the demands for positive discrimination in favour of the 'gifted', usually middle class, with little break in the discursive continuity). The task of educators was to strip away all non-educational mechanisms whereby social advantage was allocated, 'revealing' an essential educational subject beneath. Economists agreed with psychologists about the concept of natural individual 'ability'. Marshall was interested in Galton's early studies of genius and hereditary. As Vaizey stated, ' "intelligence" in the economics of education corresponds to "land" in

classical economics' (Vaizey 1962: 113). Human capital as a natural
resource: this was educational common sense.

> It was assumed, at least in the discussions of intelligence testing circulated
> to teachers, that the precondition for school success was a type of pre-social
> 'natural' talent, and that ultimately the social distribution of school success
> could be explained in these terms, once the distorting effects of economic
> factors on school provision and participation had been lessened or removed
> (McCallum 1990: 34).

The attempt to remove these social effects, understood as 'barriers'
to the expression of individual ability, was the engine of educational
policy for half a century. Yet it was driving into a cul-de-sac, because
the very qualities ascribed to 'individuals' were not only over-deter-
mined by the financing of schooling and its institutional structure and
patterns of social group use; these individual qualities were socially constructed by the technologies of psychology and education. None of
these effects could be rendered 'neutral'. The government of education
had been charged with the elimination of the consequences of itself.
Equality of opportunity was a circular task, in which the educational
worm was doomed to follow the marks left by its own tail.

It was the job of teachers to apply the economic resources devoted
to the educational project in a manner that was as efficient in the
utilitarian sense, so as to maximise the amount of merit that was produced. W. Connell (1993: 51–55) notes that the meritocratic system
was underpinned by four main instruments: intelligence testing,
streaming or tracking in the classroom, public examinations, and the
division of labour between academic and non-academic schools. A
battery of tests and sorting techniques were developed to ensure that
teachers would discover talent, and there would be adequate discrimination between all of the students in the controlled environment of
the classroom. 'Throughout the 1950s, and even beyond, the criterion
of intellectual ability dominated curriculum planning' (Bessant &
Spaull 1976: 85), and later – though there was a growing unease about
IQ testing – the focus on individual differences and individualisation
increased.

There was a ready-made measure of the success or failure of equality
of opportunity policies. That was the extent of equality of positional
outcomes by social group: the degree of social mobility, the success of
the socially disadvantaged in further education and in entry to the professions. Thus a second engine of policy was to reform the equality of
opportunity instruments themselves until their social neutrality (measured by equality of outcomes) was evident. Equality of opportunity policies became locked into a dynamic of self-criticism and ceaseless

reformation, and an inherent conflict between educational science and social objectives was established.

There was never a consensus on the extent of social redistribution and institutional change required to secure a fair and scientific competition based on equality of opportunity. Where and to what extent should the state intervene? Three often contradictory definitions of equality policy emerged. First, there was equality of government expenditure per student. This was almost universally endorsed as a base line entitlement, but was understood variously as the starting point or the termination of equality policies. Second, there was equality of total material resources per student. This required governments to apply more than average resources to students – or communities – with less than average resources of their own, leading to programs of positive discrimination. This was also flexible: it could function either as a substitute for universal provision (targeting), or as additional to it (redistribution). In the 1970s positive discrimination took the latter form, becoming the main mode of equalitarian reform. Third, there was equality in overall educational conditions, so that all institutions were rendered equivalent in positional terms. This would have required a universal system of schooling and the abolition of selective private schools, and a profound reduction in the intensity of positional competition.

The mainstream political debate lay between the first and second notions of equality. In Australia the conservative parties tended to be associated with notions of equal entitlement, while Labor tended to be the initiator of positive discrimination, but these lines became blurred and programs eventually became a hybrid of both. During World War II the Commonwealth Labor Government introduced subsidies for university students in science faculties whose parents earned below a certain income level. In the wake of this scheme there was a sharp rise in the proportion of first year science students from government schools, from 32 per cent in 1939 to 45 per cent in 1943. The proportion from Catholic schools also rose, from 13 to 19 per cent. At the same time the average school leaving mark of first year science students at the University of Melbourne rose from 243 in 1939 to 357 in 1943 (Anderson & Vervoorn 1983: 67; McCallum 1990: 105–106, 115). This sealed Labor's commitment to positive discrimination and income-based schemes.

The Menzies conservative governments after 1949 distributed scholarships on the basis of academic merit rather than income. Menzies advanced the education of the middle class in the private schools and universities, rather than searching for 'genius born of low parentage' as Marshall had put it. Nevertheless, by 1970 his second successor as

Coalition Prime Minister, John Gorton, was talking about equality of opportunity, at the highest level of government (Roper 1970: 11).

The equalitarian expectations of education became almost universal on both sides of politics (Aitkin 1981). Drenched in popular politics and the language of democratic rights, rooted in the principle of fairness already naturalised in the legal system, rising to the widespread aspirations for upward mobility while promising a just science in social selection; equality of opportunity had become hegemonic.

The 'revolution in rising expectations'

In sum, one of the defining characteristics of Australian society in the three decades after World War II was the formation of expectations related to education. Education was expected to contribute to economic growth and development, to the broadening of the character and reach of modern citizenship, to rising living standards and quality of life, to widening opportunities, to greater equality and social reform, and to a growing number of individual futures. Improved living standards themselves contributed to growing expectations and allowed more families to keep their children at school. Just as political citizenship and economic consumption were becoming blended in government, so the social and economic arguments for education were blended and interchangeable. Democratic reform in education was defined as equal opportunity to accumulate wealth and rise up the social ladder (Partridge 1965). The rising level of formal education paralleled the rising threshold of 'necessary' consumption. It seemed the stairway to heaven was within everybody's reach.

The politics of this 'revolution in rising expectations' were shaped in the joining of human capital theory and equality of educational opportunity, a combination which achieved a high level of sophistication in the influential policy discourse of the OECD. Education was understood as both a system of rational social selection and as a system of ordered justice, one in which efficiency and equality had been combined. Equality would maximise the pool of talent, while investment in human capital would increase social equality by raising general educational levels. Education was to be resourced according to the principles of equality of opportunity, and these resources were to be deployed rationally by educational psychology, thereby optimising the investment. It was true that the private rates of return on investment in human capital would rise if income differentials increased, suggesting tensions between economic and egalitarian objectives, between relative and absolute advance, and between general and individual prosperity, but for a time these tensions were suppressed (OECD

1981b). It was assumed that economic needs would be best met by 'an undifferentiated expansion of education – one which was not formally and deliberately targeted on particular manpower needs and particular social groups' (Jones 1989: 3). It was *social* investment. The *individual* human capital calculus, with its market implications, was not operational in educational provision. Individual human capital remained a metaphor, albeit one that was a powerful engine for growth.

Equality of opportunity and human capital theory had different constituencies. Human capital theory appealed to economists, industrialists and newspaper editors, and the politicians that it turned into the organisers of prosperity. Equality of opportunity had the sweeping democratic appeal: it offered everyone dignity and social worth, and a share in prosperity, and it was made for popular politics. Karmel (1962) argued that it would be possible to persuade people to increase tax payments solely to improve public financing of education, and for the next decade he was correct.

There was much campaigning to heighten and focus demands for education (Bessant & Spaull 1976; Smart 1978). The political significance of educational resources was triggered by deficiencies in capital works, shortages of qualified staff and large class sizes in the 1950s and early 1960s. Between 1950 and 1970 the average student–teacher ratio in government primary schools fell from 32 to 27, and the secondary ratio fell from 20 to 17 (ABS 4202.0) but though the resourcing of schools improved it always seemed to lag behind needs. In the mid-1960s the mobilisations for education began to become stronger and more confident. The campaigns for funding of government schools were not directly linked with the campaigns for state aid to private schools, but both pointed towards more funding, and an expanded Commonwealth role. The agitation for resources and the growing expectations of education fed on each other. (Later, they were to collapse together). In some States there seemed to be a perpetual crisis in education.

The rising popular expectations destabilised governments: it was ironic that these same rising expectations had been partly created by governments. 'By the late 1960s Australian education, especially at the school level, was entering a particularly turbulent phase. Both socially and politically, education rapidly became a dominant, perhaps even the dominant, public issue during this period' (Smart 1978: 97). Whitlam remarked later that 'the most intense political debate in Australia during the 1960s was not about Viet Nam, it was about education' (Whitlam 1985: 291).

The full dynamic of expanding places, growing expenditures and rising expectations was now apparent. The task of secondary schools had shifted, unevenly and by fits and starts, from selection to universal progression. Their goal – itself a natural outcome of the logic of equality of opportunity – was now to maximise the cohort able to proceed to higher education. What was the limit to the size of this cohort? Broad brush metaphors about investment in human capital provided no basis for limiting government expenditure on education: rather, the human capital argument implied the continual expansion of provision. From the point of view of governments, the essential fiscal–political service had been performed by those restrictions on participation that used the measurement of 'ability' as the basis for differential resource allocations. This limitation on expansion could at least be justified within the terms of equality of opportunity. The problem here was that as the number of qualified students rose, so did the thresholds of 'ability' and expectation. The tension between selection and universality, inherent in any meritocratic regime, was now apparent. In 1939 only one student in every 100 proceeded to university, and Cunningham, the first director of the Australian Council of Educational Research (ACER), argued this was 'a substantial under-utilisation of talent'; at least 10 per cent were capable of university study (McCallum 1990: 114). In 1962 John Vaizey, the economist of education, stated 15 to 20 per cent could succeed (Vaizey 1962).

Each lifting of the threshold showed more clearly that 'ability' and 'educability' were not natural but were historically relative, determined by administrative and political requirements. As long as education remained publicly funded, there was no clear basis for restrictions on spending. The broad support for increased taxes and increased expenditure meant that education could only expand to meet demand, and the level of demand was rising. For a while, demand directly controlled the pace of expansion. The Commonwealth Government's labour-power planning policy in higher education 'amounted to little more than confident statements about unlimited growth, and it was this optimistic vision which had to serve the function of a rationale for the expansion of higher education' (Anderson & Vervoorn 1983: 27). Governments had lost control of the fiscal politics of education. At the same time, the youth revolt of the late 1960s suggested that the homegenising function of education had also partly broken down. Keynesianism, student power and the counter culture reinforced the sense of an education sector spinning out of control, a sense the emerging New Right was able to augment and exploit (Buchanan & Devletoglou 1970).

The rising popular demand for education was driven above all by aspirations for upward mobility. The early 1970s study of *Educational opportunity in South Australia* noted that fourth year students' occupational ambitions reflected those of their fathers only to a degree. 'The *upgrading* of aspirations amongst the students by comparison with their fathers' actual occupations is remarkable' (Blandy & Goldsworthy 1975: 18). Individual aspirations for education began to become universal. Perhaps it was in this sense that education constituted a common culture. But the total expectations of education were impossibly high.

> The mid-1960s represented the high point of faith in education and the expectations of that period now seem hopelessly unreal, even ludicrous. Education was expected to establish an equal society, maintain economic growth and promote national prosperity, while at the same time providing everyone with higher incomes, interesting jobs and a pleasant middle-class life (Bennett 1982: 165).

An immense aggregated burden of hope and ambition had settled on the education system, particularly the secondary schools where the individual futures were assigned. 'To meet these aspirations would require a change in the structure of the economy of staggering proportions within the space of a generation', (Blandy & Goldsworthy 1975: 18) in order to provide the necessary opportunities. But like the continuing expansion of tax revenue and government education, the continuing growth in professional labour depended on the maintenance of the long economic boom.

Notes

[1] The Priorities Review Staff noted that work oriented courses and certificates predominated in education. This was probably inevitable, it stated, given that 'the demand for tertiary education exceeds its supply. But with an adequate supply of graduates, other forms of tertiary courses should be developed' (PRS 1973: 17). The policy makers of the early 1970s did not imagine that when the supply of graduates rose above the demand for traditional graduate jobs, the student demand for 'certificates' would increase rather than decline; and education would become more vocationally oriented rather than less.

[2] The private teachers' colleges played a minor role, enrolling 2576 students in 1973 (ABS file data).

CHAPTER 3

The Karmel report and educational equality

> 'Education is the key to equality of opportunity. Sure, we can have education on the cheap, but our children will be paying for it for the rest of their lives. . . . We believe that a student's merit rather than a parent's wealth should decide who should benefit. . . . Education should be the great instrument for the promotion of equality.'
>
> *Australian Labor Party leader Gough Whitlam,* Policy speech, *Blacktown Civic Centre, Sydney, 13 November 1972, p. 5 & p. 12.*

Prelude: The Karmel report (1973)

Schools in Australia, the report of the Interim Committee for the Schools Commission chaired by Peter Karmel, was released in May 1973 to almost universal acclaim. The committee knew the newly elected Whitlam Labor Government would support its recommendations, and held nothing back. Few government reports have secured such an impact. Within two years, the funding recommended by the Karmel report had lifted Commonwealth spending on schools from $364 to $1091 million and transformed the material position of all schools, private and government. The report settled the Commonwealth's role in school education and laid down a system of classifying and funding private schools that was still intact more than two decades later. Its Disadvantaged Schools Program was the high-water mark of efforts to eradicate poverty through education, and the prototype for later programs of positive discrimination and targeting to raise participation. Discursively, its reach was almost as long; the Karmel notions of equality of opportunity, diversity, choice, devolution and participatory citizenship left deep marks in schools and government. It captured the hearts and minds of the younger activists who had begun teaching between

46

the late 1960s and the mid-1970s. The climax of the Whitlam policies (chapter 2), the influence of the Karmel report was to long outlast them. It became *the* moment of modernisation in Australian education. Since the mid-1960s the government schools had increased their share of enrolments to nearly 80 per cent. The independent schools remained a small minority sector and the Catholic schools were in decline. Nevertheless, since 'state aid' began in 1963 the private schools had enjoyed growing Commonwealth support, including operating funds from 1969. At first sight the Karmel committee appeared to favour the government sector. It extended operating funding to that sector, so that forty years of campaigns for federal funding finally achieved their goal; and of the proposed funds for 1974 and 1975, 69.8 per cent was allocated to government schools and 27.2 per cent to private schools, with the rest in joint programs. The government school teacher unions hailed the report. Their long opposition to state aid to private schools was forgotten. In a letter to the *Sydney Morning Herald* Australian Teachers' Federation (ATF) President Ray Costello wrote that:

> The report has our complete support. We believe the philosophy and recommendations of the committee members represent the most important development in Australian education this century. The Karmel committee's report represents a giant step forward in Australian education (Costello 1973).

Only the organisation for the Defence of Government Schools (DOGS) maintained its condemnation of state aid. The ATF slogan was 'government schools first', meaning no private school should receive state aid until all of the needs of government schools had been met. The generous Karmel grants to government schools cut the ground from under this position; and the 'needs' based funding formula, under which a school's recurrent grant was determined by its level of economic resources, made it difficult to oppose support for poor Catholic parish schools. Although the NSW Teachers' Federation was a strong opponent of state aid, when the Karmel report was released the Federation's journal *Education* hailed it as a 'major breakthrough'. During the federal election of 1974, the Teachers' Federation leadership threw its weight behind the Whitlam–Karmel programs. Senior vice-president Van Davy called for 'a conscious vote for the greatest thing that ever happened to Australian education'. But 'to laud the government's education policy had one inescapable consequence. It nullified the Federation's traditional opposition to state aid' (O'Brien 1987: 121).

In 1976 an OECD review team remarked on the unusual importance of the private schools in Australian education, and noted that 'criticism of the non-government sector and of the public subsidy to institutions in this sector appeared to us remarkably muted' (OECD 1977: 38). Within six years, under the Fraser Coalition Government, Commonwealth funding of private schools doubled in real terms while funding of government schools fell by 18.9 per cent, the private school share of funds rose from 25.7 to 46.4 per cent, the private sector was undergoing unprecedented expansion, and the government schools were facing crisis. The state aid debate had broken out again, and the teacher unions were vociferous critics of government policy. Yet Fraser had not abandoned the Karmel framework, but manipulated that framework so as to shift the balance within it. The great renovation of the private schools under the 'needs' policy, and the great expansion in demand for private schooling which followed, undermining the comprehensive character of the government systems, occurred within the terms and conditions of the system of funding established in 1973.

I. Government and private schooling

Pluralism and community

Anderson (1992) identifies four conditions that favour the development of a large and influential private school sector. First, 'a mainly comprehensive public secondary system' with little differentiation on taste or quality grounds. Second, 'powerful, centrally directed educational administrations' providing 'little opportunity for community participation in decision making' which might allow the needs of particular groups to be managed by themselves. Third, religious and ethnic heterogeneity. Fourth, substantial state aid to private schools. Of the seven Anglo-American and Scandinavian countries Australia is the only one which rates 'high' on all these conditions.

There are three kinds of private schooling in Australia. First, 'the elite schools which, although comprising a relatively small fraction of the private sector, loom large in social importance and in the public image ... an elite school is one that recruits from the elite sector of society, and helps to reproduce it'. Second, schools 'committed to the maintenance of particular subcultures' based in religion or ethnicity. Third, reform or 'alternative schools' which rest on particular educational notions of community or individual development. Two further categories of private school, profit-making and charity schools, are largely absent. In addition to private schools there are the 'community schools', would-be comprehensive government schools 'designed to accept all children in a particular community or locality' and 'agencies of social cohesion' (Anderson 1992: 218–221). Using Anderson's framework, the Catholic school systems are ambiguous. They are grounded in the 'subcultural' maintenance of Catholicism and sometimes ethnicity, they might claim differentiation on grounds of quality, and they share with government schools the responsibility of serving all of the children in a particular locality. They might be either 'private' as in Australia, the Netherlands or France, or 'public' as in Britain and New Zealand.

In most OECD countries there has long been a dual system of government and private institutions in schooling, but aside from the Netherlands and Belgium, where the private sector shared a common system of regulation with government schools, among OECD countries only Spain has a larger private sector than Australia. In countries where the private sector is confined to a minor role in 'subcultural' maintenance there is no necessary tension between the mission of the private sector and the comprehensive character of government schooling. In countries such as Spain, Australia and France, with well developed differentiation on the basis of both subculture and social position, the dual system contains an endemic tension. Anderson describes it as a conflict between community government schools and a 'pluralist' private system. Private education is not a single system in itself, being a heterogeneous amalgam of individual institutions and systems, but all parts of the private sector reduce the comprehensive character of government schools; for the government and private schools draw from a common pool of enrolments and are both contending for community standing and governmental support.

> The public (community) and private (elite) school sectors can be thought of as two parts of a single system. They are not islands, separate from one another, but dynamically interacting sub-systems, each influencing the other through transactions across a shared boundary (Anderson 1992: 231).

A system based on free moving choice between schools, especially one in which positional competition is endemic, tends to exacerbate tensions between community schooling and pluralism. Ironically, the weakening of comprehensive schools could also weaken the conditions under which choice may flower. 'Of importance is the learning of tolerance which is central to the curriculum in a pluralist society. Thus there is the contradiction that the exercise of tolerance through subsidising choice of schools may reduce the opportunity for the children in a pluralist society to learn tolerance' (Anderson 1992: 223).

There are two methods whereby the tension between community and pluralism can be resolved. First, pluralism can be contained *within* the framework of the government school system: when choice becomes choice of learning program rather than choice of school, and operates within individual schools or within a cluster of non-competing neighbouring schools, both community and pluralism are served. Second, a unified market of competing schools can be established, across the sectors; dissolving the community schools altogether.

State aid in Australia

Commonwealth assistance to private education began with a 1951 Liberal–Country Party Government decision to provide financial assistance for denominational colleges at universities. In 1952, following a suggestion of the headmasters' conference, Prime Minister Robert Menzies introduced tax deductions for school fees, up to fifty pounds. In 1954 donations to school building funds also became tax deductible; from 1956 the Commonwealth paid interest on the loans used to finance school buildings erected by private schools in the ACT under direct Commonwealth administration (Smart 1978). In the United States the first amendment to the constitution prevented direct aid to religious schools. In Australia an almost identical constitutional provision provided no impediment, although the point was not legally tested until the 1970s, by which time state aid was established.

Menzies resisted the mounting pressures for direct state aid to private schools in the States until 1963, when he suddenly announced that the Commonwealth would provide funding for science blocks in both private and government schools, along with a new program of Commonwealth secondary scholarships. The science block program helped to alleviate the costs of modernising. The grants were proportional to secondary enrolments and favoured the leading private schools which had high retention rates. Between 1964 and 1971 the private schools received 37 per cent of science block monies. Because Commonwealth secondary scholarships were based on competitive tests they also favoured the private schools (Davey 1978: 38, 68–69). This introduction of state aid in 1963, exacerbating a split in the Labor Party and strengthening Menzies' support from Catholic voters, has been well documented (see for example Bessant 1977; Smart 1978; Whitlam 1985; Jackson 1985). Though many government school supporters continued to oppose it, political party support for state aid soon became bipartisan. Despite differences in character between the community-based Catholic parish schools and the small, exclusive group of elite private schools, the political alliance between their leaders turned into a long-term partnership. The potential support base of the would-be comprehensive government schools was bisected twice, by class and culture. The Catholic sector provided the state aid alliance with a mass base able to match the mobilisations of government school supporters, and between them the headmasters' conference and the Catholic hierarchy commanded great lobbying power. After 1963 assistance to private schools expanded rapidly. In 1968 the Commonwealth began grants for school libraries, and separate deputations from the headmasters' conference and Catholic education requested a program of recurrent grants. This was introduced in 1969, for private schools only. In 1972 general capital grants were introduced for both sectors (Table 3.1). State governments also introduced state aid; for example Victoria began per capita grants in 1967, two years before the Commonwealth. As Jean Blackburn, a member of the 1973 Karmel committee later remarked, both levels of government used state aid as 'a vote catching ploy. The result was a political auction, not a public policy' (Ashenden 1987a: 61).

II. The Karmel report

Radical egalitarianism

By the late 1960s radical egalitarians, grounded in a militant professionalism that conflated the democratisation of power structures and rewards with curriculum reform, were gathering support in education, especially in government schooling in Victoria. Teacher educator Doug White stated in *Australian capitalism: towards a socialist critique* (1972) that educational expansion was little more than a modernisation strategy, and more attention should be paid to the kind of education people received.

Table 3.1 Commonwealth grants to private schools 1968–69 to 1972–73, constant 1984–85 prices

	Science laboratories* $m	School libraries* $m	Per capita grants $m	Schools in ACT and NT $m	All programs $m
1968–69	52.0	7.5	–	4.4	63.9
1969–70	54.7	31.8	51.7	7.6	145.8
1970–71	52.8	53.6	98.0	8.9	213.3
1971–72	40.8	37.0	111.7	11.3	200.8
1972–73	34.4	33.3	140.9	11.7	220.3

* These programs were available to both private and public schools but private schools benefited disproportionately (see text). The Science Laboratories Program terminated on 30 June 1975 and the School Libraries program on 31 December 1974.
Source: CBCS, undated.

There is now a radical wing to the modernisation trend which at times goes beyond modernisation: I refer to teachers and some other educationists who, while actively dismantling the old central system of bureaucratic regulation, external examinations and inspectorial systems, have gone ahead to produce the beginnings of a different kind of education (White 1972: 239–240).

The radical egalitarians worked from the notion of equality of respect for all persons as worthwhile in themselves. This was incompatible with all forms of competition and positional ranking, including the formal grading and selection of students for university entrance. Whereas equality of opportunity drew attention to the social structures in which people enjoyed status, prestige and economic rewards, equality of respect considered people independently of those goods and their distribution. 'It is arguable that the principle of equality of opportunity (as opposed to equality of respect) rests on an abstract conception of the "individual" whose opportunities are to be equalised, imputing to them a certain range of self-interested and competitive wants and interests' (Lukes 1973: 125–127). Equality of opportunity assumed that people were driven by egoism and material goals. Equality of respect rested as much on fraternity as on liberty. The goal of a fair competition became less important.

The Victorian Secondary Teachers Association (VSTA) secured the abolition of school inspectors, increasing the autonomy of individual schools and teachers, and pressed for reforms in certification. It received some support from Ron Reed, the director of secondary education in Victoria, who envisaged secondary school as 'a non-competitive, non-selective cycle, to be completed by the near totality of young people'. VSTA leader Bill Hannan argued in 1970 that 'competitive education is a contradiction in terms'. People should not have to compete for the right to know, which should be universal. Knowledge advanced because people shared it (Hannan 1985: 92, 151–154, 167–179).

> It may well be a fact that a competitive system requires an artificial incentive. It is not, however, an established fact that in order to work, people need the incentive of competition. To advocate competition as a necessary incentive is simply to draw a vicious circle, in which the alleged incentive eventually becomes the purpose (Hannan 1985: 176).

In the circumstances this was a powerful philosophy, the more so because the struggles for equality of opportunity provided the radical position with a continuing source of recruits. As practical politics, radical egalitarianism was less effective. Dreams of upward mobility continued, even among some militant teachers: it was hard to sustain anti-competition as either personal lifestyle or collective goal. Nevertheless, in Victoria a minority of government high schools developed an alternative curriculum and alternative credential at year 12 stage. In 1972 the VSTA put forward a proposal for a ballot in place of the existing mechanisms of tertiary selection.

The ballot threatened to overturn the very systems of competition and merit. Hannan argued in 1972 that: 'A democracy must be committed to universal education ... "ability" very often means simply affluence, race or social class. When we want to select, we must have a more neutral device than "ability" measurement. A ballot, or some variant of random selection, is such a neutral device.' He saw the ballot as a temporary step until universal access to higher education was achieved, although it might continue to be useful for selection into 'a few essential but very expensive kinds of training' (Hannan 1985: 56–58). The proposal generated furious resentment in conservative educational circles; but little popular support was evident, and there was dissent inside the VSTA.

Thus the goals of the radical egalitarian reformers remained distant and were never translated into actual government programs. Yet they gathered enough support to fire the later conservative campaigns in schooling, about standards and control, and they uncovered flaws in the practice of equality of opportunity itself. The presence of selective private schools undermined even the modest versions of educational equality. Equality of opportunity required a universal approach, but its educational technologies were only applied systematically to those institutions directly controlled by the state: government schools, but not the private schools and not the universities. 'The meritocratic and scientific appearance of educational participation was in contrast to the apparently spontaneous gathering of merit within the social world of the private grammar schools' (McCallum 1990: xv, 59). Fairness was never established. Wilenski later concluded that to lift the educational level of all the disadvantaged, Labor would have needed to restructure the entire schooling system by abolishing the distinction between public schools, Catholic schools and independent schools, mixing all the students in common comprehensive institutions. 'Obviously this would have directly challenged one of the support systems of the existing power structure in Australian society and would have been strongly resisted' (Wilenski 1983a: 45). Even in that setting, where merit would be at its zenith, the project of separating individual characteristics from their social setting was bound to be defeated. The characteristics of the strongest groups would continue to prevail. Only the abolition of positional competition in education could have secured equality of outcomes by social group.

The Karmel report's construction of equality

Some government policy statements have effects. Governmental prob-lems are not given but need to be constructed, and in such a way the official agenda appears as self-evident and the intervention of govern-ment a reluctant necessity (Beilharz 1987). The languages of policy, and the knowledges constituted in policy statements, define the posi-tivity of government and limit what is 'sayable' on the terrain of its operation. In this manner the political and economic concerns of gov-ernment and business are brought into conjunction with program administration and its techniques for governing the citizen–subject. Government political discourse is also more than rhetoric. 'It should be seen, rather, as a kind of intellectual machinery or apparatus for rendering reality thinkable in such a way that is amenable to political deliberations' (Rose 1993: 289).

> All government depends on a particular mode of 'representation': the elab-oration of a language for depicting the domain in question that claims both to grasp the nature of the reality represented, and literally to represent it in a form amenable to political deliberation, argument and scheming . . . Language here serves as a *translation mechanism* between the general and the particular, establishing a kind of identity or mutuality between political rationalities and regulatory aspirations. . . . Language, that is to say, provides a mechanism for rendering reality amenable to certain kinds of action (Miller & Rose 1990: 6–7).

While some policy statements are marginal to government programs others can be very important. The report of the Whitlam appointed Interim Committee for the Schools Commission (Karmel 1973) was the most influential of all the education reports in the postwar period, and the massive funding increases which followed its release were the high-water mark of equality of opportunity policies in Australian education. The report established a common resource standard in schooling, fixed well above the levels of funding then prevailing in the government and Catholic school systems. This common standard promised to provide a fairer educational competition, as well as a better quality education and more generous opportunities for all. The Karmel committee connected to the radical egalitarian and progressivist values of the time, such as redistribution and positive discrimination, devolution, self-determin-ation, and equality of respect, securing a discursive leadership among the younger generation of teachers – although it reworked these themes away from any system-level confrontation with positional inequalities and governmental authority. In its refusal of vocational

values and consequences, in the absence of references to national economic goals, the Karmel committee fixed its star above a policy land-
scape very different to what followed. Yet the report also signified the
limits in equality of opportunity programs. It drew those limits explicitly, and it laid the groundwork for the redefinition of equality programs that later followed.

The Karmel committee referred to the classical indicator of equality of opportunity – the same average level of achievement in each
social group, so that education no longer reproduced social inequalities. The committee also understood equality of opportunity to mean
an equal starting point in the educational 'race'. The question to be
determined was whether schooling programs should set out to equalise all of the conditions governing student achievement and if not,
which factors would receive governmental attention. In the outcome,
the report focused only on selected economic conditions. The
Karmel committee's main objective was to secure equal in-school economic resources for every child, taking both private and public
resources into account. Here the committee moved away from the
Commonwealth's previous notion of equal government grants per
child, a basic entitlement to be supplemented by school communities' own private efforts. It preferred what was known as the 'needs'
approach. It supported positive discrimination in favour of schools
classified 'disadvantaged', establishing what became the long running
Disadvantaged Schools program; and urged the withdrawal of Commonwealth funding from the wealthiest private schools (the committee's proposal for redistribution). It applied a common resource
audit in which all schools were treated alike, whether government,
Catholic systemic or independent private.

Recognising as it did that schools were more or less powerful as
attractors of resources, the Karmel formula 'equalised the schools, from
the point of view of their consumption of resources . . . To many contemporaries this seemed a very just approach' (Fomin & Teese 1981:
191). As it turned out, the withdrawal of funding from a small number
of wealthy private schools was defeated in the Senate and Karmel
resource equality was never fully implemented. But if the committee's
whole policy had been adopted, students would have still been unequal
with other students, and schools unequal with other schools. Even to
equalise measured economic resources per child, the committee would
have needed to prohibit resource provision above the common standard, and include home-based resources; and there were other, less
tangible factors that contributed to differentiation of student success,
including family and community attitudes to education; language;
gender; not to mention the culturally specific character of the

curriculum, favouring some groups above others; and the washback into education from segmentation and hierarchy in the labour markets and professions.

The committee avoided this broader, more dangerous policy terrain by refusing the fuller implications of the objective of equality of outcomes by social group.

> It is almost certainly the case that schools alone cannot effect the degree of environmental change necessary to enable all groups of children to reach an equal *average* level of educational attainment . . . Such a position goes considerably beyond that envisaged in the attempt to make environmental influences more equal, an attempt which might still result in unequal outcomes between social groups . . . The doctrinaire pursuit of equal average outcomes for all social groups could be so expensive as to be unacceptable in terms of alternatives foregone . . . A further danger is that outcomes might be obtained by retarding the most academically able in order to reduce the range of difference (Karmel 1973: 22–23).

Even within the limits of the committee's definition of equal starting points, there was an internal flaw: the same amounts of additional government money had different meanings in different school contexts: the additional monies helped the government schools, but they did more than that for the private schools, they enabled the Catholic schools to survive, and the elite private schools to flourish, providing a powerful counter-model to the strategy of equality of opportunity through a system of comprehensive government schooling. The Karmel committee 'extended equality to the sector generating inequality' (Fomin & Teese 1981: 190); and the committee went further, highlighting the resource concentration and by implication, high quality of the leading private schools, describing them as worthy of imitation by all schools (Karmel 1973: 12).

By normalising the selective schools – so strengthening their competitive position at a key moment of education policy making – the committee undermined its own modest and contradictory reading of equality of opportunity. Not only was the system of positional domination to remain untouched, it was explicitly confirmed. Consistent with this, the committee signalled a desire to jettison the meritocratic project. It agreed that 'equality of opportunity as it has been interpreted in Australia has emphasised methods of selecting educational elites in ways presumed to be objective and fair'. But it wanted to work away from this question of composition of the elite. A focus on equality of outcomes was deficient, it stated, because 'it admits only one criterion of excellence – an academic one – and assumes that everyone should value the same thing'.

In a remarkable passage the Karmel committee used concepts of diversity, participation and personal growth to deflect concerns about unequal power and wealth and undermine the politics of redistribution. By asserting the equal worth of all human circumstances it adapted to prior social inequalities and abandoned the classical equality of opportunity project.

> The school does not exist to grade students for employers or for institutes of higher learning. Nor should it regard higher education as the only avenue to a life of dignity and worth. . . . An equal valuing of people based on their common humanity might lead to quite different interpretation of equality of opportunity. Such an interpretation would emphasise the right of every child to assistance in developing a variety of socially desirable attributes which might both afford him personal satisfaction and contribute to an improved quality of community and cultural life. To be able to relate to others, to enjoy the arts both as a participant and as a patron, to acquire physical grace and to exercise developed mental powers in all aspects of living might be valued as means to a more generous and fulfilling life. The cash returns to these attributes and the access they give to power would then become an incidental rather than a determining reason for valuing them (Karmel 1973: 23–24).

The committee's egalitarian alternative to positional competition was not the deconstruction of advantage, but its oblivion; in the flowering of a hedonistic, cultivated individuality, amid a cultural pluralism somehow floating free of relations of power. In this late Keynesian celebration of individual lifestyles, financed by government, there was a strange statist echo of the counter-culture. Yet in calling up the counter-culture the Karmel report uncoupled itself from the radical associations of equality politics. For example it avoided altogether the thorny question of selection and exclusion in the upper reaches of schooling. The subsequent triennial report of the Schools Commission followed a similar persuasion. The criteria of instrumental outcomes, places in higher education and the labour market; and the comparisons between individual and group success, should be set aside, the Commission stated in 1975. Schooling was important in its own right, and everyone could succeed within it. 'Schooling is not a race; its major objective is not to identify winners and losers, but to give maximum assistance to all young people growing up' (SC 1975: 7).

In an insightful early response to the 1973 report, titled *Create your own compliance*, White comments that 'the Karmel report plays down the talent selection and upward social mobility aspects of education, without abolishing them. Equality is now seen as equality of diversity . . . equality comes across not as a right to obtain resources, or access to power, or to socially favoured jobs. Equality is access to enjoyment and participation' (White 1973: 43–44).

The competent citizen

The Karmel report sought to rework not only the resourcing of schools within a national system of schools, but the behaviour of parents, and the character of school communities. Here the deliberations of the Karmel committee intersected with the radical campaigns for school-based decision making, and the growing politicisation of the parent groups, but it sought to relocate local educational radicalism in a larger reconstruction of the government of state education, in which the external regulation of schools by centralised government departments would be partly replaced by self-regulation. The report argued vigorously for self-governing schools that responded directly to their parents and school communities. It favoured 'less rather than more centralised control' over schools. It believed in a 'grass-roots approach'. Responsibility should be devolved as far as practicable to educators, in consultation with parents. 'The openness of the school to parents is a means both of extending its educational influence and of reinforcing pupil motivation', it stated. 'As responsibility moves downward, the professionals in schools must expect to share planning and control with parents and interested citizens, safeguarded by limitations where professional expertise is involved.'

Equality, diversity, participation and local identity were meshed together. Here equal rights were to be achieved through a process of participation and self-determination in which all choosing subjects, and all of their choices, were on an equivalent plane. 'Better ways will not necessarily be the same for all children or for all teachers. This is an important reason for bringing responsibility back into the school and for allowing it to be exercised in ways which enable a hundred flowers to bloom rather than to wither' stated the Karmel committee, echoing the Maoist terminology then fashionable among teachers. The Priorities Review Staff emphasised the Karmel committee's focuses on innovation, diversity and the decentralisation of decision making, which 'should, if successful, cause substantial improvements in the quality of education', it stated (PRS 1973: 11).

The fact that choices might involve the vertical ranking of schools, with unequal implications for the social value given to different students' education, was avoided. But the Karmel committee was unabashed in valuing the free initiative, variation and responsiveness it saw as characteristic of private schooling (Karmel 1973: 10–14; Matthews & Fitzgerald 1975: 32). The 1978 report of the Schools

Commission took the arguments further. 'Each school needs to make its own adaptation to its particular community; it needs to be free to do so and encouraged to do so'. Significantly, the report added that 'devolution of financial responsibility is crucial to real devolution' (SC 1978: 7–11, 118).

The Karmel report's emphases on participation, inclusiveness and devolution were a sign of governmental things to come; in which both education and social advantage ceased to be seen as caused by social structural factors, and became understood as merely individual; while equality of opportunity to rise up in the world was reduced merely to universal rights of access, measured by participation in *any* form of education or the labour markets (or life itself). White comments that 'equality had, in the late sixties and early seventies, come to have a new meaning. It had come to mean, to play an active part in the making of one's life – equality of access to decision making, equality in social relations, as well as equality of access to material resources' (White 1987: 22).

The 1975 report of the Commission saw equal rights in terms of universal rights to the acquisition of skills, including the skills of self-management and individual responsibility required to be an active citizen–worker. 'A basic plateau of competence is required by all children if they are to become full citizens able to exercise options' (SC 1975: 7). Like other notions of equality, equal rights of citizenship could take different and contrasting forms according to the context. On one hand, 'endowing children with the status of citizenship, making them full and equivalent members of a community, was a profoundly progressive recognition of a principle of equality, and one ultimately in conflict with the principles of inequality that lay at the heart of a capitalist economic system' (Rose 1990: 122–123). On the other, when citizen competence was stripped of concerns about power structures and distributional inequalities, and aligned with the requirements of employers, it no longer constituted a rallying point from which to attack the *status quo*. Here the Schools Commission kept its options open. Bartos notes that in the succeeding years it veered between the two notions of equality, one based on access, 'the extent to which different social groups had access to post-school options'; and the other based on competence, 'a number of learning outcomes which equity demanded all young people achieve' (Bartos 1993: 167–168).

The notion of equality as the right to individual competence, and access to education, rather than incomes policy or job creation, as the means to personal empowerment, was the one that became dominant. Turning students into self-regulating individuals in possession of generic skills and vocationally specific competencies was compatible with national economic policies for a higher skilled workforce and with educational equity defined in vocational terms, no longer constrained by the Karmel committee's reservations about positional competition. Social group inequalities dropped off the main agenda, except that participation rates by social group were used to measure progress towards universal participation. Group inequalities were no longer to be overcome by removing the causes in the social structure, as the earlier reformers had hoped. The solution now lay in individual recruitment into the lower positions in the education system, supported by the Karmel committee's notion of equal but different.

III. The Karmel report and private schooling

The calculation of resources

The Labor Party's commitment to 'needs based' funding of schools in all sectors, determined by their measured level of economic resources, helped it to secure victory in the 1972 elections; and Whitlam claimed the party had put the state aid debate behind it (Whitlam 1985: 297–305, 328). In the rhetoric in and around the Karmel report, the committee and Government talked of the need to open up schools, to transcend 'obsolete' differences between school sectors and between States; to consider the education of all Australian children, to assess their needs in common, and to secure the meeting of those needs for years to come (Karmel 1973: 48). The Karmel report cut across the accumulating improvisations of the earlier policies, setting the financing of private schools on a comprehensive and long-term basis. By allocating more funding all round with the greatest share going to government schools, the report normalised support for all schools in the public mind and 'solved' the political tensions engendered by state aid. For the private schools, the Karmel report completed the process begun with science grants ten years before. It enabled private schools to consolidate and strengthen, and pursue their social projects with growing success. Only in the longer term was it apparent that by reversing the growth in the public sector's share of enrolments, the committee had dealt a fatal blow to the capacity of the government systems to sustain a comprehensive role.

The heart of the report was the common system of 'needs based' resource accounting and the application of that system to all schools. All schools were described in terms of the quantity of their economic resources, as measured by past levels of operating expenditures per student, from both government and private sources. An index of socio-economic disadvantage was also applied, to enable small additional grants to the poorest schools. The committee then established common resource targets, later known as the 'Karmel targets', applying to all schools in all sectors. Its objective was to provide funding to all schools whose resources were below this designated minimum level of resources. A school's 'need' for resources was measured as the difference between its existing resources and the Karmel targets; these targets were fixed at more than one-third above average government school resources, and two-thirds above Catholic school resources.

In this manner the government and Catholic schools were locked into the Karmel settlement with the promise of successive annual increases in operating funds. There was a small number of private schools which had already achieved the committee's target resource standard, and the report recommended that for them state aid should be phased out. For the two years 1974 and 1975 the report recommended $1.16 billion for government schools and $0.45 billion for private schools, representing altogether 0.6 per cent of the Gross National Product. Because most Commonwealth funding was previously applied to the private schools, the effect was to increase government school funding by $1.0 billion, while private school funding rose by merely a net $0.13 billion (1984–85 prices, Karmel 1973: 141–145). Government schools appeared as the main immediate beneficiaries of the Karmel policies (Table 3.2).

The Karmel report's largesse concealed what were, from the viewpoint of the comprehensive government school project, significant limitations and problems. First, the data on operating resources were provided by the schools and systems themselves. The private school accounting of private resources was selective; the Karmel resource accounting was incomplete. 'While non-government schools have shown a willingness to comply with government auditing requirements, they have shown less willingness to disclose assets and private revenue' (Praetz 1983: 41). It underplayed the resources available to private schools, exaggerating their needs and artificially boosting the size of their grants. Private school assets and resources such as buildings, and properties paid for with nominal leases; government income for capital works and loans servicing; and exemptions from rate and land tax, and payroll tax were left out of the Karmel resource calculations altogether.[1] There was nothing to stop a private school running down its private income, enabling it to replace part of its tuition charges with government grants, and thus cheapening the private cost of student entry. This was to have important long-term consequences.

Table 3.2 Additional Commonwealth funding for schools as presented in the Karmel report*, two years, 1974 and 1975 current prices

Program	Government schools $m	Private schools $m	Joint programs $m	Total* $m
General recurrent funding	175.9	21.3	0	197.2
General building funding	100.0	16.0	0	116.0
Libraries	33.3	6.7	3.8	43.8
Disadvantaged schools	43.8	6.2	0	50.0
Special education	43.5	0	0	43.5
Teacher development	0	0	10.3	10.3
Special projects	0	0	6.0	6.0
Information systems	0	0	0.2	0.2
All programs	396.5	50.2	20.3	467.0

*When existing Commonwealth programs for schools were taken into account, private schools received an additional $112.1 million in recurrent funding in 1974 and 1975, plus $1.7 million for libraries and $15.7 million in general building funds. Government schools received $64.0 million more in building funds. Existing legislation provided further grants for science laboratories, libraries, and other school buildings, and programs for Aboriginal students, and English as a Second Language (Karmel 1973: 144).
Source: Karmel 1973: 141–143.

Second, the report in the main ignored its own dictum that 'more equal outcomes from schooling require unequal treatment of children' (Karmel 1973: 22). The Karmel resource accounting was premised on equality rather than positive discrimination; the special program for disadvantaged schools was relatively weak, amounting to only 9.5 per cent of the total recommended grants for 1974 and 1975; and it could scarcely compensate government school communities for imbalances in the economic resources located in the home and brought to bear on education, not to mention the inherited cultural capital of the elite families. By limiting its compass to selected school-based resources, while tolerating higher private resources in the elite schools, the Karmel strategy could only produce a slight narrowing of resource differences. The absolute resources of government schools were lifted, but their comparative position, even in economic terms, was not greatly advanced by these mechanisms.

By seeking to establish a stable settlement between the established forces, the Karmel committee ensured that the historic subordination of government schooling could not be addressed. By reducing the inherent differences between the school sectors to economic differences between individual schools, of either sector, the Karmel framework submerged the positional differentiations between government schooling, elite private schooling, and the Catholic parish schools, and the tensions between government and private schooling were suppressed from view. The system of resource accounting facilitated the myth that all schools were involved in a common task in the education of children, and differences in their social roles and clientele should be ignored. This seemed egalitarian, but it helped to legitimate those later comparisons between government schools and elite private schools which ignored differences in their tasks, in the resources of their communities and the heterogeneity of their students, so that such comparisons inevitably favoured the elite private schools. But the tasks of the schools, and thus the effects of the Karmel grants, differed by sector. Government schools carried the costs inherent in educating the whole community, and were already almost entirely dependent on public monies; and after the committee's increases, these schools remained largely dependent on State governments.

While the Karmel grants improved the absolute material standards of government schools, and strengthened their function as the apparent site of equality of opportunity, those grants did not improve the relative social role and position of government schools. Not so the grants to private schools. The whole private sector was re-energised by the Karmel settlement, and elevated *vis-à-vis* the government sector.

The private schools after Karmel

The leading independent schools had an old claim to be 'public' schools (a descriptor used in both Britain and some of the Australian states), dignifying their projects of cultural maintenance, educational excellence and training for positions of leadership as a kind of public favour, a service to Australian history and social destiny. The elite schools believed that those projects required the fullest independence from government controls; they were 'public' in their claims for finance and prestige, but 'private' in the face of broader obligations and democratic pressures. In 1973 the contemporary support for equality of opportunity presented these schools with a credibility problem. Here the Karmel report's system of common resource accounting, placing them on the same plane as other schools, allowed them to be democratised in appearance without democratising in substance.

> The solution to the problem of the continued viability of the private school, and with it the direct, almost domestic system of reproduction which it supplied to its clientele, lay in appropriating not only public funds, but a distinctive identity as a public institution, the maintenance of whose distinctiveness in some way became a public duty not a private cost (Fomin & Teese 1981: 185).

The proposal to phase out funding of the wealthiest private schools suggested that it was the elite schools that were the chief losers in the Karmel settlement, and so it was stated in the debates of the day. Not so. Towards these schools the report was almost entirely positive. It did not decry the concentration of private effort in those schools, still less their social project of elite formation and reproduction, and stopped short only at public subsidisation above its chosen threshold. Even this excluded only a handful of the wealthiest schools. In a report permeated by discussion of equality, the elite schools' dominance of senior secondary prizes, of the most favoured university courses, and of access to the professions, was not a problem. Their own influence in the framing of the academic competition, from which they derived such prestige, simply passed without comment. The Karmel report established a framework in which the material privileges of the elite schools and, by implication, their traditional status, could appear as socially neutral and within the reach of all schools. These schools were presented as exemplary, worthy of imitation by all other schools. 'The committee . . . appreciates the high standards which some non government schools have reached often after years of effort. Ideally the committee would like to see all schools raise to this high standard' (Karmel 1973: 12). There was little prospect that the playing fields, swimming pools, orchestras or language laboratories of the great private schools could somehow become common to all schools; and no prospect whatsoever that the positional status conferred by these schools could become general, whether by dint of educational effort, good management, or community sacrifice. The report's notion of the private schools as the site of innovation and choice further valorised them as 'public' goods.

> The representation of the private schools as an 'alternative' system within a broader system, and thus, potentially, as a site of free initiative, variation and responsiveness, was to prove in the future a very advantageous definition, under whose aspect government schools would necessarily appear drab, uniform and unresponsive (Fomin & Teese 1981: 187).

Thus the Karmel report freed the elite schools to pursue the private interests of their communities, under government cover and without interference. When the conservative party majority, by threatening to block the Schools Commission legislation in the Senate, forced the restoration of the base grant received by the 'category A' schools, this again underlined their national prestige and educational value, even while restoring the older, universal form of state aid. If this development sat uneasily with the needs policy, it did not undermine the structures set up to administer that policy; still less the main premise of the Karmel settlement: Commonwealth financing for both wings of the dual system of schooling.

In the Catholic schools the Karmel grants were crucial to survival and restoration. But these grants also carried the seeds of future growth and development, in both the Catholic systems and the other non-elite schools. The effects of the post-Karmel increase in per capita grants to schools, combined with the 1974–75 decision to replace tax concessions for school fees with a tax rebate at a lower level, was 'to produce a massive shift in government subsidies from the household to the school'. This reduced the private capacity to pay for the more expensive forms of private education, but enabled expansion in the number of private school places, and the cheapening of their private cost (Williams 1984). The committee was little concerned as to where this might lead. Policies that were primarily intended for the renovation of the Catholic schools were to be used by the Seventh-day Adventists and the Lutherans to set up school systems of their own. This open-ended tolerance of growth ensured that in future the proportion of government funds going to the private sector would expand, and government schools would face increasing pressure from a growing range of low cost alternatives. The committee set no limits on private sector expansion. It believed aggregate private school enrolments should be raised to the 1972 level, through 'new and expanded non-government schools', but gave little thought to how enrolments would be stabilised at the point.

> In the absence of any directive from the Government on the degree to which grants ought to be provided for the expansion of the non-government sector, the committee has taken the view that it would be reasonable to make funds available to enable the non-government school sector to maintain its share of enrolments at the level existing in 1972. Any variation from this position would, in the committee's view, require a policy decision on the part of the Australian Government (Karmel 1973: 78).

For any government to prescribe a particular distribution of enrolments was to direct the 'free choices' of self-regulating private individuals in an overt manner, and to politicise the very question of the relation between the sectors which the Karmel report was meant to bury. Not surprisingly, no such 'policy decision' was made, and future enrolment shares were determined *de facto* rather than *de jure*. But the committee showed little concern about the possible consequences of private school expansion. Once, briefly, it acknowledged the dynamics of the dual system:

> 2.13 There is a point beyond which it is not possible to consider policies relating to the private sector without taking into account their possible effects on the public sector whose strength and representativeness should not be diluted. The uncoordinated expansion of the private sector could lead to a wasteful duplication of resources (Karmel 1973: 12).

Here again the issue was evaded: by definition, an expansion already sanctioned within the report could not be described as 'uncontrolled'. And immediately, the report took a contrary tack. The concerns about waste, duplication and the erosion of government schools were sublimated into a vision of the 'drawing together' of private and government schools in a new integrated system, in which all schools would be autonomous and equal in diversity; a vision in which the tensions in the dual system would disappear: a vision premised on the further extension of state aid, to full funding and the reconciliation of private schooling with free state education.

> As public aid for non-government schools rise, the possibility and even the inevitability of a changed relationship between government and non-government schooling presents itself. The level of resources in all schools having access to public funds would be determined on essentially common criteria. Moreover, as an aspect of the accountability which must be a feature of aid, the standards of non-government schools will come under public scrutiny and the levels of aid related to those standards will bring about a position where the role of fees in the financing of schools will have to be re-examined . . .

> 2.14 The committee sees positive advantages in this drawing together of the public and private sectors, based, hopefully, on a greater degree of independence in government schools and not on a decrease in the independence now open to schools outside the government systems. . . . the committee recommends the joint planning and operation of facilities by people engaged in schooling in an area, whether they be in government or non-government schools. Such developments when taken together with changed patterns of funding open up the possibility of the eventual development of a school system itself diverse, where all schools supported by public money can operate without charging fees (Karmel 1973: 12–13).

With this utopia on the boardroom wall, as it were, it was easier for the different members of the post-Karmel Schools Commission, drawn from the various private and government system interests, to sit comfortably at the table with each other. 'The Commission early recognised that little would be accomplished if serious efforts were not made to develop policy positions which would be acceptable to all members of the Commission' (McKinnon 1982: 139). For the rest of the 1970s the Commission was to flirt with the integration of government and private schools, without any real encouragement from the Catholic bishops, and less from the headmasters' conference; and without securing any real increase in the public obligations of private schools such as some open enrolments, or public representatives on governing bodies. Nonetheless, the Commission could justify to itself any and every increase in private school subsidisation, not only as a matter of right, but as an advance towards its own imaginary of an enlarged, loosely integrated and consensual public system, a system that never developed.

Effects of the Karmel settlement

The Karmel report's vision was positive sum, in that by educating all individuals to the fullest possible extent, the contribution of each to the nation would be enhanced. Yet by sidestepping the nature of the dual system, it laid the basis for the relative strengthening of the middle and upper echelons of the positional structure of schooling, the future subordination of the mass of students in government schools, and the weakening of the comprehensive public education project. Three years later the Commonwealth report on *Poverty and education in Australia* (Fitzgerald 1976) was to describe the dual system of schooling as the medium whereby those educational disadvantages based on social class were perpetuated. But while it would have been politically almost impossible to abolish state aid, the Karmel committee and the Labor Government *did* have choices other than those they took. Given the weak resource position of most private schools, the Commonwealth was in a strong bargaining position. As the later Schools Commission chair, Keri McKinnon, put it: 'without doubt, the non-government system, within a year or two, would have been in a state of collapse had the funding not come' (McKinnon 1981). The Government might have limited private sector growth. It might have obliged private schools receiving aid to become more socially comprehensive and financially accountable. It might even have made entry into the government system a longer term condition of continued funding. McKinnon later stated that in 1974 the Commission could have insisted on 'substantial administrative controls', but it 'sought to avoid unnecessary restrictions or conditions' (McKinnon 1982: 144).[2]

The Schools Commission and the Karmel policy framework were maintained by the Fraser coalition Government of 1975 to 1983. Where it innovated, the Fraser regime did so within the logic of the Karmel mechanisms. In 1976 it reintroduced the automatic linkage between Commonwealth grants to private schools and the level of State spending on government schools. From 1977 to 1981 there were three successive increases in the proportion of government school costs on to the private sector. The number of categories of private school were collapsed from eight to three. While making these changes the Fraser Government increased the per capita grants received by the most affluent schools by 144.9 per cent at primary and 160.2 per cent at secondary level. The Catholic systems received increases of 66.3 per cent (primary) and 65.9 per cent (secondary). Between 1975–76 and 1982–83, Commonwealth funding of government schools fell by 18.9 per cent in real terms, but funding of private schools rose by 100.3 per cent. It was the fastest growing area of all Commonwealth spending (Table 3.3).

Within the 'needs' based assessment established by the Karmel committee, schools learned to manipulate their entitlements by placing part of their income in separate funds outside the needs assessment; allowing private income in the form of fees and contributed services from religious orders to decline; channelling part of the additional money into school or school system expansion rather than per capita resource improvement. In the outcome private schools expanded the number of places and improved the quality of education at the same time, and still increased their level of government funding. Remarkably, despite the growth in Commonwealth allocations to private schools, the 'needs

Table 3.3 Commonwealth spending on private schools 1975–76 to 1982–83, constant 1984–85 prices

	$m	%
1975–76	354.8	–
1976–77	401.2	+13.1
1977–78	435.9	+ 8.6
1978–79	466.3	+ 7.0
1979–80	469.8	+ 0.8
1980–81	526.1	+12.0
1981–82	612.1	+16.3
1982–83	710.8	+16.1
change between 1975–76 & 1982–83	+ 356.0	+100.3

Source: CB papers.

gap' between government and private schools actually *increased*, providing a continuing argument for funding increases. In 1974 the measured average recurrent expenditure per Catholic primary school student was 80.8 per cent of average recurrent expenditure per student in government schools. By 1981 this proportion had fallen to only 71.5 per cent (CSC 1984: 132–133).

The late Keynesian dynamics of funding growth and expanding provision survived in policy on private schools long after austerity had come to other sectors of education. The rapid growth of funding continued into the mid-1980s, driven by electoral politics and facilitated by public officials often compliant with the demands of the private school supporters. Unlike most OECD countries, a majority of the decision makers influential in public education – politicians, businessmen, bureaucrats, academics – educated their children outside the state system and had nothing invested in it. By 1982–83, the last Fraser budget, the private schools were receiving 49.2 per cent of all Commonwealth grants to schools although they educated only 24.1 per cent of students. The number of new private schools was rapidly increasing – subsidised by a generous Commission policy in which any and every private choice of school was funded at government expense – and the private sector's share of total school enrolments was rising. From a highpoint of 78.9 per cent in 1977 the government sector's share dropped to 75.6 per cent in 1983. By 1990 it had reached 72.1 per cent.

The Karmel report was notable not only for its innovations but for its continuities. The committee repeatedly presented its report as a departure from past policies. As a Labor Party initiative it probably handed more money to government schools than a conservative government would have. But the States were the main financiers of the government sector. It was the private sector where the Commonwealth's role had always been instrumental, and decisive. Here the report was in continuity with Commonwealth policies since 1951. It locked the Government into a long-term commitment to the satisfaction of private 'needs' and 'choices'. By attempting to remove funds from the elite schools, it became partner to the government school supporters, sharing with them an egalitarian project. Yet the private sector was the ultimate beneficiary of the Karmel report. What appeared as the committee's partial negation of state aid was actually its consolidation and reaffirmation, on a grander plane. If the government–private division had once appeared a barrier to modernisation by precluding the education of the mass of the people, it seemed this was no longer the case. But the price of a dual government and private system of schooling, in which social support was shifting to the private side of the system, a shift underwritten by government funding, was market segmentation and growing inequality.

It was never officially admitted, but it was becoming apparent to all, that in schooling some forms of citizenship were more equal than others. Beneath the rubric of equal but different choices, scripted so well in the Karmel report, the private schools steadily elevated their margin of social superiority. The differentiation of citizenship-information, whereby the products of schooling were ranked in a hierarchy at the point of entry into higher education and the labour markets, was well fitted to the more competitive era that followed the Karmel report, and the more individualistic values that guided post-Whitlam public policy.

Notes

[1] Similarly, in Britain there was a 'large number of indirect subsidies going to private schools'. Their charitable status provided 'exemption from income tax, corporation tax, capital gains tax'; and they received a 50 per cent rate reduction and other benefits (Blaug 1981: 33–35).

[2] In 1987, reviewing the private–government schooling debate, Karmel stated that since private schools received government funds, they should become more accountable. Private schools were not necessarily better. However, his own children had attended private schools. 'We said, "We won't sacrifice our kids to our principles". But if all the well-motivated people did it, it would leave a residue in the government system'. He sighs. "I guess that doesn't say much for our principles" '. Karmel stated that in his view the tensions in the dual system were insoluble (Button 1987).

PART II

THE ANTI-CITIZEN 1975–1990

'It is not individuals who are set free by free
competition; it is, rather, capital which is set free.'

Karl Marx, Grundrisse,
Penguin, Harmondsworth, 1973 (1857–1858), p. 650.

In 1975 Keynesian economic management collapsed, and the broadening of citizenship through public programs began to fall away. Given that citizenship had been identified with the extension of careers and consumption it was probably inevitable that when growth and full employment faltered and opportunities dried up, social competition would increase and solidarity would decline. This was fertile ground for the market liberal economists in the New Right such as Hayek and Friedman. The agenda of government was reset (chapters 4 and 5). At the high point of the 'anti-citizen' in the second half of the 1980s greed was good, government was corporatised, the public interest had become the global economic market, and official support for the education programs of the 1970s had begun to collapse (chapter 6).

CHAPTER 4

The New Right and public policy

'Once the principle is admitted that the government
undertakes responsibility for the status and position of
particular groups, it is inevitable that this control will be
extended to satisfy the aspirations and prejudices of the
great masses. . . . in the existing state of public opinion
nothing else would be practicable. But what to the
politicians are fixed limits of practicability imposed by
public opinion need not be similar limits to us. Public
opinion on these matters is the work of men like
ourselves. . . .'

> *F.A. Hayek, speaking at the founding conference of the New
> Right at Mont Pelerin, Switzerland, in 1947, reproduced in F.A.
> Hayek,* Individualism and economic order, *University of
> Chicago Press, Chicago, 1948, pp. 107–108.*

Prelude: A sudden discontinuity in government (1975)

Keynesian policies postponed recession rather than abolishing it. In the
second half of the 1960s in the developed world, the rate of industrial
profit began to fall (Mandel 1978), and 1974 and 1975 saw the first
common international recession since the 1930s. Production, investment and employment collapsed. Inflation climbed, ruling out the
Keynesian solution of using public spending to reflate the economy.
The United States' real GDP fell by 0.5 per cent in 1974 and 1.3 per
cent in 1975. As Table 4.1 shows, in Australia growth slowed rather
than fell, but inflation was above the OECD average.

The Australian Government's first response was to reaffirm Keynesian economic strategies. In the 1974–75 budget many new Labor programs were introduced and outlays rose by 19.9 per cent in real terms,
the largest increase since the war. The Commonwealth budget deficit
was 3.8 per cent of GDP. 'The expansion in the public sector contained
in this budget is designed to take up the slack emerging in the private

Table 4.1 Key economic indicators, Australia and OECD, 1971 to 1977

Growth since previous year:	1971	1972	1973	1974	1975	1976	1977
	%	%	%	%	%	%	%
Australia GDP	5.0	3.4	5.6	1.9	1.8	4.0	0.9
Capital formation	7.0	−1.5	4.8	−3.1	−0.6	4.4	−0.9
Employment	2.4	1.4	2.8	2.1	−0.4	1.4	0.9
Consumer prices	7.2	6.0	8.4	16.2	17.9	14.6	10.3
All OECD GDP	3.5	5.4	6.0	0.8	−0.1	4.6	3.8
Capital formation	5.2	7.6	8.2	−4.8	−6.0	4.7	6.3
Employment	0.5	1.3	2.2	1.1	−0.7	1.3	1.6
Consumer prices	5.8	5.4	8.3	14.1	10.9	8.8	8.5

Source: OECD 1991: 191–207.

sector', said the 1974 budget speech. In the next twelve months unemployment worsened. This would normally have required another fiscal stimulus. But instead, the norms of economic policy themselves were altered. The monetarist assumptions popularised by Milton Friedman and F.A. Hayek replaced Keynesianism (see below). In the 1975–76 budget further planned new programs were abandoned and outlays grew by only 5.1 per cent. The new Treasurer, Bill Hayden, said the public sector was 'crowding out' the private sector.

> We expect that as the expansion of public sector activity is restrained, the opportunities for private sector expansion will improve . . . We are no longer operating in that simple Keynesian world in which some reduction in employment could, apparently, always be purchased at the cost of more inflation. Today it is inflation itself which is the central policy problem. More inflation simply leads to more employment (CBP 1975).

Commonwealth spending on schools and higher education was frozen, triennial budget commitments were suspended, the trend to universal pre-school was halted and the planned open university never began. In most other OECD countries, too, governments halted or reversed the growth of expenditure, taxation and deficits. By the late 1970s views about the public sector had changed, and the concentration of resources in a sector not subject to market forces came to be seen as harmful to efficiency (chapters 4 and 5). This was becoming translated into a radically different policy discourse in education (chapter 6). The emergency measures of 1975 had become the cornerstone of a new era.

I. The change in the policy framework

Monetarism and markets

Monetarism was little known outside the economic journals until the beginning of the 1970s, when it began to emerge as a strategic alternative to Keynesian economic management. The monetarists believed inflation could be controlled by limiting the sources of monetary growth, including wage increases and the public sector borrowing requirement (PSBR). Unlike neo-classical economics, monetarism shared with Keynesianism an interest in the manipulation of economic aggregates, but its implications were different from Keynesianism. The Keynesians had failed to account for the effects of government financing. Monetarists argued that higher public output absorbed physical resources needed by the private sector, and higher public borrowings caused interest rates to rise, choking off private borrowings, investment and production. This brought reduction of the budget deficit to centre stage, either through reduced expenditure, or increased taxation. Monetarism stressed the need to reduce social spending.

The monetarists also argued the economy was not as controllable as the Keynesians had believed. There was a 'natural' rate of unemployment which could only be reduced by distorting 'natural' market forces, with dire effects (Heald 1983: 33–55). This knocked away another prop of the Keynesian programs. It also foreshadowed a future role for education as a substitute for employment: the goal of 'full education' would come to replace full employment.

Monetarism was eventually discarded. After the institution of floating exchange rates it became impossible to track the national money supply, and even before that, the manipulation of monetary aggregates rarely had the predicted effects. Nevertheless, the importance of monetarism was not economic but political. The significance of monetarism lay in its anti-Keynesian role, in association with the emerging New Right and claims about the primacy of markets. 'Monetarism was the battering ram that made the breach' (Gamble 1986: 32–38). By explaining government intervention as the *cause* of the mid-1970s recession, rather than the solution, monetarism turned Keynesianism on its head and established a narrative foundation for the market liberal position. Milton Friedman was the leading theorist of the money supply, but along with other market liberals he now became sceptical about the efficacy of money policy alone. He began to emphasise the need for more thorough-going reforms in the economic 'fundamentals', before inflation could be eliminated (Bosanquet 1983: 52–58).

To market liberals all alternatives to markets were flawed, particularly non-market programs in the public sector. In an influential series of articles in the 1975 and 1976 *Sunday Times*, Bacon and Eltis reasoned that only 'industrial' production sold in a market was productive of wealth, and the level of employment in industry determined the total level of productive activity. The relative growth of labour in the 'unproductive' non-market services was therefore responsible for Britain's economic decline. 'Growth requires that the unproductive sector be smaller so that part of the surplus of the productive sector can be invested.' Bacon and Eltis noted between 1961 and 1975 employment in education grew by 85 per cent, more than any other sector, although participation ('real outputs') increased more slowly. They recommended user charges and tighter control of expenditure (Bacon & Eltis 1978: vii–xi, 1–15, 31–32, 79, 86). Opposition leader Margaret Thatcher agreed. On 25 July 1978 she told the House of Commons that

> If our objective is to have a prosperous and expanding economy, we must recognise that high public spending, as a proportion of GDP, very quickly kills growth . . . We have to remember that governments have no money at all. Every penny they take is from the productive sector of the economy in order to transfer it to the unproductive part of it. That is one of the great causes of our problems (House of Commons 25 July 1978, in Thompson 1984: 281).

Two years later President Ronald Reagan said in his inaugural address that 'in this period, government is not the solution, it is the problem . . . It is time to check and reverse the growth of government' (Sawer 1982: 1–19). The Reagan politic combined smaller government with a renascent capitalism fed by 'supply side' economic policies. Supply siders claimed too much attention was given to restoring financial stability, and not enough to awakening enterprise. They wanted tax cuts and the deregulation of the 'obstacles' to enterprise, because taxation stifled entrepreneurial initiative and worsened inflation. Supply side economics required still deeper cuts in spending, and the creation of markets and an enterprise culture.

Thatcherism and Reaganism completed the transition to the new era. These were governments led by market liberals and conservatives. Aspects of the Keynesian programs survived, but they were dominated, and partly absorbed, by newer practices under the sign of the New Right. Slowly at first, and then with gathering speed, the relations between citizens and government, and the relations between citizens, began to alter.

Explanations for the change

In 1975 and after, Keynesian policies were abandoned and replaced by new policies shaped by market liberalism, and the character of government programs began to change. A little before, in the the intellectual discipline of economics, Keynesian economics in universities and government was displaced by market liberalism. What are the explanations for this great change, both sudden and profound, whose effects are still being felt?

In the early 1970s the conditions that sustained Keynesian government were disappearing. Keynesian economic management could only be practised on a national scale within an international economy in which the degree of openness remained limited, and fixed exchange rates set the limits within which domestic economic activity could fluctuate. The collapse of the Bretton Woods agreement on fixed exchange rates in 1971 removed the main constraint on expansion of the money supply. Countries could increase domestic demand freely, while allowing their currencies to depreciate in order to keep costs in line with their competitors, opening the prospect of unlimited inflation. Further, in the more open economic environment the multiplier effects of a public sector stimulus were liable to produce a surge in imports, rather than increased domestic production, exacerbating domestic inflation and balance of payments difficulties. Tendencies to inflation were compounded by the quadrupling of oil prices in 1973. The rate of real wage increase had peaked in the early or mid-1970s (it varied between the OECD countries), when profit margins were already narrowing.

After the effects of these changes had accumulated, the crash of 1974–1975 sent shock waves through public policy and the corporate world, and the international financial institutions (public and private) pressured every national political system, demanding the abandonment of Keynesian 'pump-priming' as a policy tool. At the same time, the recession narrowed the fiscal and political margins of government. The recession increased demands on government services and transfer payments, but the tax base had declined, and business support for state expenditure slumped along with the economy. From the point of view of most business firms programs in areas such as welfare constituted unproductive consumption and a waste of social capital. The recession reduced support for programs that in normal time might have been seen as productive but made no direct contribution to wealth creation, such as vocational education.

The popular political base of Keynesian programs had also weakened. Expectations of government had climaxed in the early 1970s, but there was now a growing gap between expectations, and the capacity and willingness of both governments and taxpayers to pay. Small business had been hit by both recession and government. In the last financial year of the Whitlam Government (1975–76) the Pay As You Earn (PAYE) income tax paid by individual wage and salary earners was unchanged due to recession and unemployment, but other individual income tax, including the provisional tax paid by small business and the self-employed, rose by 16.0 per cent in real terms (CBP).

During the long boom there had been a strategic centralisation of government on grounds of economic policy. Economic growth had become the dominant indicator of national well-being, and the terrain of the 'economic' broadened to include areas once regarded as 'non-economic'. In these conditions, the changes of 1975 and after in the master discourse of economic policy were quickly generalised across all programs.

Rise of the New Right

These factors explain why Keynesianism was giving way, and why sweeping policy changes were possible, but do not explain why the new policies took the *particular* forms they did, or why the New Right had a major impact. ('New Right' is used here in the British and Australian rather than the North American sense, as a political movement uniting market liberals and mainstream political conservatives, but excluding the morally based fundamentalist conservatives concerned about issues like school prayer and abortion who are usually included in the American New Right).[1]

When the opportunity suddenly appeared in 1975, after almost three decades of patient, flexible political work the New Right organisations and supporters were ready. The New Right began at a conference organised by the economist and political philosopher F.A. Hayek at Mont Pelerin in Switzerland in 1947. The work of New Right think tanks in Britain and the United States expanded in the 1960s. Leading market liberals such as Hayek, Friedman and James Buchanan began to become recognised public figures.[2] Friedman's work had a great impact on economic policy in the early 1970s. Buchanan developed an influential economic science of politics, public choice theory.

By 1975 the intellectual leaders of the New Right had become leading critics of Keynesian orthodoxy. Friedman was the high priest of monetarism. Hayek predicted run-away inflation as early as 1959, and had long polemicised against full employment policies (Hayek 1948a; 1967c; 1978c). The New Right had both an explanation for the problems facing Keynesianism and an alternative set of policies. Most importantly, the New Right organisations and networks had by then secured broad support in business and industry, particularly the global companies, financial corporations and international regulatory institutions. Its organisations were located at points of exchange between business, the universities, the media and government, and played both expert and polemicist. The think tanks were 'a society of like-minded people reinforcing each other's pre-conceived notions and rejecting any thinking that does not fit the mould – practising what consultants call the art of "directed conclusions" ' (Desai 1994: 32).

The primary concern of the New Right was not to support one political party against another, but to reconstruct and control the terrain on which all mainstream politics took place. It directed one set of efforts to public opinion, and another to 'opinion-makers and decision-makers, newspaper editors, commentators, politicians, academics'. It was adept at both the 'grass roots' and the 'tree tops' (Carey 1987: 11–14).

The Australian New Right developed more slowly, and derived its activities from its British and American predecessors, except for a distinctive interest in industrial relations (Kelly 1992: 111–123). North Atlantic market liberalism reached economics, government and the media before the local think tanks began to work on public opinion. Friedman and Hayek played individual roles. Hayek's 1976 visit to Australia included 60 seminars, lecturing engagements and other appointments in 35 days. He was interviewed on national television and met the Prime Minister, the Deputy Prime Minister, the head of Treasury, the Chief Justice of the High Court and the major business leaders (Hayek 1979b: 1, 57–59). Friedman toured Australia in 1975 and 1981. *Free to choose* (1980) sold very well in Australia.

By the end of the 1970s the Australian New Right was playing a prominent role in public life. In a frank interview in *The Sydney Morning Herald* in 1985, Hugh Morgan, Managing Director of Western Mining Company and a board member of most Australian New Right organisations, stated that the think tanks were funded by business to control and work the political agenda. The issues he wanted on that agenda were 'the education system, the growth of the public sector, the power of the trade unions and the arbitration system' (Sheehan 1985).[3]

The shift in public policy was matched by the equally sudden changes in the discipline of economics. During the ascendency of Keynesian macro-economics, neoclassical micro-economics had survived, and the norms of perfect competition had been retained at the core of the discipline. Keynes did not challenge the goals of what he called 'classical' liberalism. His disagreement was on grounds of realism, on whether market competition could reproduce itself unaided by demand management.

But if our central controls succeed in establishing an aggregate volume of output corresponding to full employment as nearly as is practicable, the classical theory comes into its own again from this point onwards . . . there is no objection to be raised against the classical analysis of the manner in which private self-interest will determine what in particular is produced, in what proportions the factors of production will be combined to produce it, and how the value of the final product will be distributed between them' (Keynes 1936: 378–379).

There were gaps between Keynesian macro-economics and neoclassical micro-economics, creating openings for change. The achievement of the Chicago school of economists such as Friedman, and of the Austrian political economists such as Hayek was to re-knit orthodox micro-level economic analysis with liberal political economy, while jettisoning orthodox macro-economics. This enabled the market liberals to claim that 'the findings of modern positive economics provide support for free market policies' (Gamble 1986: 29–31). The outcome was a heady brand of crusading neoclassical economics, with a broad sweep similar to that of the socialist project, offering even the small local accountant a world-historical role in the defence and extension of 'the market'. Meanwhile, economic managers in government were finding points of agreement with the small accountant and her/his scepticism about Keynesian intervention. In the Australian Government the 'Treasury line' was fixed by the early 1970s: 'pervasive confidence' in the efficiency and equity of markets, opposition to direct intervention in market transactions, expenditure restraint and balanced budgets, a greater concern about inflation than unemployment (Langmore 1992; Whitwell 1990).

The emerging economic and political orthodoxy was readily translated into government policies through the lobbying and networking efforts of the large corporations. The New Right was always a formation of the business and propertied classes. Hayek stated the mission of the New Right was to be the political brains of the *bourgeoisie*, given that 'the propertied class, now almost exclusively a business· group, lacks intellectual leadership and even a coherent and defensible philosophy of life' (Hayek 1960: 128). The think tanks were sustained by corporate sponsors. In Britain, the bedrock political support for Thatcherism was in the finance sector of the City of London, and the Council of British Industry (Jessop et al 1984). The New Right advocated a set of policies closely attuned to business: it opposed unionism, supported wage cuts, and called for cuts in government programs little used by the owners and managers of the large companies. (Export-based companies had little interest even in the effects of transfer payments on domestic economic demand.)

More than that, the New Right totally supported the *status quo* in wealth and property, being opposed to any and every government-instigated redistribution, and called for the removal of all government regulations limiting business. It was the great entrepreneurs who were competitive, who played the market, who wanted to colonise and modernise the world in their own image. The universals of market liberalism were the particulars of the business class.

These same universals of market liberalism were also becoming the universals of government. In his study of management Fligstein notes:

> The relationship between the state and the large firms has generally been to serve the interests of the firms. At times, state agencies have been captured by corporate interests and policies are made for their benefit. The state can, however, act as a mediator between interests and in its own interests, and the problem of deciding what is occurring is an empirical question (Fligstein 1990: 9).

In the 1970s the large companies and governments were moving closer together. Reflecting on the Whitlam Government's period in office, Wilenski noted the leading companies retained 'a privileged position' because 'vital decisions on the size, nature, direction and location of investment (and thus on the well-being of society as a whole)' were in business hands. The small government movement was a backlash from 'powerful and privileged elements' affected by redistributive programs, or threatened by needs-based services and social equality. They wanted 'to challenge the ability or legitimacy of state activity in changing market outcomes, and to remove from the public policy agenda a range of issues as inappropriate for government intervention' (Wilenski 1982: 48). Perhaps Wilenski over-estimated the threat to property posed by Keynesian policies, but the New Right *was* responding to the 'threat', real or imagined, of the modest social ownership inherent in the mixed economy and universal welfare.

II. Government remakes itself

Competitive national economy

It was not until the reform programs of the 1980s that the full transformative potential of the new framework became clear. Strikingly, like Keynesian modernisation, New Right modernisation became advocated by governments drawn from both sides of politics: Republican or Democrat in the United States; Labor or conservative in Australia and Britain. The market liberal shaped policy agenda became common to all OECD countries, although each national government handled policy implementation according to its own political imperatives. Conservative and Republican governments were more aggressive in identifying themselves as New Right, but when the Labor governments of Australia and New Zealand were in office, and the Mitterand Socialist regime in France, they implemented similar policy settings: low inflation and the abandonment of full employment as a practical goal; financial deregulation and partial trade liberalisation; slow growth or actual reductions in the size of the public sector; the move from universal services to targeting in social policy; user pays, contracting out and other forms of marketisation, and corporate management in government.

Retreating from the late Keynesian version of citizenship as quality of life, in which the growing range of choices were underwritten by government itself, financed from taxation revenue, the post-1975 governments emphasised the market and individual effort as the primary sources of satisfaction. There were differences between the Laborist and conservative governments. In Australia the Liberal–National Party Government of 1975 to 1983 set out to weaken the role of unions and reduce real wages, while the Labor Government of 1983 to 1996 used the unions as tools for governing wage costs, training reforms and industrial militancy. There were also differences in the extent of reliance on discourses of equity in social policies, albeit fewer differences in the content of those policies. But overall, bipartisan similarities were more important than partisan differences.[4]

It was timing, not party, which ensured it was conservatism in Britain but Labor in Australia that was in office at the highpoint of New Right influence. Kelly describes Labor's adoption of the new orthodoxy, joined to its own prices and incomes policy, in the late 1970s. Whitlam's successor as ALP leader, Bill Hayden, argued that 'Labor must achieve economic management superiority over the Liberals'; and 'a successful economic policy required confidence and support from what Labor called "the big end of town" – the centres of corporate and financial power'.

Labor began to accept as the source of its economic ideas the international orthodoxy. This was represented by the treasury, the finance department and the prime minister's department in Canberra, the economics profession, and the prescriptions disseminated to industrial nations by the International Monetary Fund (IMF) and the Organisation for Economic Cooperation and Development (OECD). . . . It wanted to follow the experts and the experts were a new generation of Canberra based economists who believed in the efficiency of markets and deregulation (Kelly 1992: 23–24).

At the same time, national government was shaped by more than monetarism and market liberalism: it was also affected by the circumstances in which it found itself; by the need to provide for social order and equity in the face of unemployment, and the collapse of full-time youth labour market (which placed limits on the potential for market deregulation), and by global pressures in an increasingly crowded world economy. In Australia, exports were declining even in relation to the rest of the OECD (Table 4.2), and a sharp deterioration in mineral and agricultural prices brought on a severe balance of payments crisis in 1986.

Here the emergence of the distinctively New Right-influenced mode of government regulation was accompanied by the growing global mobility of capital. Telecommunications and air travel collapsed barriers of time and distance; and a small number of global companies achieved remarkable economic penetration and cultural integration across the world. Market liberalism rode these trends. In sharp contrast to the Keynesian years, the mainstream modernisation strategy was the borderless world market. Giddens defines globalisation as 'action at a distance' (1994: 4). Market liberals argued for maximum international exposure to facilitate global business and cultural influences ('international best practice'). The Business Council of Australia agreed: its own leading member companies were globally based: their interests transcended national GDP. In the 1980s the Labor Government in Australia became an enthusiast for this position (Kelly 1992), deregulating the exchange rate and international currency transactions; licensing foreign banks; providing greater freedom for foreign investment and foreign purchase of domestic equity; and the partial deregulation of lending and credit.

These reforms more effectively locked the Australian Government into the control systems of the global economy. For example, the

Table 4.2 Change in exports of goods and services, OECD, 1976 to 1983

Country	Change in exports in real terms, from previous year (%)							
	1976	1977	1978	1979	1980	1981	1982	1983
Australia	8.8	0.6	3.4	11.5	−1.5	−3.8	6.3	−2.4
Japan	14.5	10.5	0.0	7.6	17.1	14.2	3.9	1.8
All OECD	9.0	5.8	6.6	9.4	7.2	5.3	−1.5	0.3

Source: OECD 1991: 199.

deregulation of the exchange rate and currency dealings in 1983 transferred part of the control over fiscal policy from the national government to players in the international financial markets. The
commitment to smaller social programs and tax cuts were signifiers of
economic rationalism. Money market dealers disciplined national fiscal
policy by devaluing the Australian dollar in response to deficits or
spending considered to be 'too high'. Devaluation increased the total
cost of overseas debt repayments, and a run on the dollar threatened
a balance of payments crisis. Likewise, the international credit ratings
agencies took 'fiscal responsibility' into account when setting the risk
level of government debt. The higher the government deficit, the lower
the credit rating, and the higher the interest bill on repayments, again
increasing the deficit.

As the House of Representatives Committee on Infrastructure noted,

> If public spending is viewed unfavourably regardless of its intrinsic merit,
> increases in public borrowing may well work towards higher interest rates.
> However, lower levels of public borrowing may not lead directly to lower
> interest rates because Australian interest rates now seem to be more deter-
> mined by overseas rates plus a risk premium related to market perceptions
> of our growth and trade prospects.

Higher interest rates also increased the cost of servicing private overseas debt. 'While Australian overseas debt remains high, this country is
especially vulnerable to market opinion' (Langmore 1987: 86).

Market liberal deregulation created the very economic relationships
imagined by the theory; except that the deregulation of finance led not
to the abolition of central controls, but the replacement of government
control with control by a small number of private companies and international regulators. Globalisation weakened the capacity of national
governments to determine the *content* of national policy agendas, now
often steered from a global distance. But globalisation also empowered
national authorities, who became the interpreters of global agencies
and market requirements, and the arbiters of local reform. The two
systems of control, national and global, reinforced each other.

The Australian Government shared the OECD policy consensus that
the weaknesses of OECD countries were essentially 'structural', deriving
from deficiencies in 'the capacity of economies, institutions and societies in general to adjust to changing circumstances, to create and
exploit new opportunities, and on that basis deploy and redeploy
resources'. 'Responsiveness' and 'flexibility', speed and effectiveness in
the face of competitive pressures, became the watchwords of economic
policy; and the site of reform was moved from the macro-economic

settings on which Keynesianism relied, to the detailed micro-economic workings of production and exchange. The new strategies, hammered out in global meetings and conferences in the mid-1980s, had a considerable impact on Australia.

The OECD placed economic competition at the centre of its modernisation vision. 'Ultimately, whether firms respond to the opportunities arising from technological advance, as well as to broader changes in economic circumstances, depends largely on the intensity of competition', it stated, though it warned 'the move to a more competitive economy will not be painless, even in the context of improved economic performance – and a continuing process of adjustment involves "losers" as well as "winners"' (OECD 1987a: 37, 48).

It was believed that if the micro-economic 'impediments' to the functioning of markets could be removed, a return to sustained growth was in prospect. The capacity for economic adjustment was affected by 'the supply and allocation of the factors of production, the market for goods and services, and the taxing, spending and regulatory functions of the public sector'. The OECD emphasised changes in government and their effects on efficiency. Problems caused by government included 'the extension of spending commitments well beyond the margin provided by economic growth', and rising levels of taxation. Health, education and welfare programs had outstripped 'management capabilities'. The allocation and deployment of public sector resources had escaped 'the control of market processes'. There was a need for new cooperation between government and business; a shift in the financing of services from government to private individuals; and a change in the public/private balance of activity. Government programs needed transparency, flexibility and accountability and 'a continued search for cost efficiency in public management' (OECD 1987a: 16–45).

Structural adjustment and economic performance (OECD 1987a) also saw education as one key to improved labour productivity and technological advance, and the inculcation of flexibility, responsiveness and competitive behaviours. Chapter 7 will examine the micro-economic reform of education in greater detail.

On 25 May 1988 the Australian Government signalled the extension of micro-economic reform to the public sector and the commercialising of public enterprises. In the next decade there was a great transformation in the systems and methods of government, in which the changes brought about in the New Right era came to fruition. Government moved beyond the early emphasis on small government and the 'anti-citizen', to the reconstruction of the citizen as an *economic citizen* and the creation of a 'productive culture'.

Social policies

Esping-Andersen (1983) identifies three models of government service provision: market, residual and universal. 'Market' services are provided on full-cost basis to everyone, so that the best services are enjoyed by those with the most money. 'Residual' services are free or low cost services targeted to lower income groups unable to afford higher quality market based and often privately provided services. Residual institutions lack broad tax-payer support. 'Universal' systems in this sense are comprehensive of the whole population, providing common services of uniformly high quality, and competition between service providers (and users) is weak or non-existent. Universal services are entitlements common to all citizens: they provide both a shared form of identity and a platform on which individuals can build their separate lives. Politically, universal systems are underpinned by social solidarity, benefiting as they do from the presence of the more powerful social groups.

During the long boom in Australia the debate lay between universal and residual, and over time the universal element was enhanced. But at the special 1980 OECD conference on 'The welfare state in crisis' OECD Secretary-General, Emile van Lennep, emphasised that 'methods of achieving social objectives should not be allowed to undermine the economic system which produces the means' (OECD 1981a: 9). While social policies continued to incorporate the whole population, there was an OECD-wide movement away from universal non-market government programs, and towards targeted programs. As Beilharz notes, 'democracy is a more expensive universal than justice' (Beilharz 1989: 87, 96). The goals of abolishing poverty and maintaining full employment were abandoned as incompatible with low inflation, labour discipline and smaller government. Papadakis (1990b) describes a shift to the conception of a mixed economy of welfare based on public, voluntary, commercial and informal sectors. Policy sets varied between countries: Thatcher's Britain moved well down the New Right path, while the Scandinavian countries retained elements of universalism. Australia operated closer to the British end of the spectrum. The OECD argued for a combination of targeting and market mechanisms.

> The forces of an entrepreneurial and competitive market economy could also be put to more active use in the implementation of many social policies ... As these activities need to be conducted with maximum efficiency so as to minimise wastage of highly strained public resources, it

is sensible to consider enlisting market forces, competitive stimuli and capital market control in the provision of these services (OECD 1987a: 337–338).

Market approaches to social policy were more than an extreme form of residualisation. They were an alternative form of incorporation to that of universal services. Everyone had the right to participate in the market society, and faced the same rules. At the same time, markets required the partial suppression of social solidarity and the naturalisation of inequalities, breaking from the welfare state. The New Right critics of universal health, education, welfare and transport services, and universal transfer payments, argued that these programs constituted a regressive income transfer to affluent recipients. It was ironic that the argument against social solidarity was based on the now unfashionable egalitarianism. (The use of egalitarian logic was selective; it was never invoked against supply side tax policies that benefited the upper income groups). But this argument was important in detaching laborists and social democrats from universalism, and moving policy opinion one step further to the assertion that the state should no longer subsidise members of the community capable of paying privately. Thus policy was shifted, from redistribution to marginal welfare provision.

Here Pareto's neoclassical welfare economics provided governments with a set of policy tools which automatically excluded redistribution. Paretian welfare was defined as the welfare of individuals, rather than society, group or class. The individual was sovereign in judgements about her/his welfare; and 'if any change in the allocation of resources increases the welfare of at least one person without reducing that of any other, then the change should be considered to have increased social welfare'. An allocation of resources was Pareto optimal if no one could be made better off without making at least one person worse off. This ruled out all programs which subtracted from any one individual's welfare, thus privileging the *status quo*. Strictly, Paretian welfare economics ruled out taxation on the grounds it was coercive. 'The Pareto criterion does not sanction making the poor better off, however large the potential gain, if this also means making one rich person better off' (Heald 1983: 86, 108, 122–123). An education system with high levels of inequality might still be Pareto optimal. The Paretian criterion meant that in education, even programs to assist the disadvantaged were ruled out, unless they were *entirely ineffective* in improving the relative educational outcomes of disadvantaged students(!).

In Australia after Whitlam the main change in social programs was a widespread reversion to targeting, using income tests and sometimes asset tests. From 1978 all aged persons were subject to an income test. Facing a demographically driven increase in pension payments, the Commonwealth Government's long-term strategy was to support the development of employer/employee funded private superannuation. After 1987 family allowances were means tested. Tertiary student allowances were subject to increasingly restrictive parental and personal means tests. A range of further support was free of charge only to those who had already passed a pension means test. In some areas government support was withdrawn altogether. In children's services in 1979, the Victorian Government provided for 44.6 per cent of children in care, and the private sector 55.4 per cent. By 1986 the State cared for only 15.5 per cent, and government funding of both private and public institutions was much reduced (ACOSS 1989: 19).

In unemployment programs a common safety net was retained, but the introduction of a job search allowance in 1989 restricted unemployment benefits to teenagers, as it was subject to a parental income test for 16 and 17-year-olds (Chapman 1992: 77–78) and for some others the continued receipt of benefits was made conditional on structured training. The Government also developed wage subsidy programs, part-funded by employers, resting on the labour market itself. Thus the Government extended and intensified its management of the behaviour of unemployed people, while transferring to employers part of the responsibility for their support. The welfare role of private institutions was expanded by subsidies to private training.

The trend away from universalism led Esping-Andersen to characterise Australia as a 'liberal welfare state', 'designed to preserve and protect the labour market and the traditional norms of the work ethic', a country in which the labour market rather than the state was the basic provider (for more discussion see Castles 1985; Beilharz et al 1992). But there had also been a departure from the old model. Whereas tariff protection and industrial regulation had provided a common bulwark against fluctuations in the world market, now market essentialism and global economism were dissolving the earlier tradition. Old solidarities had fallen away. Self-reliance based on isolated individualism was on the rise.

Corporate management

In his overview of the evolution of corporate management in the twentieth century, Fligstein remarks that:

> The perspective that managers and entrepreneurs develop can be called a conception of control ... these actors want to control their internal and

external environments . . . Conceptions of control are totalising world views that cause actors to interpret every situation from a given perspective . . . At the centre of conceptions of control are simplifying assumptions about how the world is to be analysed (Fligstein 1990: 10).

Corporate management in government and in quasi-government institutions such as universities developed as a cluster of techniques in which the work of these organisations was codified as a form of economic production, and public administration was refashioned on the basis of 'leading edge' business practices, with competition, market incentives and negotiation. Centrally regulated planning, program budgeting, product definition, output measurement and cost control, were coupled to a system of local managers with operational autonomy, tethered to the centre by accountability protocols. Desired organisational achievements (targets) were specified in the form of 'product-like entities'. Often these were 'given a cost-value and placed within a real or imagined market', with a price per 'product', to be recovered by charging participants, who became defined as 'consumers'. Organisational activities were divided into programs, based on specific output targets and specific budgets (Considine 1988; 4–18). Corporate management used a number of techniques of audit and accountability: program evaluation, regular performance evaluation of individuals and departments including managers at all levels, and later, quality assurance and other forms of bench-marking. Accountability cemented the authority of managers and managerial techniques, while these techniques made aspects of work 'thinkable and calculable and thus manageable' in new ways (Townley 1993).

At the same time, these new techniques hid other aspects of the organisations from view. Considine notes that corporate management privileged relatively quantifiable activities, over more intangible activities such as staff training. More generally, it became difficult 'to discuss, plan or evaluate public sector action according to any non-economic and non-quantifiable criteria', including indicators of redistribution or other forms of equity, or to develop accountability to the 'public' (Considine 1990: 173). Corporate management facilitated accountability only to managers.

The 'public' was imagined as an economic rather than democratic identity, as a consumer, taxpayer or property holder rather than participant or citizen. For example public corporations were viewed by their managers 'from the standards of the imagined stockholder or investor wishing to maximise the market value of his or her assets' (Considine 1988: 8). Public service norms based on bureaucratic rules and procedures, and notions of service and dedication, were eclipsed. Structures based on representation or direct democracy, which might destabilise managerial control or undermine efficiency targets, were supplanted or radically reduced.

Corporate management allowed ministers, senior managers and line managers to develop more effective and detailed control within hierarchical systems, while remodelling the structures of local autonomy. The senior executive group decided what was to be produced. The standardisation of output through program budgeting and output measurement, and the integrated handling of costs and resources across the organisation, allowed priorities to be directed from the centre, so that local units conformed to the central agency worldview. Local managers were made personally liable for the achievement of program objectives, and together with their conditions of work, this tied their interests to head office. Under these conditions devolution and local autonomy could be increased, often on the basis of negotiated 'output' contracts, without forgoing centralised control over the organisation's activities. Devolution simply meant that local units were made responsible for the centrally determined outcomes. 'Devolution has been made possible by a new emphasis on aggregate financial controls and the limits within which departments operate' (OECD 1990b: 11–20). Resources could be shifted around 'without obtaining clearance from up the line', but only into 'more narrowly circumscribed areas of expenditure' (Considine 1988: 8–9, 13).

The new breed of generic managers were trained to assume management functions in a wide variety of organisations or agencies, without grounding in local histories or practices. They rejected 'the long established belief' among policy makers that public administration and market corporations followed 'substantially different logics' (Considine 1988: 7). In Pusey's sample of members of the Commonwealth senior executive service, 67 per cent considered the similarities between senior executive work in the public and private sectors were more important than the differences. Only 16 per cent agreed that 'higher administration in the public sector is fundamentally different from what business executives do' (Pusey 1991: 122). In government programs and universities, managers' pay and conditions were moved closer to business practice, including limited term contracts, incentive based recruitment and remuneration, performance management and improvement techniques. It was believed that insecurity would drive more efficient performance. Managers were subjected to simulated business indicators. Output and cost targets replaced profit targets; and systems of competition between institutions, between units of institutions, and between individual managers were developed.

The Australian Government developed a homogeneous group of managers with common techniques and outlooks modelled on those of private enterprise. Private sector management consultants were used to normalise the corporate ethos. When corporate management was extended to post-school education in the late 1980s, and then to government schooling, it was shaped by the then fashionable currents in business circles. Global business was imbued with the finance conception of efficiency, in which the firm was an asset used to obtain short-run returns and keep the stock price high. This highlighted short-run economic indicators, and immediate market judgements of competitive position (Fligstein 1990). In education, where markets were imperfect or non-existent, this created the 'need' for measures of competitive standing to fill the vacuum. Quality assurance, widely practised in business, quickly took root in education.

Marketisation

Marketisation refers to the development of market relations through privatisation and/or commercialisation. *Privatisation* involves the transfer of government enterprises, institutions or programs from government institutions to the private sector. By the second half of the 1980s in Australia there was a bipartisan consensus on the need to privatise the public airlines, communications, water, power and other utilities. *Commercialisation* means the introduction of competition and/or market exchange in publicly-owned institutions, through internal reform or by contracting out some activities to market-based providers.

While never strongly supported at the popular level, marketisation was attractive to governments. The introduction of competition strengthened efficiency pressures and management control. Consumers could be used to discipline the work of professionals, with less resistance than when control was exercised bureaucratically. Marketisation enabled governments to reduce funding without having to debate spending cuts, for example through user payments, and to introduce vertical product differentiation undercutting demands for egalitarian distribution. Whereas regulation tended to encourage the supply of high price/high quality products or services, deregulation allowed a wider range of price/service options to emerge. The onus for high quality services could be shifted from government to 'user'. More generally, by transferring activities from politics to management, market reform narrowed the scope of public policy and reduced the political pressures on governments. 'In a command system envy and dissatisfaction are directed at the rulers. In a free market system they are directed at the market' (Friedman & Friedman 1980: 27).

By deregulating and commercialising, rather than privatising, governments could re-order production without renegotiating their own authority. Thus rather than minimising government, market reform often minimised the *non-market* objectives and activities of government. The ultimate role of agitation for privatisation was often to create the discursive conditions for market reforms within government, for example in education. In government services the OECD supported some privatisation, but focused more on commercialisation:

> The best way to stimulate flexibility is to strengthen existing social programs by offering incentives that allow competition and market forces to contribute more to their efficiency . . . autonomous, medium-sized service organisations geared to economic incentives and control mechanisms could play a greater role and usefully complement the services provided by the public sector. However, the need for greater flexibility and responsiveness to changing needs must be met within the framework of existing systems, most of which are public (OECD 1987a: 321).

One way of establishing a simulated market dynamic was to use competitive bidding for production contracts, in both commercial and non-commercial services. The tendering process allowed governments to steer outputs from the distance while evading responsibility for the effects on users and employees. Another method was user payments. Here the commercial approach was incompatible with pricing systems designed to secure equality of cost or access across the whole citizenry independent of region or social group; and governments became increasingly hostile to cross-subsidisation and non-commercial objectives, especially in public utilities in electricity, gas, water, mail and telecommunications services. It was argued that equity should be pursued through targeted subsidies not prices, and that less than full cost pricing caused 'over-consumption'. Definitions of social equity and citizen right were reconstructed to fit the new policy framework. In 1987, arguing against the cross-subsidisation of telecommunications, the OECD stated that 'common sense notions of equity . . . the principle that an individual consumer should not be charged for resources that he or she has not consumed – dictate a preference for cost-based pricing' (OECD 1987a: 308–309). This was *market*-based equity.

III. Fiscal policies after 1975

Smaller government

After 1975 the New Right fiscal imperatives – minimise outlays, reduce taxation, eliminate government deficits – dominated government and public policy, though the formal objectives were rarely achieved. The New

Right treated smaller government as a universal panacea for almost every economic and social ill, although there was no empirical evidence linking the size of government to the rate of economic growth. In Australia spending, taxing and size of the government workforce were already below OECD averages (Table 4.3). Yet the 'need' to reduce spending to increase international competitiveness became a truism, indicating the success of the New Right in setting the terms of debate.

Langmore comments the Commonwealth Treasury used whatever were 'the convenient arguments of the moment' to justify cutting outlays. It was argued that public spending was inflationary; that it crowded out private investment; and that it worsened the balance of payments and increased foreign debt, although Australian government deficits and government foreign borrowings were relatively low. Langmore notes that in 1991 Australia had 'the lowest level of general government debt of any country for which the OECD publishes figures'. Australia's gross debt on general government was only 15.6 per cent of GDP, compared to 36.7 per cent in Britain, 43.9 per cent in Germany, 58.5 per cent in the USA and 63.4 per cent in Japan (Langmore 1992). Between 1975 and 1990 Australia's deficit on general government was below the OECD average in all but two years. The public sector share of foreign debt declined from 35.7 per cent in June 1980 to 26.5 per cent in December 1988 (Howard 1989; OECD 1991: 204).

The size of the deficit problem was exaggerated, by including the costs of government capital investment as a charge against current revenue, rather than the common international practice of depreciating those costs against a separate account. This created a 'restrictive bias' in fiscal policy. In the Commonwealth Treasury in the 1940s 'the practice of charging capital expenditure against current revenue, in

Table 4.3 Outlays and receipts of government as a proportion of GDP Australia and OECD, 1970 to 1990*

	Government outlays: GDP share			Government receipts: GDP share		
	Australia	OECD Europe	Total OECD	Australia	OECD Europe	Total OECD
	%	%	%	%	%	%
1970	26.8	36.6	32.3	26.6	36.6	31.1
1975	33.4	44.3	38.1	29.0	39.6	33.1
1980	31.6	44.8	37.2	30.1	41.4	34.6
1985	36.5	49.0	39.7	33.8	44.3	36.2
1990	34.8	47.6	39.2	35.3	43.9	37.1

Source: OECD 1991; 1994 update.

defiance of accounting conventions applying at that time, developed as a means of disguising budget surpluses' (Whitwell 1990). In 1983 two academics from the Brookings Institute remarked during a study of the Australian economy that the purpose of this bookkeeping manoeuvre lay in 'frightening the *bourgeoisie* by exaggerating the deficit problem' (Langmore 1987: 88–90).

Nevertheless, the fiscal imperative operated as a powerful universal. Government became less a question of providing for needs, more a question of minimising costs and providing for tax relief. The goal of the smallest possible deficit could always be invoked, whether to trump proposals for additional spending or new programs, to facilitate the termination or restructuring of programs for non-fiscal reasons, or simply to discipline the government. Tax reductions, rather than social spending, were seen as the principal avenue for government-driven improvements in living standards. Politicians converged around promises to lower taxes. The allure of lower taxes, and the negative-individualist heroics of the tax revolt, provided New Right policies with their main element of popular support.

Regular surveys by the Australian National University (ANU) Research School of Social Science identified the change in opinion. In 1967 almost three-quarters of respondents wanted more services rather than tax cuts. By 1987 more than three-quarters preferred tax cuts to more services (Table 4.4). A similar survey by Papadakis (1990a: 18–20) found that without the undecideds, 71 per cent preferred tax reductions to more spending.

Nevertheless, this general stance was *not* replicated in all program

Table 4.4 The choice between social spending and tax reductions, 1967, 1979 and 1987

Q. 'If the government had a choice between reducing taxes or spending more on social services, which do you think it should do?'

	1967 %	1979 %	1987 %
Spend more on social services	71	38	23
Reduce taxes	29	62	77
Total*	100	100	100

*Don't knows have been distributed among the other two groups.
Sources: Aitkin 1981: 44; Bean 1989.

areas. The ANU surveys found that in the cases of education, health and old age pensions, a majority supported more spending even if it meant more taxes. Support for education spending was especially high. Papadakis found that 55 per cent of respondents opted for increased spending with higher taxes. Other opinion polls indicated continued support for education spending (Shapiro & Papadakis 1993). In education the fiscal imperative faced a counter imperative. To render it ineffective, economists, New Right commentators and some officials began to argue here was no necessary link between more resources and better educational outcomes (see chapter 9).

Fiscal outcomes

Between the mid-1970s and the early 1990s federal outlays increased a little slower than GDP, although State government spending grew faster. But by the end of the 1980s the fiscal climate was completely different to the early 1970s. Government spending still operated as something of a Keynesian stabiliser during recessions (see Table 4.5), but except for welfare benefits and labour market programs, the old Keynesian dynamic of spending growth and expanding functions had been broken.

The conservative parties under Malcolm Fraser took office in December 1975 as one of the first governments in the world formally

Table 4.5 Commonwealth budget outlays, 1975–76 to 1995–96, constant 1984–85 prices

Fraser Coalition Government $m		Hawke and Keating Labor Governments $m	
1975–76	47 570	1983–84	60 493
1976–77	47 181	1984–85	64 675
1977–78	48 659	1985–86	66 348
1978–79	48 673	1986–87	66 344
1979–80	47 716	1987–88	64 088
1980–81	49 513	1988–89	61 032
1981–82	51 422	1989–90	61 294
1982–83	55 808	1990–91	65 061
		1991–92	68 608
		1992–93	72 470
		1993–94	74 311
		1994–95	78 082
		1995–96	78 504

Source: CBP.

committed to New Right policies. Fraser dropped Whitlam's programs in housing and urban and regional development, transferred some health functions to the States, enabling a 25 per cent reduction, and between 1975–6 and 1979–80, social spending, aside from welfare programs, fell by 26.0 per cent while GDP rose by 11.5 per cent. The ratio between all social spending and receipts from Pay As You Earn (PAYE) taxation, the main tax on wage and salary earners, fell from 1.57 in 1975–76 to 1.07 in 1981–82. PAYE revenue rose by 41.9 per cent (Table 4.6). This deterioration in the benefit/cost ratio of public programs helped to fragment the pre-1975 consensus about the role of government, and underpinned the New Right-inspired 'tax revolt' of the late 1970s.

In 1980 the Government created the Committee for Review of Commonwealth Functions (the 'Razor Gang') to fundamentally change its role. The Razor Gang proposed the sale or lease of government enterprises, contracting out of government activities to the private sector, reductions in industry assistance, rationalisation of teachers' colleges, university fees and loans (withdrawn after opposition) and some transfer of health and education programs to the States. The research and publications activities of the Commonwealth education agencies, which were implicated in the political dynamics of expanding programs, were either reduced or truncated.

When the Hawke Labor Government took power in March 1983 it was positioned to become a small spending government, and in 1984 the Prime Minister announced his 'trilogy' of fiscal commitments, promising not to increase outlays, taxation or the deficit as a proportion of GDP, and to reduce the deficit in money terms. In three successive budgets from 1986–87 spending fell in real terms through cuts in grants to the States, economic services, general public services and defence. Commonwealth outlays fell dramatically from 31.3 per cent of GDP in 1984–85 to 25.8 per cent in 1988–89. Receipts fell from 28.4 per cent in 1987–88 to 25.3 per cent in 1991–92. Tax rates on corporations and middle to high income earners fell, and targeting reduced social outlays. By 1988–89 the ratio between social spending and taxation had dropped to 1.18. From 1987–88 to 1990–91 there were budget surpluses totalling $17.9 billion, the first for three decades (see Table 4.7). After the floating of the dollar, this confirmed Labor as a government of the New Right.

Later these surpluses provided a political breathing space that enabled the Government to increase social spending by $11.2 billion in the recession from 1990–91 to 1992–93, including training initiatives

Table 4.6 Commonwealth social spending compared to PAYE taxation*
1975–76 to 1987–88, three year intervals, constant 1975–76 prices

	Social spending	Net PAYE revenue	All social spending	Net PAYE taxation	Ratio of social spending to PAYE tax
	$m	$m	1975–76 = 100.0		spending/tax
1975–76	23 796	15 325	100.0	100.0	1.55
1978–79	23 993	17 505	99.6	114.2	1.37
1981–82	23 241	21 744	96.5	141.9	1.07
1984–85	30 710	22 331	127.5	145.7	1.38
1987–88	31 552	24 985	131.0	163.0	1.26

* PAYE refers to Pay As You Earn Taxation. The ratio in column six is derived from the total expenditure on social programs (column one), divided by total PAYE revenue (column two).
Source: CBP.

Table 4.7 Commonwealth budget surpluses, 1987–88 to 1990–91

	1984–85 prices $m	% of total outlays
1987–88	2061	+0.7
1988–89	5893	+1.7
1989–90	8036	+2.2
1990–91	1907	+0.5

Source: CBP.

for the long-term unemployed. Labor managed to increase its own social spending while restraining public outlays, by the simple device of transferring the cost of small government to the States. Between 1983–84 and 1993–94 the Commonwealth social welfare budget expanded from $11.1 to $27.2 billion and from 6.6 to 10.3 per cent of GDP; spending on unemployment and sickness benefits rose 3.1 times in real terms. Between 1975 and 1984 alone, the number of people receiving pensions and benefits, excluding family allowances, rose by nearly a million. Commonwealth general revenue (untied) grants to the States fell sharply, declining by $4.4 billion in real terms in the eight years to 1991–92 and from 21.7 per cent (1983–94) to 12.5 per cent (1993–94) of outlays. This affected the capacity of the States to provide educational and other services.

The growth of Commonwealth welfare programs did not signify a broadening of the social base of the public sector. On the contrary, because of the shift from universal approaches to targeting, and growth in programs such as unemployment relief that were focused on minority groups, the range of beneficiaries shrank and the basis of social solidarity was eroded. Papadakis (1990a) finds that the minority programs such as unemployment relief were less popular than the quasi-universal programs in health and education that were being squeezed by the growth of transfer payments. Between 1975–76 and 1993–94 welfare spending increased from 23.1 to 36.6 per cent of Commonwealth outlays. Education funding was at 8.5 per cent of total outlays in 1993–94, the same level it had been in 1975–76, Common-wealth education funding fell behind the rate of enrolment increases (see chapter 9).

The fiscal imperative strengthened the hand of management in all social programs. A failure of efficiency was interpreted as a failure of control. System managers developed global expenditure and cost savings targets as mechanisms for imposing fiscal discipline (OECD 1987b). Within programs and institutions, managers used output and efficiency objectives to drive restructuring. The result was an implosion of efficiency pressures, exacerbated by the top-down structures typical of fiscally-driven systems in bureaucratic organisations. In the longer run this increased the relative attractiveness of devolved market-based systems (chapter 9) to state-employed professionals and local managers. Self-financing was one escape from the remorseless efficiency pressures.

Notes

[1] In the United States market liberals are often described as 'libertarians'. However, American fundamentalist conservatives (unlike those of Australia) emphasise individualism and markets. The two kinds of 'New Right' are not far apart.

[2] For a good short account of the British New Right see Desai (1994).

[3] A comprehensive history of the Australian New Right has yet to be written, but there are useful data in various chapters, magazine and newspaper articles, and pamphlets, notably Carey (1987), and including Duncan (1984), TNC (1985), MacMillan 1985, Jay (1986a; 1986b), Sheridan (1986), StC (1987), Moore & Carpenter (1987), Williams (1987), Dusevic (1990). In Australia the think tanks were small but influential, especially the Centre for Independent Studies, the Monash University based Centre for Policy Studies, later the Tasman Institute, and the Institute of Public Affairs in Victoria (IPA). The IPA was reborn as a New Right organisation during the 1980s and in its new guise it set the policy agenda of that state's conservative government from 1992 onwards, substantially influencing its education policies.

[4] In an analysis of ALP government and its relation to the New Right, Knight et al (1993: 12–15) argue that the similarities between Labor governments and Thatcher governments should not be privileged at the expense of the differences, claiming that the Conservatives' support for privatisation distinguished them from Labor's strategy of corporate managerialism. But both sides of politics supported privatisation *and* corporate managerialism, although the pace of privatisation was somewhat slower in Australia than in Britain during the 1980s. In New Zealand the Labour Party was more free market than most conservative governments. 'The extraordinary feature of the Labor decade was precisely that it involved an attempt to modernise Australia and to modernise the Labor Party, but at the risk of emptying out the Labor tradition' (Beilharz 1994: x).

CHAPTER 5

Individual and government

'Underlying most arguments against the free market is a lack of belief in freedom itself. The existence of a free market does not of course eliminate the need for government. On the contrary, government is essential both as a forum for determining the 'rules of the game' and as an umpire to interpret and enforce the rules decided on. What the market does is reduce greatly the range of issues that must be decided through political means, and thereby to minimise the extent to which government need participate.'

Milton Friedman, Capitalism and freedom, *University of Chicago Press, Chicago 1962, p. 15.*

Prelude: A small cloud on the horizon (1968)

In 1968 real GDP in the OECD region was increasing at 6.3 per cent per annum, unemployment was 3 per cent and inflation was 3.9 per cent (OECD 1985): after two decades of boom conditions, economic growth was more or less taken for granted, and there was little sign of the problems to come. The late Keynesian consensus continued, on both sides of politics. Yet it was a troubling time for conservatives, the year of near revolution in Paris; the peak of the peace demonstrations and the radical student movement in the United States; President Lyndon Johnson's sudden decision not to seek re-election and to negotiate a ceasefire in Vietnam; the assassination of Martin Luther King, and the riots in Watts and other American cities. The 'sexual revolution' proceeded apace. The counter-culture was at its height.

In the midst of these crumbling certainties, the British Conservative Party chose a rising parliamentarian called Margaret Thatcher to deliver the Conservative Political Centre party conference lecture at Blackpool. By custom the lecture was used to outline the speaker's fundamental beliefs and the directions Conservatism ought to follow. Thatcher set herself against the Keynesian policy framework of the time. 'The great mistake of the post-war period has been for the government to provide or to legislate for almost anything.'

Economic growth had fuelled the expansion of government, driven by vote buying, so that people had become accustomed to receiving benefits at no cost. Governments funded their programs by printing more money, instead of controlling the money supply. The welfare state had become 'extensive and all pervading'. The rapid spread of higher education had equipped people 'to criticise and question almost everything'. Government was 'more and more remote from the people' and showed 'increasing authoritarianism'.

Thatcher cited polls showing that two-thirds of people wanted more say in the running of government. She argued not for democratisation and the freedoms of the politically active citizen, but for depoliticisation; freedom of the individual from constraint by the state: negative freedom, economic freedom rather than political freedom.

> But the way to get personal involvement and participation is not for people to take part in more and more government decisions but to make government reduce the area of decision over which it presides and consequently leave the private citizen to 'participate', if that be the fashionable word, by making more of his own decisions. What we need now is a far greater degree of personal responsibility and decision, far more independence from the government, and a comparative reduction in the role of government (Thatcher 1968, in Wapshott & Brock 1983: 275).

People should be encouraged not to rely on the state but to enrich themselves by their own efforts. 'The Conservative creed has never offered a life of ease without effort. Democracy is not for such people. Self-government is for those men and women who have learned to govern themselves' (Wapshott & Brock 1983: 270–281).

It was a startling doctrine, a claim for a dramatic shift in the Conservative Party. But market liberalism was unfashionable. In 1968 'Thatcherism' was only a small cloud on the horizon, and the warning was scarcely noticed. Few at Blackpool that day could have imagined that these perspectives would come to shape government in the industrialised world – that Thatcher and others like her would absorb the market liberalism of Hayek, Friedman, Buchanan and the public choice school and others into a power–knowledge system of rule that was designed to remake the social world as competitive markets.

I. Market liberal power/knowledge

Market liberalism as a political project

Market liberalism was designed for criticising, seizing and wielding power, and for using power to remake the world in its own image. Like Keynesianism before it, market liberalism was joined to power and had practical effects. 'Theories here do not merely legitimate existing power relations but actually constitute new sectors of reality and make new fields of existence practicable' (Miller & Rose 1990: 7). Rose (1993: 283) states that market liberalism[1] should be considered not as a political philosophy or a type of society but as a 'formula of rule'. Market liberalism was a means of criticising and reprogramming government. It provided a means of analysis, a set of guidelines for reform, and a model for government and society to become. The market liberal compared the liberal ideal of free competition and 'economic man' to every existing practice. Not surprisingly, these practices were found wanting, needing incessant reform until the moment that the ideal state was achieved.

Yet the political implications of market liberalism were conservative as well as radical, because it took as given the legal and economic *status quo*. Like its corporate political supporters, market liberalism was imbued with a kind of restless, relentless traditionalism. It was a crusading *status quo*, that functioned as a line of defence, as a standard of criticism, and as a norm to be created.

Market liberal power/knowledge was always normative in character. Market liberal explanations in economics, political science and public administration were designed to persuade and convince people to a viewpoint, to shape people's behaviours. The normative character of the market liberal project was often made explicit.

In the founding text of public choice theory, *The calculus of consent* (1965), Buchanan and Tullock stated that 'we are not directly interested in what *the* state or *a* state actually is ... but propose to define quite specifically ... what we think a state ought to do'. To Buchanan and Tullock 'the only purpose of science is its ultimate assistance in the development of normative propositions'. In the speech he made while receiving the Nobel Prize for economic science, Buchanan castigated fellow economists for their lack of political purpose. 'They seem to be ideological eunuchs', he complained. 'Their interest lies in the purely intellectual properties of the models with which they work' (Reisman 1990: 1). In their work Buchanan and Tullock assumed that all people were *homo economicus*, making rational economic choices with the sole objective of maximising their individual utility. The two theorists acknowledged that in the real world not all behaviour was 'economic', groups existed as well as individuals, not all choices were rational, and their theory had a limited capacity to provide representative generalisations. Nevertheless, they stated that, provided *homo economicus* applied to some behaviour some of the time, the model still had 'positive worth', because it became possible to predict trends in marginal behaviours, and by applying theory in the form of policy, to screen out elements inconsistent with the model, and begin reshaping behaviour along the lines imagined (Buchanan & Tullock 1965: 3, 30, 82, 265–267, 297, 308).

Hayek was more circumspect about the normative character of his work. He wanted to naturalise as much of market liberalism as possible by moving it out of the realm of political and intellectual controversy and into a privileged zone of pre-given truths. His theory of the spontaneous order argued that, left unattended, human beings would naturally develop *homo economicus* and free competitive markets. Societies based on market competition were superior and would force out other societies. The legal structure of the market, private property, stability of possession and transfer by consent were laws of nature (Hayek 1967d; 1978b). The teleological character of the argument was obvious. It had limited credibility even in market liberal circles. Buchanan commented that Hayek's theory of the spontaneous order had done 'great damage' by obscuring the need for political intervention. 'I have no faith in the efficacy of social evolutionary process . . . Evolution may produce social dilemma as readily as social paradise' (Buchanan 1975: 167). But Hayek did not maintain this 'spontaneist' position consistently. Elsewhere he acknowledged that market liberal behaviours were not natural, and had to be created (Hayek 1979a: 75–76). Otherwise there would have been no 'need' for the New Right.

Market liberal individualism

The objective of the market liberals was to create the social conditions in which their particular brand of individualism would be universalised; in which the democratic political citizen would be replaced by the individualist economic 'anti-citizen'.

Hayek set himself the task of purging liberalism of its social democratic accretions by stripping it back to classical liberal axioms, using these to constitute the New Right's domain of normativity. This was a highly individualist reading of the classical liberal tradition, working through Hobbes and Locke in the seventeenth century to Adam Smith, Hume and Spencer, without Adam Smith's recognition of moral bonds and altruism (Hayek 1960; 1978b). The market liberals distinguished themselves from the democratic tradition of the French revolution, and the liberal social democracy of John Stuart Mill and Keynes, which had joined active citizenship to state intervention in the labour markets, investment and distribution. Notwithstanding references to Adam Smith's invisible hand, the distinctive features of market liberalism were drawn from Spencer's cynicism about government and democracy, and Hobbes' idea of the state of nature, of 'masterless man' warring for power, wealth and glory in a market economy (Macpherson 1968: 11–12), in which

> the *Value*, or WORTH of a man, is as of all other things, his Price; that is to say, so much as would be given for the use of his Power: and therefore it is not absolute; but a thing dependent on the need and judgement of another (Hobbes 1651/1968: 151–152);

and without the restraints of the law, the life of man would be 'solitary, poore, nasty, brutish and short' (Hobbes 1651/1968: 186). The distinctly Thatcherite dyad of free market and strong state can be read in Hobbes.

The starting point of market liberalism was the property owning individual with inviolable command over 'his' private economic sphere, protected by property law (Hayek 1967b). 'The recognition of property is clearly the first step in the delineation of the private sphere which protects us against coercion; and it has long been recognised that a people averse to the institution of private property is without the first element of freedom' (Hayek 1960: 140). The market liberals were normative and methodological individualists. They wanted a social order based solely on individuals linked by contract and exchange; and consistent with this objective, the tools they used to explain reality were individualist in nature.

To the methodological individualist all social phenomena were explained 'wholly in terms of facts about individuals' (Lukes 1973: 110). There was no such thing as 'society' distinct from individuals. Wealth was not created by societies and distributed to its individual members: it was created by individuals, and 'society' could only take it away (Joseph & Sumption 1979: 85). Individuals were motivated only by self-interest and self-love. Remarkably, they argued that there was no 'general altruism' or social solidarity, unless expressed for selfish purposes (Hayek 1960: 78–79). In market exchange, the interests of the other party were *necessarily* excluded from consideration (Buchanan & Tullock 1965: 18).

The market liberals defined freedom as negative freedom, meaning the freedom of individuals and their property *from* coercion by external agents, usually meaning the state. They rejected the notion of positive freedom, meaning freedom *to* exercise choices or achieve wants. Hayek argued that freedom was economic rather than political. He rejected notions of self-determination or empowerment, a view of freedom he associated with Dewey, the most influential modern philosopher of education. He also argued against the notion that freedom was a matter of enabling material conditions, on the grounds that this opened the door to collective responsibility and state interference in private property. To Hayek, individuals should take full responsibility for their own fate. Poverty was not a reduction in freedom, providing that the poor were free to enter into market exchange. 'Money is one of the greatest instruments for freedom ever invented by man' (Hayek 1944: 19, 67, 76).

Market liberalism therefore rested on an individual versus the state – or market versus the state – dualism, corresponding to its negative versus positive freedom dualism.[2] In this framework, there could be no middle way between state 'constructivism', planning and egalitarianism on one hand; and markets, voluntary cooperation and freedom on the other (Hayek 1979a: 151; Friedman 1962: 13). As a means of coordinating individual preferences, markets were seen as *necessarily* superior to political democracy.

This doctrine handed control to 'competitive' individuals and organisations; that is, those with significant weight in the market. But market liberalism did not problematise relations of domination; whether rich over poor, employer over employee, or man over woman, except domination by the state. Remarkably, the market liberals defined private corporations as *non*-coercive. Joseph and Sumption (1979: 53) argued 'the power conferred by private wealth is not a power to coerce others. It is not backed by unlimited political force. It is not concentrated.' And again: 'private wealth like political power may corrupt, but unlike electoral power its corruption does not harm others'. Methodological individualism meant the institutional character of corporations was ignored; the individual economic control exercised by business leaders was seen as benign, and the natural state of affairs. At the same time, union power *was* seen as coercive because it interfered with private property (Hayek 1960: 267–269).

The existing distribution of property, wealth and incomes was placed beyond reach. This created a problem: how could the pre-given distribution of resources be justified? Buchanan created the notion of a founding social contract in which an original property settlement was established from which all else evolved, but admitted there was probably no such thing (Buchanan 1975: 50). Hayek's theory of spontaneous evolution attempted to naturalise property as the outcome of past market activity: he argued that justice lay not in distributional outcomes, but in the freedom from interference ·of the markets that produced those outcomes. In this view there could be no such thing as a just distribution or redistribution (Hayek 1967c). But Hayek's position rested on a priori judgements either assuming 'the acceptability of existing distributions', or having redistributive implications which he refused to acknowledge (Kukathas 1989: 172, 272).

Government and democracy

Friedman argued the role of government was to preserve law and order, maintain property rights and enforce private contracts; to foster competitive markets, and to counter those 'neighbourhood effects' (negative 'externalities' resulting from the operations of a free market) that were important enough to require government intervention. Anything beyond that was fraught with danger (Friedman 1962: 34). This did not imply a weak or minimalist state. The market liberals supported the legal authority of the state, and its monopoly of coercive functions (Hayek 1960: 21), and intervention to produce negative liberty and competitive markets.

> We need a strong state to preserve both liberty and order . . . The state has, let us not forget, certain duties which are incontrovertibly its own: for example – to uphold and maintain the law; to defend the nation against attack from without; to safeguard the currency; to guarantee essential services. We have frequently argued that the state should be more strongly concerned with these matters than it has been . . . What we need is a strong state determined to maintain in good repair the frame which surrounds society (Thatcher 1980, quoted in Heald 1983: 322).

To Hayek the coercive powers of government should be separated from the administration of programs (Hayek 1979a: 41–42). The marketisation of programs allowed governments to do this while still retaining control over outcomes. Buchanan's ideal was the 'protective state', designed to maintain the orderly functioning of markets. Its functions were automatic, established in 'constitutional contract' and not a matter for ongoing political debate or decision (Buchanan 1975: 162–163). Hayek wanted to cement the rule making and rule enforcing authority in the legal rather than political wing of government, and to severely restrict the functions of government outside this sphere.

The New Right did *not* see citizen participation in political decisions as a desirable end in itself. A major theme was 'the necessary limits of democracy and how different areas of policy can be removed from democratic control' (Gamble 1988: 52). To Hayek 'the resolutions of a majority are not the place to look for superior wisdom. They are bound, if anything, to be inferior to the decisions that the most intelligent members of the group will make after listening to all opinions' (Hayek 1960: 110). He separated freedom from democracy. Economic freedom, in the mode of individualism and negative freedom, was a higher value than political freedom as democracy. Economic freedom was necessary to political democracy, although not sufficient for it. But democracy was neither sufficient for economic freedom, nor necessary to it. A liberal regime did not need democratic rights(!): 'it is possible that an authoritarian government may act on liberal principles' (Hayek 1960: 103–116; 1979b: 35).

On the grounds of these principles, the market liberals argued for a major reduction in the functions of government.

Hayek supported certain universal government services that assisted the functioning of markets, such as roads, statistics and maps, standards of measure and quality certification. But public works could be contracted out, and communications and the money system should be denationalised (Hayek 1960: 264, 298). Where government maintained a continuing role the market liberals wanted to break the nexus between public services and government institutions. Private producers should be free to compete. 'What is objectionable is not state enterprise as such but state monopoly' (Hayek 1960: 224). Government activity should be conducted on the same basis as private enterprise, without subsidies, special tax concessions or other forms of assistance. The market liberals also supported the devolution of public provision and funding: 'for there to be a meaningful devolution of decision-making powers, there must also be an appropriate devolution of finance and provision' (Reisman 1990: 168; Hayek 1978b: 145). This was a formula for the full commercialisation of government production.

Buchanan argued for user charges because these would reduce frivolous consumption and promote efficiency. He proposed the individualisation of public costs and benefits, whereby each taxpayer would have a specific transactory relationship with government, and people could individually opt out of both the costs and the benefits of government programs (Buchanan 1975: 39, 174–176; Reisman 1990: 170–171). Thus the relationship between citizen and government was imagined as an individualised tax-spending transaction, in which there was no qualitative difference between public production for the common good, and private production and consumption.

In relation to social policies Friedman argued that governments should protect people who were not 'responsible individuals', but he suggested that the welfare safety net should take the form of tax exemption rather than services (Friedman 1962: 192). Hayek rejected the use of equality as a measuring stick for policy. Social programs should treat all members of society in the same way (equity), but they should not aim for social equality. The correction of inequalities interfered not only with private property and negative freedom, but with the natural course of evolution. Economic inequality was inevitable, and gross inequality was highly desirable. An attack on inequality was an attack on the property of the 'economically most advanced classes' who were the motor of evolutionary progress.

Nor should the harsher effects of market competition be eased, as this would reduce individual incentives. 'To suffer disappointment, adversity and hardship is a discipline to which any society must submit' (Hayek 1960: 47; Hayek 1979b: 31). The struggle for relative advantage was essential to social order. People who were equal, who were no longer struggling to dominate each other, were no longer subject to control.

> Egalitarianism . . . is wholly destructive because it not only deprives the individuals of the signals which alone can offer to them the opportunity of a choice of the direction of their efforts, but even more through eliminating the one inducement by which free men can be made to observe any moral rules: the differentiating esteem by their fellows (Hayek 1979a: 170).

Buchanan argued that both inequality and exploitation were inevitable. This was fortunate he stated: 'in a world of equals, most of the motivation for trade disappears' (Buchanan & Tullock 1965: 304; Buchanan 1975: 11). To Hayek and Buchanan any economic redistribution should only occur on the basis of *unanimous* agreement; which in practice made redistribution impossible to achieve. Buchanan called this the 'unanimity rule'. When taxation reduced an individual's assets without consent, 'coercion is apparently exercised upon him in the same way as that exerted by the thug who takes his wallet in Central Park' (Buchanan & Tullock 1965: 42).

These arguments about the 'necessity' of inequality and the impossibility of social solidarity were not popular and were tempered in later New Right polemics. Roger Kerr, Director of the New Zealand Business Round Table, stated that citizenship was inherently hierarchical whereas economic markets were not. The political system favoured 'the already strong and influential, those who are articulate and well endowed with cultural power', whereas the market system had 'powerful equalising tendencies' (Kerr 1992: 3).

Friedman (1962: 35–36) developed a long list of functions governments should vacate, including parity price support for agriculture, tariffs and export restrictions, output controls, rent/wage/price controls, regulation of minimum wages, regulation of communications, social security programs financed from compulsory levies on wages, licensing of professions, consumer protection, publicly owned and operated tolls, and national parks. Hayek reserved some of his harshest criticisms for government social programs. In 1960 most welfare programs were 'a threat to freedom' because 'though they are presented as mere service activities, they really constitute an exercise of the coercive powers of government and rest on its claiming exclusive rights in certain fields'. Dependence on public pensions was likely to lead to 'concentration camps for the aged unable to maintain themselves'. By 1976 'the prevailing belief in "social justice" is at present probably the gravest threat to most other values of a free civilization'. Keynesian social justice policies had destroyed liberal limits on the role of the state. Redistribution and progressive taxation were 'the crucial issue on which the whole future of society will depend'. 'Unlimited democracy' had led to the uncontrolled expansion of government. Society was hostage to 'the momentary passions' of 'the multitude'. (Hayek 1960: 42–93, 256–308; Hayek 1976: 66–67, 153). Buchanan argued that majority coalitions in government used government programs to improve their living standards, financed by taxes on the minority and the denial of negative freedoms.

Hayek, Buchanan and Friedman all called for constitutional reforms to limit the scope of politics and the size of government, including a flat tax on all incomes, balanced budgets and limits to government's share of GDP (Friedman & Friedman 1980: 301–309; Reisman 1990: 88, 128–129, 165). Hayek suggested a narrower franchise. The scope of public programs should be controlled by an upper house, based on 15-year terms and once in a lifetime suffrage (Hayek 1979a). In the lower house, public servants, and the recipients of 'public charity' such as the aged and unemployed, had a vested interest in government programs. They should be denied the vote. Hayek noted in *The constitution of liberty* that 'it is useful to remember that in the oldest and most successful of European democracies, Switzerland, women are still excluded from the vote and apparently with the approval of the majority of them' (Hayek 1960: 443).

Public choice theory

Public choice theory was a new system of knowledge developed in the zone between politics and economics, where Keynesianism, lacking a theory of the state, was weak. It assumed that the individual, whether as political or economic citizen-consumer, was an atomised chooser whose only concern was self-interest.

It was a creed perfectly attuned to the culture of 'greed is good' that gained such currency in the second half of the 1980s. Public choice theory became widely used in applied economic research and policy analysis. It used a quasi-economic methodology based on neoclassical economics, joining this to economic axioms about *homo economicus* and competitive markets, and certain distinctive axioms of its own. These axioms, which were never grounded empirically, constituted a singular narrative about political behaviour, in which there was an inherent tendency for government programs to expand, and taxation to increase. Majority coalitions were formed by politicians around elections ('logrolling'), in collaboration with those government officials and professionals with a vested interest in government programs ('producer capture'). All groups conspired together to support each other's programs, and voters had an incentive to be 'free riders' who benefited from government programs without paying their share of the costs (Buchanan 1975: 156–161). The Friedmans employed a similar argument (Friedman & Friedman 1984) in their denunciations of government-provided education.

This core narrative of public choice theory was a powerful tool for criticising existing government activities.[3] Barry (1990) remarks on Buchanan that 'his most important single achievement is his destruction of the idea that public officials necessarily promote the public good'. The notion of 'producer capture' was used to divide public sector workers from the beneficiaries of their programs: rapacious voters were redefined as virtuous taxpayers, paralleling the New Right-inspired political shift from public spending to tax reduction, and from democratic politics to managed markets. At the same time, the methodology of public choice theory laid the basis for transition to a corporatised and marketised form of government, based on negative freedom and contractual relations.

For Buchanan and Tullock there was no 'public interest' separable from the interests of single individuals. Group decisions were the sum of the individual decisions, combined by a decision-making rule. Consistent with negative freedom, the individual benefits of government action were defined as *negative costs*: 'the minimisation of costs rather than the maximisation of some difference between benefits and costs becomes the criterion for organisational and rule decisions' (Buchanan & Tullock 1965: 12, 35, 87, 132, 284, 315). In the zero sum and individualised calculus used by public choice theory, the negative of a negative (the absence of costs) was treated as the logical equivalent of a positive (the provision of benefits). When one person minimised their individual tax payments, this made the *same* net contribution to the public good as did government social programs providing common benefits. Buchanan's norm was the private individual with little need for collective action.

In public choice theory there could be no such thing as a positive-sum collective program that expanded the horizons of everyone. All interactions were zero-sum: if someone gained, someone else had to lose either by paying more taxes or receiving fewer benefits.

The discursive framework of market reform

The market/state dualism (Dow 1990) at the heart of market liberalism moved between two contrary forms: absolute opposition between market and state, and absolute identity of market and state. These two forms corresponded to two different tactical moments; the liberal critique of government (opposition) and liberal positivity and the remaking of government (identity). Thus when non-market government institutions or programs were criticised, they were positioned as *separate from and opposed to* the ideal market, the 'other' to this market, highlighting the allegedly anti-market characteristics of government, and drawing attention to the need for reforms. At other times, the real differences between government and market corporations were suppressed, and institutions of government were treated as if they were *identical* to market corporations; those qualities of government that could be rendered equivalent to corporate behaviour were brought to the fore.

Seizing on the positivity of government-as-corporation, the market liberal reformer could reconstruct the whole of government on market lines. In public choice theory Buchanan and Tullock began by treating the activities of governments as if they were market economic activities. Neoclassical economics was based on the logic of choice for the self-interested, utility maximising individual. This enabled economists to screen out all social effects of market production and exchange. The public choice theorists now transposed that individualising method to the domain whose distinctive purpose was the organisation of the social and the collective, the domain of government. 'Political decision-making is viewed, in the limit, as analogous to the determination of the terms of trade in an exchange' (Buchanan & Tullock 1965: 322).

The individualistic approach or method tends to obliterate any logical distinction or difference between the 'public' and the 'private' sectors of human activity. Collective action, along with private action, is motivated by individually conceived ends, and all action proceeds only after a mental calculus is performed by some individual or individuals. As decision-making or choosing bodies, individual human beings remain fundamentally invariant over the range of both private and public activity (Buchanan & Tullock 1965: 316).

In applying market oriented measures of efficiency, the market liberals found, not surprisingly, that non-market institutions produced identifiable economic costs without identifiable economic benefits. This 'discovery' underpinned the market liberal arguments about the need for marketisation and corporate reform. It was a circular argument, in which both the 'problem' and its 'solution' were identified by setting aside the non-market purposes of government programs, deriving from citizenship, common human rights and the welfare state, such as universal health and education, and cross subsidised universal services in transport and communication. For example, Buchanan and Tullock deliberately left out factors relating to political obligation and other 'moral' aspects of government (Buchanan & Tullock 1965: 309–311). For them the state was no longer understood in the Keynesian sense as the bearer of a combination of economic objectives and social objectives. Further, those market economic objectives that were not reducible to *individualised* costs and benefits (for example the monetary system, the legal regulation of contracts, vocational training), were also left off the list of benefits, appearing only as costs. As Domberger and Piggott noted in relation to proposals for privatisation: 'The theoretical case for public ownership has traditionally rested on . . . the properties of resource allocation in the economy as a whole. In contrast, the case for private ownership rests on the incentives and constraints that the market provides to promote efficiency within the firm' (Domberger & Piggott 1986: 147).

The comparison was further tilted to the market side, because they compared *actual* government programs with an *ideal* market. 'Measured against that utopia, it is not surprising that state provision can hardly compete' (Hindess 1987: 142–143). This meant that market failure could be downplayed, while government failure stood out in the boldest possible relief. Market generated requirements were understood as rational, neutral, objective and benign, while government requirements became intrusive, capricious, dangerous and potentially corrupt. Choice was defined in market-individual terms, obscuring the question of the material capacity to exercise choice, and the role of government in enhancing that capacity. In this framework it became inevitable that governments suppressed choice while markets enhanced it, and any and every step towards the marketisation of government was *ipso facto* the advance of efficiency and freedom. 'Once the central message is accepted, privatisation has few logical bounds: not only where performance is judged to be unsatisfactory but also to prevent now unsatisfactory performance deteriorating in future through the manifold inherent deficiencies of the public sector' (Heald 1983: 316).

There was a further, remarkable twist to these arguments. Buchanan argued that not only had government fallen short of market criteria, it had fallen short of its *own* traditional criteria of public service and public interest. He complained that 'persons who control collective decision-making' used this as 'a means of generating directly enjoyable and divisible private and partitionable goods rather than producing genuine public goods[!] which benefit all persons in the community' (Buchanan 1975: 50). Having created the negative norm of a market-based government by arguing that all government officials were necessarily *homo economicus*, and there was no such thing as genuine public goods, Buchanan then attacked the failure of governments to meet the (hitherto impossible) norm of altruism. Both a normative market and a normative public sector were used to criticise the existing functions of government. Having established this framework of judgement, it was a simple matter for public choice theory to 'prove' that government was an unrestrained leviathan that was neither disinterested and enlightened, nor responsive to need or right, and unconstrained by either market discipline or virtue. The subtext was that democratic controls could never work.

Thus the Keynesian understandings of 'public' and 'private' were inverted. The true public interest became the invisible hand of the market, and marketisation was presented as the way to render 'the public sector for the public', as the 1979 Conservative Party platform stated (Heald 1983: 316). The absence of traditional public goods would be 'met' by reforms that would eliminate them altogether.

The strategic brilliance of this contrary discourse lay in the manner in which it spoke at the same time to those who expected more from government, those who were cynical about it, and those who wanted less, and arranged those differing viewpoints into a narrative sequence in which Keynesian 'big government' was the past and the universal free market was the future, drawing people from one to the other. Public choice theory returned to the ideals of public good and public service, 'proved' they had failed, explained why, and provided a solution for that failure. For the old ideal of public intervention in the 'public interest', now tarnished, it substituted the new ideal of the market. In this manner the New Right used even the denial of social democratic utopias as a generative force. It required its supporters to relegate their egalitarian ideals to the past, but without discarding all the pleasures and resentments that those ideals could bring.

II. Liberals and conservatives

New Right conservatism

New Right conservatism was different to liberalism. It was centred on property rather than markets. To Roger Scruton 'the ascendancy of consumption belongs, not to the essence of property, but to its pathology'. Property and individuals were not natural or spontaneously formed, but depended on historical and social conditions. 'Individual freedom is the great social artifact which in trying to represent itself as nature alone, generates the myth of liberalism.' However, there were no limits to the state, whose justification lay only in itself. Social order required 'the continuous attention of authority' and the maintenance of class distinctions. Scruton also argued for the primacy of politics over economics. 'Economics stands to politics in much the same relation as neurology stands to personal affection' (Scruton 1984; Kitson 1990; Hayek 1960: 401). Conservatives understood relations of power.

At first sight these two conceptions of the state, its conservative celebration and its liberal negation, were wholly incompatible. But the ambiguity of the state/market dualism allowed the New Right to assert state control, while denying citizen's rights, closing down public programs and abandoning government intervention to alleviate poverty or redistribute income. The outcome was a hybrid discourse, in which the liberal refusal of the state became displayed as the very banner of the state machine.

These plural liberal-conservative foundations provided the New Right with tactical flexibility; it could 'switch the grounds of its legitimations at will' (Levitas 1986: 11). But there was also a deeper symbiosis, in which each side of the alliance adopted some of the norms of the other. The market liberals absorbed the conservative concerns about social order, weaved into market liberal arguments against Keynesian and egalitarian policies and in favour of market reforms.

Hayek stated that negative freedom could only be maintained where conventions and traditions made human behaviours predictable. Correspondingly, the market was seen as an instrument for maintaining stable and predictable human behaviour (Hayek 1948d: 24; Kukathas 1989: 11, 175). Thus Buchanan blamed Keynesian economics for 'a generalised erosion in public and private manners, increasingly liberalised attitudes towards sexual activities, a declining vitality of the Puritan work ethic, deterioration of product quality, explosion of the welfare rolls, widespread corruption in both the private and the government sector, and finally, observed increases in the alienation of voters from the political process' (Buchanan & Wagner 1977: 65). The reciprocal was this: although conservatives had long been concerned about the corrosive effects of capitalist markets on existing traditions, property and authority, and rightly so; now, in the face of the danger of the welfare state, communism and social democracy, many conservatives were persuaded that when properly controlled, markets would function as defenders of property and tradition, rather than their negation (Gray 1986: 87). For example market reforms in government could be used to depoliticise key sectors, such as education and to close down policy debate.

Many conservatives now embraced the liberal motifs of markets and competition. Perhaps this signified the ascendancy in the Anglo-American business class of the finance sector, mobile capital, global assets; and the financial conception of efficiency where value was determined by competitive position. Social efficiency and elitism were conflated, market competition and social hierarchy were combined, and each was seen a condition of the other. As the leading market liberal and Liberal Party economic spokesperson, Jim Carlton, put it:

> We must aim for a society marked by competition as well as cooperation, whose achievement is heightened by the absence of restraint on high fliers, where 'elite' is not a dirty word and people are not levelled by false notions of equality. It is only by encouraging the talented and industrious that the whole society is lifted out of mediocrity, allowing the least able to be elevated with the least difficulty (Carlton 1985: 40).

Starting from these premises, orthodox conservatives could support crusading, reconstructing governments of the Thatcher kind, in which the critical zeal of market liberals was combined with conservative expertise in relations of power. Both market liberals and conservatives agreed on the need to reduce the scope for democratic accountability and public debate by increasing management and/or markets. Both supported the separation of the formal political agenda from the system of control; so that control would be exercised at least partly *outside politics*, by tradition and by spontaneous market processes, both of which Hayek considered to be prior to politics (Galeotti 1987: 168, 173–174). A fence was to be built around 'politics', ensuring that any renegotiation of the *status quo* will take place elsewhere, and the outcome would be determined by economic power and social position. Might would become right, and the 'contagion' of democracy (Scruton) would be contained.

Thatcherism and national decline

The model of government nurtured under Thatcher in Britain, from 1979 to 1991, developed this liberal-conservative symbiosis to the highest degree, and created forms of government and models of public program that provided influential models throughout the world, especially in Australia and New Zealand. Stuart Hall (1988a, 1988b, 1991) argues that Thatcherism was a form of politics designed to secure and maintain political hegemony in the Gramscian sense, 'to gain ascendency over a whole social formation, to achieve positions of leadership in a number of different sites of social life at once, to achieve the commanding position on a broad strategic front'. Central was 'the constructing and winning of popular consent' (Hall 1988a: 53). The objective was a new political alignment. Thatcherism conflated Keynesianism, social democracy, socialism and communism, so that the campaign against the welfare state became part of the global crusade against communism. 'Thatcher made no secret of her wish to see socialism destroyed as an effective force in Britain, and a two-party system organised in which both parties fully accepted the legitimacy of capitalism and the market' (Gamble 1988: 219), a goal that was achieved.

Its passage into the state was crucial, but Thatcherism was not 'state bound'. Sovereign power was deployed in a complex manner, with specific strategies in relation to the finance sector, the media, the business world, education and other sectors. Thatcherism worked at the level of people's identities and attitudes (their subjectivities). It was designed to change people's behaviour and the character of their relationships with each other. Its subject positions embodied the core conceptions of competition, enterprise and individual responsibility (Hall 1988b: 45–53). This reconstruction of subjectivities was at the core of the reforms in education and other social programs. The new consensus was secured by isolating certain groups, including at different times the 'new class' professionals in state programs, the unemployed, and welfare recipients; by symbolic dualisms such as productive/unproductive, and wealth creation/distribution; and by a contrived sense of inevitability expressed in slogans like 'there is no alternative' and 'life wasn't meant to be easy' (the first slogan was associated with Thatcher, the second with Australia's Liberal Party Prime Minister of 1975–1983, Malcolm Fraser).

Thatcherism led the rewriting of political discourse, not just in parliament, government and the media, but in everyday circulation. 'I heard large numbers of people stop talking the language of labourism, the welfare state, social democracy and suddenly begin talking another language of cost effectiveness, value for money, choice and freedom' (Hall 1988b: 61).

The link between government and subject was secured by narratives about the nation, in which enterprise was equated with patriotism, installing market liberalism in private-national identities. The invisible hand became the hand of national interest: in this framework, Keynesian programs were not only uneconomic, they were unpatriotic.

Above all, at the core of both Thatcherism and Reaganism was the pervasive narrative of national decline, resting again on fear and blame: the causes of decline were unions, government intervention, import protection, egalitarianism (Joseph & Sumption 1979), social programs, public schooling and so on. The narrative of decline carried great weight in Britain and the United States, because of the need to make sense of the weakening Anglo-American global economic dominance. Perhaps it was a sign of the derivative nature of Australian politics that a local version of the narrative so easily took root, although there was no lost empire to lament. Nevertheless, there *was* a basis for national economic insecurity. First, there was the ongoing weakness of the local capitalist class, a derivative class that was starved of capital and overshadowed by foreign control in key sectors of the economy. 'We suffer the pleasures of a *bourgeois* culture without the vicissitudes of a vigorous modernist entrepreneurial *bourgeoisie* to hold it up' (Beilharz 1994: 6). Second, the deterioration of commodity prices and of wool as a staple meant that Australia's share of world trade was falling. Australia had the third highest income per head in the world in 1950, but by the early 1980s had fallen out of the top ten.

The 1986 claim by the Treasurer, Paul Keating, that Australia was in danger of becoming a 'banana republic' dominated subsequent debate and locked the Australian polity into the common Anglo-American narrative. The presumption of decline and the need for vigorous national reconstruction was the platform for the major reforms in education and other programs in the second half of the 1980s.

Post-Foucauldian accounts suggest that larger changes in the mode of government are composed inductively, through the accumulation of smaller changes at the micro-level in particular governmental technologies (see for example Rose 1993: 285). However in the period after 1975 this sequence was reversed. The Keynesian programs continued into the late 1970s, although their political base had fallen away, and they were the target of disappointed expectations and growing popular frustration. The initial New Right breakthrough was at the peak of state administration, and in the 'master discourse' of economic policy. A new system of control was created, and over time it worked its way into any and every program area.

Notes

1 Rose (1993) refers to 'advanced liberalism'. The term 'neo-liberalism' is also used.

2 Hunt argues that when freedom is defined as self-determination, the negative/positive freedom dual collapses. 'If freedom is understood as a capacity to pursue one's interests, it seems obvious that such a capacity can be increased, on the one hand, by my acquiring resources for action, and on the other hand, by removing constraints or obstacles in the way of action. Freedom is one thing but it has what may be termed positive and negative conditions' (Hunt 1991: 296). Freedom has no essence, only social and historical forms; but the crucial distinction here is between Hayekian freedom separated from relations of power, and freedom as defined by Marx, Foucault, Dewey and others who see it as implicated in power.

3 The British television series *Yes, Minister* and *Yes, Prime Minister* were a public choice account of government and political behaviour.

CHAPTER 6

The New Right and education

'Competition has got a bad name in education circles in
recent years, but competition is itself a good thing.
Moreover, competition is a fact of life. We live in a highly
competitive environment, whether we like it or not. School
education should help children to learn to cope with
competition, it should teach them how to succeed, how to
cope with occasional failure. It is futile and cowardly and
ultimately self-defeating for schools to attempt to abolish
competition . . . We all know that the Japanese school
system is highly competitive and we all know that this can
produce stresses for students. But our own system has
become far too uncompetitive so that bright students are
not challenged.'

'*Our education: nothing short of disaster*', *editorial in* The
Australian, *6 January 1988.*

Prelude: 'The lies they tell our children' (1985)

On 25 January 1985, as parents were preparing for the beginning of
another school year, the *Business Review Weekly* carried a worrying
cover story on the deficiencies of government schools. Retention to
the end of schooling was low in Australia, compared to other nations,
it found. The national pool of talent was being 'artificially con-
stricted'. The schools were producing 'a large number of unemploy-
ables'. 'If the education system was viewed as a business', wrote editor
Robert Gottliebsen, 'it would represent an enterprise that performed
very badly' (Gottliebsen 1985: 27–28). On 28 January *The Australian*'s
editorial writer joined the argument. 'Education in this country',
stated *The Australian*, 'has for too long been plagued with the lazy
philosophy that teaching is not about the basics'. On 30 January the
Australian Financial Review editorial writer commented that higher
spending and smaller classes, usually seen as methods by which

schools could be improved, might not necessarily be tackling the standards problem at all. Certain economic evidence from the United States suggested that there was no correlation between levels of spending and the 'outputs' of schools.

Much the same kind of articles had been appearing since the mid-1970s; it was normal fare for the beginning of the school year, although this time there was a little more than usual. However, the main debate had not yet begun.

On 2 February *The Australian* published an article by Greg Sheridan. It began with maximum exposure on page 1, under the heading 'The lies they tell our children'. It continued under 'Vipers in the nation's classrooms' in the body of the newspaper. 'All around the country, teachers are giving our children a diet of intellectual poison', asserted Sheridan. In order to encourage children to stay on at school, government school teachers (who had just been slammed by *Business Review Weekly* for low retention rates) were running an entertainment-oriented curriculum, destroying academic standards and undermining national competitiveness.

Worse – and here Sheridan drew on the accumulated techniques of American cold war era propaganda – government school students were being indoctrinated. They were taught to despise their country, and hate the world of their parents. Homosexuality was being presented as a positive life-style, yet Enid Blyton was banned. Echoing the arguments of the Reagan Government's *A nation at risk* (Gardner 1983), Sheridan branded government education as a 'major' subversive influence. The many-sided theme of subversion and teachers as agents of subversion, with its threats to intellectual rigour, to parent control, to established values and to the national interest, dominated his argument.

> Large areas of the State education system have been captured by mediocre talents who adhere to a variety of fruit-cake ideologies with little regard for serious scholarship which conflicts with their views. . . .
> Syllabuses in the social sciences and values-related areas are being taught which are deeply hostile to Australia, to the US, to capitalism, to European civilisation, to industry, to Christianity . . . Australian sex education courses have adopted attitudes plainly in conflict with the majority of parents. . . .
> In general, Australian education is a disaster. It is as if the whole Government school system has had a collective nervous breakdown, and no longer has any idea of its real identity (Sheridan 1985a).

Sheridan stated later that 'The lies they tell our children' in *The Australian* 'really had its genesis in my reading the American book "Why they are lying to our children". I felt intuitively, and also from what I know about Australian education, that the accusations it made about American education would be true of Australian education' (Sheridan 1985c). Sheridan's article was also similar to 'Subtle and sinister, this infiltration of our pupils' minds', written by Brian Cox (1982), former editor of the *Black Papers*, for the British *Daily Mail* three years before.

Sheridan had failed to back his claims with solid evidence, but this turned out to be immaterial. The article was captivating. The prose was lurid and the images shocking, fearful and menacing, locking onto the already-existing parental anxieties about moral security, child safety, unemployment and career prospects. Compared to Sheridan's careful, balanced articles in the 1990s on Australian foreign policy, the style and content of his 1980s articles on education were completely different. But there was something about the issue of standards in schooling that tapped a deeply sited vein of war propaganda in public debate, turning conservative public commentators into moral crusaders.

Judging by the reactions to Sheridan, it was also an issue that sold newspapers. Letters flooded in to *The Australian*. Sheridan had his critics, but also supporters such as mining company executive and New Right leader Hugh Morgan, and Professor Lauchlan Chipman of the Australian Council of Educational Standards. Sheridan published more articles (1985b). The debate raged on, through talkback radio and other newspapers. Senator Susan Ryan, Commonwealth Minister of Education, joined the fray. The New Right-generated 'crisis' in education had become a national issue of the first rank.

Along with the campaigns on 'big government' and smaller taxation, education was one of the areas where the New Right built popular support. The different parts of the New Right had varying concerns. Employers wanted a vocationalised curriculum. Cultural conservatives wanted more discipline, tougher educational selection and a return to traditional values. Market liberals, the ultimate beneficiaries of the agitation about educational standards, wanted market reforms. But all criticised government schools and advocated 'freedom of choice', meaning more subsidies, in private schools. All were opposed to the egalitarian and progressivist strands in teaching. And all agreed that the stakes were high: education was very important. The leading market liberal Jim Carlton stated in *The Bulletin* that the New Right had 'singled out' education because of its 'primary contribution to our capacity for achievement and for our culture' (1985: 40–44).

More bluntly, British conservative Roger Scruton proclaimed that in education 'a major battle for the soul of society must be fought' (1984: 147).

I. Market liberalism and education

Market liberal criticisms of education

The market liberals defined education as they defined government, in neoclassical economic terms. All problems in education could be understood as economic problems, and could be solved by economic reforms. In 'The role of government in education', first published in 1955 and again in *Capitalism and freedom* (1962), the most influential of all the New Right tracts on education, Milton Friedman outlined an ideal education system, based on private investment and competitive markets, and used this ideal system as the grounds for his critique of existing schools and universities. Given this method of argument, it was not surprising that all problems were traced to the absence of market mechanisms; and the solution was always market reform. Nevertheless Friedman's model, critique and solutions – not to mention the circular method of argument itself – generated many imitators.

To Friedman most of the benefits of education were appropriated as monetary returns by the educated individual. In addition, elementary and general education generated 'externalities' ('neighbourhood effects'), such as shared literacy, values that strengthened social order, and the preparation of leaders, although governments did not have to pay for these externalities if parents would do so (Friedman 1962: 86–88).[1] He noted it was 'extremely difficult to draw a sharp line' between general and vocational education. Nevertheless, in vocational education, including most of higher education, *all* benefits were appropriated by individuals and there was no case for public subsidies. Vocational education was 'a form of investment in human capital precisely analogous to investment in machinery, buildings, or other forms of non-human capital. Its function is to raise the economic productivity of the human being. If it does so, the individual is rewarded in a free enterprise society by receiving a higher return' (Friedman 1962: 100–101).

Later Friedman hardened his position. Even in relation to general education 'there is no case for subsidising persons who get higher education at the expense of those who do not' (Friedman & Friedman 1980: 179–183). Further, even where governments funded education it did not follow that they should be providers, let alone monopolists. If government provision of elementary education had once been necessary, this was true no longer.[2]

Friedman and Hayek argued that with exceptions such as remote rural schools, education should be provided by competing private enterprises. If a non-market approach was used, non-profit private institutions were better than government institutions. They had little sympathy for the meritocratic project of scientific selection and equality of opportunity that had animated the builders of the post-war education systems. To Hayek the equalisation of material conditions in education, 'egalitarianism', always failed because it contradicted the 'basic instinct' of self-interest. It also breached negative freedom. 'One cannot be both an egalitarian, in this sense, and a liberal', stated Friedman. Hayek supported equality of opportunity as the removal of formal barriers, but it was impossible to fully equalise starting points without controlling 'the whole physical and human environment of all persons'. Anyway, he argued, neither merit nor individual capacity could be fully assessed. Because the circumstances influencing educational achievement were never fully known it was impossible to determine conclusively who would benefit most from further education. Friedman asked 'if what people get is to be determined by "fairness", who is to decide what is "fair"?' Better to let the market decide. Hayek argued that wealthy families should be able to confer educational advantages on their children.

> A society is likely to get a better elite if ascent is not limited to one generation, if individuals are not deliberately made to start from the same level, and if children are not deprived of the chance to benefit from the better education and material environment which their parents might be able to provide (Hayek 1960: 90).

Similarly, Friedman argued that it was 'the exceptional few' that were 'the hope of the future'. The existence of steep vertical variations in the standard of education that children received was healthy, a sign of the existence of freedom of choice, stated Hayek. Friedman and Hayek did not argue for citizenship rights in education or support the growth of educational participation as an end in itself. Hayek rejected the notion that every student should succeed. 'A society that wishes to get a maximum economic return from a limited expenditure on education should concentrate on the higher education of a comparatively small elite.' The main problem was 'the inadequate output of men of really top quality', partly because of 'the democratic preference for providing better material opportunities for large numbers over the advancement of knowledge, which will always be the work of the relatively few and which indeed has the strongest claim for public support'. Government support should not be provided to everyone 'intellectually capable' of higher education. 'There are few greater dangers to political stability than the existence of an intellectual proletariat who find no outlet for their learning' (Friedman 1962: 93–97, 195; Friedman & Friedman

1980: 134–144, 169; Hayek 1960: 87–97, 125, 223, 257–260, 379–389; Hayek 1967a: 244–245; Hayek 1976: 74, 84; Hayek 1978a: 179; Hayek 1979a: 46–61, 145–146).

This suggested that government education had produced 'too much' merit and social mobility. Thus in *Equality* (1979) Keith Joseph, one of the founders of the British New Right and later a Thatcher Minister for Education, joined the critique of merit to a defence of class segmentation:

> Rapid economic expansion and a striking improvement in the first half of this century in the standard of the state education system gave rise to a high degree of social mobility . . . The distinctive feature of English social mobility since the war has been that even men of relatively modest ability with only average ambitions have been able to put their class origins behind them and have been carried by economic expansion through the hierarchy of large companies to positions which would once have been occupied by men of equally modest ability but rather higher social status . . . On the whole, men do not like observing that higher incomes are being earned by men of their own kind. Nor are they comforted to learn that these incomes are merited by the other man's superior intelligence or skills. For when two men are being compared, the superiority of one is the measure of the other's mediocrity (Joseph & Sumption 1979: 13–14).

Thus good public education was a threat to social order. So was bad public education. Buchanan argued that schools, and other institutions 'trading in concepts', promoted social instability (Reisman 1990: 150–152). 'Few institutions in our society are in a more unsatisfactory state than schools', stated Friedman. 'Few generate more discontent or can do more to undermine our liberty.' Expenditure was rising but the 'basics' were neglected. Student test scores were declining. The average graduate was better educated 25 or 35 years before. Repeatedly, the Friedmans returned to the argument that these alleged flaws were inherent in the mode of production, in its non-market, monopoly and producer captured character. 'Professional educators – not parents or students – have increasingly decided what should be taught, how, by whom, and to whom.' Regulated salaries and uniform qualifications meant teachers were 'dull and mediocre and uninspiring'. Schools would never respond consistently to consumers, or generate ongoing efficiencies. Private schools provided competition but were discriminated against by government funding of government schools, and the opportunity for consumer choice was available only to wealthy families.

> You cannot make a dog meow or a cat bark. And neither can you make a monopolistic supplier of a service, one that does not even get its funds directly from its customers, pay close attention to its customers' wants. The

only way to do so is to break the monopoly, to introduce competition, and to give customers alternatives (Friedman & Friedman 1984: 153, 155).

In relation to higher education, the premise that the benefits were individualised, coupled with the premise that higher education was (or should be) the preserve of an elite, led Friedman to conclude that government funding of higher education must be a regressive transfer away from the average taxpayer. 'The young men and women who go to college on the average come from higher income families than those who are not in college – yet both sets of parents pay taxes. And . . . these young men and women will occupy the higher rungs of the economic ladder.' Public higher education was better than public schooling because there was more competition from private institutions. But government funding caused frivolous 'over consumption' in state universities as shown by the drop out rate (Friedman 1962: 94–96; Friedman & Friedman 1980: 127, 152–188; Friedman & Friedman 1984: 25, 142–155).

In 1970 Buchanan even claimed that free education was responsible for the student revolt sweeping through American universities. The fact that the student received 'something for nothing' had 'predictable behavioural effects'. Because the student's education had 'little or no scarcity value' there was no incentive to avoid waste. The student 'has no conception, individually, that costs are involved at all. Is it to be wondered that he [sic] treats the whole university setting with disrespect or even with contempt?' (Buchanan and Devletoglou 1970: 27). Buchanan's implication was that 'the chaos' in the universities could be ended by market reform.

Friedman's reform: the simulated market

Friedman wanted to remove 90 per cent of government funding of education. This was not politically feasible, and his 'second best' position was for a simulated education market, based on vouchers funded by government. In schooling the voucher system would operate as follows:

Governments could require a minimum level of schooling financed by giving parents vouchers redeemable for a specified maximum sum per child per year if spent on 'approved' educational services. Parents would then be free to spend this sum and any additional sums they themselves provided on purchasing educational services from an 'approved' institution of their own choice. The educational services could be rendered by private enterprises operated for profit, or by non-profit institutions. The role of the government would be limited to ensuring that the schools met certain minimum standards (Friedman 1962: 89).[3]

In higher education, Friedman stated that all institutions should charge full-cost fees. If there were to be public subsidies, the money should be allocated in the form of equal vouchers for 'the number of students it is desired to subsidise'. These vouchers would be scholarships exchangeable at any institution. Friedman opposed student assistance grants and argued that loans were not sensitive to variations in graduate income. He preferred equity investment, buying a share in the student's future earnings. 'There seems no legal obstacle to private contracts of this kind, even though they are economically equivalent to the purchase of a share in an individual's earning capacity and thus to partial slavery', he stated. One way to finance student assistance, and vouchers, was by government investment in each individual student, repayable through the tax system from future earnings.

Friedman suggested that universal voucher financing could create 'a vast new market' in education. Many new private institutions would emerge. Only institutions that satisfied their 'customers' would survive. Inequalities between institutions might increase – 'some public schools would be left with the "dregs", becoming even poorer in quality than they are now' – but, he claimed, overall quality would rise. The voucher system also provided a structure in which government subsidies could be gradually withdrawn, and the private costs of education increased (Friedman 1962: 92–105; Friedman & Friedman 1980: 163–185; Friedman & Friedman 1984: 162).

Through Friedman's vouchers, bureaucratic education systems would be instantly transformed into competitive markets. Governments could continue to shape education, its distribution, its cost, and the extent of privatisation, by controlling the licensing of schools and the terms and conditions of vouchers. Vouchers were hard to implement, but they opened a door in the imagination of policy makers, making possible the construction of markets.

Other market liberal economists popularised these ideas. In 'Vouchers for education', on the eve of the government-led education expansion of the 1960s, Wiseman rejected all public funding and provision of vocational education, and proposed vouchers for other forms of education. He called for school funding proportional to enrolments, to establish a competitive dynamic, and saw the involvement of local governments in British schooling as an obstacle to a parent-based market. He urged the national government to take control of financing and allow parents to 'contract out' of government schools. 'The private school chosen by the parents would be paid a fee by the government equivalent to the per capita grant being paid to local authorities' (Wiseman 1959/1972: 371). This anticipated the strategies that were used by Thatcher thirty years

later. Replying to Wiseman, Horobin and Smyth (1960) also anticipated the later debate:

> But would 'freedom' to spend money on this rather than that school really
> compensate for the loss of democratic control at present exercised by
> citizens over central and local government authorities? We doubt that it
> would. The extent to which consumers exercise control over many estab-
> lished businesses is severely limited, and representation on education
> authorities and school boards is an important element of a democratic
> way of life. Implicit in Mr. Wiseman's scheme is a belief that freedom to
> spend money is an adequate substitute for citizenship (Horobin & Smyth
> 1960/1972: 377).

West (1965, 1967, 1976) attacked the tradition of free education: 'it
misinforms the public and creates serious illusions' (West 1976: 35). A
universal system of private schools would provide equality of opportunity. In Australia Brennan (1971), later one of Buchanan's collabora-
tors, prepared an argument against the abolition of university fees.
Brennan built his case for more market-like arrangements on the scarcity of places. He argued that government funding of higher education
was a regressive transfer of taxation revenue in favour of relatively affluent students. 'Consumer subsidies' such as scholarships, rather than the
funding of institutions, would 'stimulate the free market' (Brennan
1971: 96–97, 135–148).

After 1975 support for market reform began to gather in Australia.
An early blueprint based on Friedman's model was Blandy's *A liberal
strategy for reform of the education and training system in Australia*, commis-
sioned by the Fraser government's National Inquiry into Education and
Training (Blandy 1979: 143–173). Blandy proposed the introduction of
a voucher based market of government and private institutions in
higher education. A regulatory body would manage the entry of new
institutions and disaccreditation of bankrupt institutions, set and
monitor standards, keep tuition fees 'within bounds', and ensure access
to disadvantaged groups. Students would receive a standard non-means
tested grant – a voucher by another name – and would be eligible for
loans to cover the gap between standard grant and fees. Needy students
could be assisted with scholarships, and the waiving of loan repayments.
Blandy also proposed a tax on former students, proportional to income
and years of study. The tax revenue would be paid into an endowment
fund, transferred to institutions in proportion to their share of
graduates.

Five years later EPAC published Fane's proposals for the privatisation
and commercialisation of Australian education. Fane argued that education was a private good, not a public good. There was no reason why

it should not be produced as a commodity. The amount of public funding should be determined by net externalities: these were 'very small', probably close to zero. While egalitarian objectives were outside his consideration ('a question for philosophers and not for economists'), Fane opposed the equal distribution of education to students with the same scholastic aptitude because this interfered with individual choice making. He proposed a market in tertiary places, whereby students scoring high marks at the end of secondary school could sell places in the most sought-after tertiary courses to lower scoring students, establishing an economically 'efficient' pattern of consumption of higher education (Fane 1984: 67–74).

In 1987 and 1988 the Centre for Policy Studies, a think tank based at Monash University, published two volumes on *Spending and Taxing* which were widely distributed in business, government, schools and universities. Each included a chapter on education. In 1987 Parish argued that government schools were 'deficient in their performance of the cognitive, socialisation and screening functions usually ascribed to education', including school discipline, academic learning and basic skills. 'Producer capture' had led to inefficiencies. Teachers lacked accountability to 'their superiors' and parents, explaining the 'drift' of enrolments from government to private schools. Rising educational expenditures had not led to better educational outcomes: smaller classes benefited teachers but not students. Parish proposed dramatic reductions in government spending. Vouchers would enable schooling to be privatised quickly, breaking the power of the education bureaucracies and the unions. And in higher education government grants should be reduced by 50 per cent over five years (Parish 1987: 95–113).

In 1988 Porter focused on market reforms in higher education. While externalities such as research and the creation of knowledge required government funding, the main benefits of tertiary education were appropriated privately. Near-free tertiary education in public institutions had 'created an attitude that it is the responsibility of government to create educational options', enabling producer capture and discouraging private effort. There was nothing to drive efficiencies. Full fees should be charged. Porter recommended vouchers, student loans in place of grants, and the reconstitution of tertiary institutions as separate legal entities capable of private ownership, takeover and merger. Australia would only benefit from additional tertiary education and research funding 'under much less centralised and more competitive arrangements for supplying tertiary education ... the regulatory and incentive structure is, we suggest, more important than dollars spent' (Porter 1988: 119–130).

II. Standards and control

The standards debate

In the 1960s and 1970s the expanding role of education, and the accompanying social and cultural changes, made the work of educational institutions more ambiguous and difficult, problematising the notion of singular academic and behavioural standards.

Mass post-compulsory education pushed against the limits of systems of curriculum, assessment and selection that had been designed to identify 'ability' in a small, homogeneous and largely exclusive clientele. The monocultural norms of the Anglo-Australian middle classes were no longer unquestioned, though they remained dominant. Newer pedagogical theories emphasised the need for teaching to adapt to the circumstances of each child; while schools were required to deal with emerging minority cultures and growing diversity in everyday life. Formal education helped to generate and identify the very diversity and relativism that weakened its monocultural traditions. 'Most moral dilemmas are ... reflections of the fact that most of us identify with a number of different communities and are equally reluctant to marginalise ourselves in relation to any of them. This diversity of identifications increases with education' (Rorty 1983: 587).

Part of this problem was that students were subject to influences often more powerful than formal education. The average student watched 15 000 hours of television per year, including half a million advertisements, while receiving 11 500 hours of formal instruction (Canberra Times 1985). From the 1960s onwards there had been an explosion of youth-specific cultures and markets, shifts in sexual behaviour, the student revolt, feminism and the ecological movements. The resulting conflicts and anxieties were readily exploited by the New Right, which often defined schools as the 'cause' of these developments. Yet the education institutions were more determined than determining. The divorce rate quadrupled between the 1960s and the 1980s and one-parent families increased from 125 000 in 1969 to 306 000 in 1982 (ABS 4101.0). Schools were required to supplement the family and the church, strengthen welfare functions, provide for the full range of students, and respond to shifts in governmental and popular opinion that were uneven, contradictory, and occurred at shortening intervals. Strategies and forms of schooling were becoming more variable, pulling the schools several ways and opening them to a growing number of constituencies.

All of these changes generated desire for the restoration of simple certainties, while also making that security impossible to reach.

In the 1970s and 1980s the desire to increase retention, and the scarcity of higher education places, led to a continuing and unresolved debate about whether the academic curriculum should be differentiated, supplemented or otherwise reformed. An increasing number of students studied subjects not part of the traditional canon. There were pressures to broaden secondary assessment to recognise a range of achievement, or to establish a common general curriculum in place of early specialisation. Reform was championed by educational progressivists, who emphasised the need for the curriculum to be relevant to each individual student, and often championed educational process at the expense of content. Like the educational egalitarians (chapter 3), progressivists were often uncomfortable with competitive assessment and student ranking. They valued self-motivation rather than an externally imposed logic of punishment and reward (Cohen 1977).

The two groups did not always agree – socialist egalitarians were wary of any move away from content – and the influence of both movements was fragmented and limited. There was a general move towards informality in government schooling, and towards comprehensive classes and away from ability streaming, but only a small number of secondary schools were consistently progressivist (Bates & Kynaston 1983: 33–34). In pockets of the government systems a socially and politically critical outlook became embedded in the curriculum – for example within the framework of the Commonwealth Disadvantaged Schools Program in New South Wales, and in certain schools in Victoria (Johnston 1993: 106–119; Hannan 1985: 63–71) – but these schools remained marginal. A 1984 study of 5000 separate 'learning situations' found that 80 per cent of student time was spent on the utilitarian learning of facts and techniques, and only 10 per cent on creative and abstract thinking, mainly in English (Little 1985).

Nonetheless the successive waves of curriculum reform, management restructuring and school devolution; the flickering changes in official language and symbols; installed a new sense of restlessness and instability. It was evident that the government of education, which once seemed so rigid, was now subject to the ebb and flow of politics.

The debates about progressivism and 'back to the basics' in the United States, and comprehensives in Britain, affected Australian education. But it was the British *Black Papers* that demonstrated the potential of the standards issue. The first issue, produced in 1969, sold 80 000 copies. Its successors focused on discipline, academic standards and market reform. By the fourth issue in 1975 the public preoccupation with standards was ubiquitous and virtually uncontested. 'Educashun isn't wurking' became a key slogan of Thatcher's 1979 election campaign, and the *Black Papers* set her early education agenda (Husen

1979: 22; CCCS 1981: 191, 200; Parkin 1984; Jones 1989). The standards issue was generative and complex. It connected to genuine educational issues, albeit filtered (and often distorted) by public debate. It responded to a multitude of social changes, simplifying and reducing those changes with powerful slogans. It had a broad populist appeal, and touched the interests of every student, parent and employer. It was about national values. But it was also orchestrated by the media, and scripted by the New Right, which had its own answers to the 'problem' of standards even before the questions were raised.

Beginning in the mid-1970s, *The Bulletin* and *The Australian* allowed themselves to function as the *Black Papers* of Australia. An analysis by the Sociology Research Group in the Faculty of Education at the University of Melbourne found that the standards debate was scarcely a debate at all. Rather, it took the form of a binary interaction between the media and the 'primary definers', a select group of institutional heads, university experts, industry leaders and politicians led by the cultural conservative educators in the Australian Council of Educational Standards: Chipman, Kramer, Partington and others. The primary definers used the media to legitimate their position, while the media used their statements to frame the debate. The same primary definers were regularly reported, using common arguments, terms and slogans. They used 'circular referencing', citing media reports of each other's statements as evidence and authority. In this manner the primary definers and media pre-constructed a consensus, and appealed to that consensus as *the* standard, while sealing off discussion of the issues from other viewpoints. Their definition of the issues was rendered universal (SRG 1979).

'Back to the basics'

The sudden increase in youth unemployment in 1974 and 1975, and the first signs of graduate unemployment, coinciding with a fall in the average salary differentials to graduates (Marginson 1995a), created a new doubt about the value of education and contributed to the decline in Year 12 retention among male students in the second half of the 1970s.

These trends provided favourable conditions for the first claims about standards. In an article in *The Bulletin* of 15 May 1976, Peter Samuels blamed youth unemployment on the failure of schools to impart 'basic skills'. He cited a 1975 survey of literacy and numeracy by the Australian Council for Educational Research (ACER). The massive response to Samuels' argument signified the emergence of a new policy agenda, sustained by the notion of *declining* standards, of an essential mission of schooling corrupted by egalitarianism, the loss of discipline and control, and 'the left-wing teachers who permeate the school and tertiary education system' (Morgan, in Sheehan 1985). The hard-headed demands for return to 'the basics', mingled with romantic images of the golden years of childhood, and the golden years of postwar prosperity, provided a clear (though not altogether practical) program for reform. Sidestepping the professional mysteries of teaching, and consistent with parent choice, it seemed to provide a common sense way to monitor and control the performance of teachers, schools and systems.

In reviewing Australian education in 1976 a team from the OECD noted that 'standards of literacy and numeracy and the effects of recent changes in secondary schools on the attitudes of young people to work and adult responsibilities was a topic on which we received much comment'. Claims that standards had fallen came from employers, parents, teachers in tertiary institutions 'and not a few school-teachers'. Often, 'progressivism and permissiveness were seen as 'the root of the problem'. But 'there was a lack of reliable empirical evidence to support these allegations', and 'the performance of the students as a whole was no worse than that of students in other OECD countries' (OECD 1977: 38, 43). The Secretary of the Australian Council of Education, and the Victorian Director-General of Education, stated that Samuels had misrepresented the ACER tests (Bates & Kynaston 1983). The ACER stated there was little in its survey findings to disparage schools. But the legend was already in place.

Nine years later Sheridan stated that 'an Australian Council of Education (ACER) survey done a few years ago reported that one-sixth of the 14-year-olds sampled were unable to read a simple sentence, while a further quarter had only partly mastered reading skills' (Sheridan 1985b). Yet the 1975 ACER report had actually stated 'we have estimated the proportion of students in normal schooling at the 10-year-old and 14-year-old levels, who were unable to read simple sentences, to be 3 per cent and 0.8 per cent respectively (Keeves et al 1976: 105). Somehow, 0.8 per cent of students was magnified into one student in six, through the distorting lens of the standards debate.

What evidence there was on longitudinal trends in literacy mostly indicated improvement over time (Little 1978), as some leading educational conservatives acknowledged. Partington noted that 'the so-called basics, the 3 Rs, have not suffered undue neglect, at least in terms of the time spent on them'. According to Start, the educational system had 'done well' in lifting everyone 'above the minimum of essential functional literacy' (Partington 1982; Start 1989). Nonetheless, trends in literacy occurred in a moving context which made comparison difficult – and for political reasons the issue could not be laid to rest. For cultural conservatives, market liberals and employers, the basic skills issue was too useful too ignore. It had strong public resonances that could be used to set off a range of other issues. This was indicated by the asymmetrical character of the 'debate'. Statements about improvements in standards, accompanied by substantial evidence, had no news value. Claims about declining standards, whether proven or not, drew maximum publicity. 'Declining standards' was a narrative and symbolism too strongly entrenched to be negated with logic, surveys, and numbers.

Employers and preparation for work

The 1979 National Inquiry into Education and Training noted 'many complaints' by employers that 'a disturbingly high proportion of school leavers had not achieved standards of literacy and numeracy that would enable them to make a satisfactory transition from school to work or further study'. Some argued there was a retreat from the 'basics' to 'softer curriculum options' (Williams 1979: 88–90). In 1985 the Quality of Education Review Committee cited the Confederation of Australian Industry, which reported that personnel officers of major companies were concerned about literacy and numeracy (Karmel 1985). Most of the data came from companies employing apprentices, rather than school or university graduates (Sweet 1979), but their problems were used to mobilise a more general business intervention in education. For the leading employers, the fundamental question was not whether today's students were better or worse, it was whether they met the needs of business tomorrow (Finn in Duncan 1987). In 1986 the Business Council of Australia, representing the larger, global companies, found that 88 per cent of its members believed business should be more vigorous in influencing 'educational objectives and practices', and 55 per cent thought standards would improve if business was more involved in educational decision making and management (BCA 1986).

These perceptions were encouraged by governments. The Prime Minister noted in 1980 that 'the education system is to blame for much of the youth unemployment in Australia ... children are sent out of school unable to read, write or add up to an acceptable standard' (quoted in Parkin 1984: 55). Similar comments were made by Fraser's Labor Party successor only four years later (Hawke 1984). Governments thereby signalled not only their alignment with business, but their desire to draw employer organisations into a privileged policy role. For their part, employers were frank: they wanted an education system specific to their own economic needs. If other and wider interests were to be met, they would have to be delivered by the invisible hand. They argued for 'relevance' and vocationalism, and while mostly tolerant of academic goals, had little enthusiasm for the traditional academic curriculum, either as preparation for work or for its 'own' sake.

In the 1986 survey the BCA companies were asked to rank the goals of secondary schools and evaluate the performance of schools in achieving those goals. Basic skills, and thinking/problem solving skills, ranked ahead of academic learning. Of the companies surveyed 83 per cent believed there was insufficient emphasis on basic skills in secondary education, but only 14 per cent wanted more emphasis on academic subjects, and 21 per cent wanted *less* emphasis. Respondents wanted schools to place more emphasis on vocational skills, preparation in work and career choices, social skills, and coping with authority (BCA 1986; IPA 1987). Employer organisations were also concerned about an alleged retreat from the study of maths and science in schools, and the attitudes of students and teachers to business. John Ralph, Chief Executive of CRA told *Business Review Weekly* that 'the child's, and later the adult's attitude to business and wealth creation is strongly influenced by the way the education system depicts business people and wealth creating production'. He wanted 'an education which stresses the links between effort and reward' (Duncan 1987: 21). Companies surveyed by the Melbourne *Herald* believed teacher attitudes were a problem. 'The education system must teach the values consistent with private enterprise and entrepreneurialism' (Herald 1988).

Cultural conservative power/knowledge

For conservatives, a strong state and cultural cohesion reinforced each other, and education underpinned them both. In *The meaning of conservatism* (1984) Scruton described education as an end in itself that should not be reduced to an instrumental role, for example in government programs to contain unemployment. However, not all children were suited to education. Universal education was both impossible and undesirable, and selection was inevitable. 'Inequality of opportunity' could not be eradicated without depriving 'the gifted child of some part of his natural understanding'. Egalitarianism in education was misguided and dangerous, and the 'contagion' of democracy had to be rooted out. Because education conferred 'the ability to communicate, to persuade, to attract and dominate', too much education made people unsatisfied with life. Class distinctions were not 'evil or unjust: they stemmed from the basic principles of social order' Scruton insisted (1984: 59–60, 147–158, 181).

Here, rooted in property and power, lay the conservative brand of educational instrumentalism. The traditional users of private schools, and of the professional faculties of the universities, defended a conservative curriculum and assessment because these older technologies of cultural acquisition and educational selection worked in their favour. The leading private schools had opted out of equality of opportunity, maintaining the right to accumulate their own superior economic and cultural resources but using system-wide competition to democratise their own success, and to institutionalise the failure of others. The demands of the academic curriculum were made 'authoritative for all students', although they represented 'the formalisation of the culture of only a few' (Teese 1986). The leading private schools saw their mission simply as the maintenance of themselves, their relationships, and their own artefacts of social life, the reproduction of what Arnold had called 'the best that has been thought and said'.

In this manner 'the private sector understood itself according to a theory of cultural distinction' (McCallum 1990: 52–55, 111–112, 135–136), a theory embedded in the 'continuous patterning' of the education system 'over generations of use around the status, culture and professional needs of the middle classes' (Teese 1986).

Gramsci states that 'every relationship of hegemony is necessarily an educational relationship'. The terms of hegemony must be continually re-established (Gramsci 1971: 350; Hall 1988b). Cultural conservatism was 'a defence of a set of ideas which have served some individuals and groups very well. Its power relies not only on whom it serves, but on its coherence, its long history, and its use of language which people can understand' (Costello 1985). It was a claim for particular mechanisms of hegemony. Conservatives supported orthodox academic disciplines and forms ('rigour') in the context of ability streaming, didactic pedagogy, unreflective curricula, authoritarian classrooms, continuous competition and the terror of failure. They saw governments, teachers, radical educationists and academics in teacher training as complicit in the erosion of the systems for producing and assigning these 'standards'. In the face of the developing mass education systems, they advocated zero sum competition and the scarcity of educational status ('excellence'). They set themselves against the Deweyan emphasis on democracy-in-community that was influential in government education, and had weakened the older conservative hegemony. It was not incidental that this defended the positional advantages of the established elites. One ACES leader described its mission in Gramscian terms:

When an establishment lacks the will and the nerve to articulate a justification for its values and to demand their imposition as far as the validity of that justification extends, then educational administrators are forced into trend spotting . . . The corrective . . . can only come from the reaffirmation of cultural hegemony by the 'mainstream' (Chipman, quoted in Little 1985).

Like Hayek and Friedman, and many educators, the cultural conservatives saw education as the producer of future social leaders, initiated in the monoculture and steeled by competition. Unlike many educators, the conservatives assumed that the pool of 'ability' was fixed, not historically based, so that the present elite was the 'natural' elite, and relative standards were the same as absolute standards. Thus inequality and under-achievement were inevitable: 'the dull, the poor and the uninterested will always be with us' (Conway 1985). Any attempt to broaden or redistribute educational achievement was an attack on excellence itself.

To claims that in a comprehensive or mass system more talent was harvested, they were at best indifferent. Comprehensives held back the 'gifted', who were the natural leaders. When education expanded the quality of schooling and university degrees eroded (Chipman 1978; 1980; 1982). Not only were the conservatives opposed to increasing the quantity of educational success, they were opposed to its redistribution on fairer lines. Any improvement in the achievements of disadvantaged groups, aside from a few 'gifted' individuals, would penalise the traditional achievers. 'If equality has meant anything at all it has meant a redistribution of resources away from those who are gifted and of superior talent to those who are less so, while at the same time downgrading the notion of superior talent' (Chipman 1978: 12).

The concern was not to maximise the educational standards of the mass, but to preserve the system of elite selection. To do this the cultural conservatives created a binary debate – you were either for standards, or for their destruction – and conflated mild social engineering of the equality of opportunity type with a radical egalitarianism that rejected all competition, ranking, and 'ability'. The policy assumption that the achievement of students from all social groups should be approximately equal was reinterpreted by the conservatives, to mean that every *individual* student should have equal achievement. This alleged levelling was much resented. 'There is within education today a philosophy that seems determined to sacrifice excellence in our young in favour of some grand egalitarianism not of opportunity but of attainment' (Barnard 1982). Education was being attacked by 'a tide of mediocrity' (Partington 1984).

The cultural conservatives understood the 'great disciplines' in the sciences and humanities as universal, and refused all educational pluralism. Here the form and content of the dominant culture, 'rigour' and monoculture, were conflated. Any departure from the traditional curriculum was a slide into relativism, and the loss of objectivity, impartial analysis, evaluative judgement, and even 'respect for precision and accuracy' (Kramer 1989).

Chipman was little concerned about the disappearance of Aboriginal languages: 'It would seem to me that you would do far more for an Aboriginal child in ensuring mastery of English, and that it may be even more valuable to teach the child Latin or Ancient Greek than the language of the parents' (Chipman 1985). 'It may be that schools should follow a fairly narrow curriculum' stated a 1985 editorial in *The Australian*. Three years later that newspaper specified a compulsory core of English, history, maths, science and a foreign language (*The Australian* 1985; 1988b). The universal character of these 'great disciplines' sustained the doctrine of education as an end in itself, and also vice versa. 'The nonsense view is getting abroad that the Higher School Certificate's only purpose is to predict university performance, whereas its purpose is to strengthen the mind in the great disciplines' (Chipman, in Sheridan 1983a).

To admit the curriculum depended on its uses was to admit it could vary with use, to fragment the authority of the monoculture, and even to question the real social instrumentalism of the curriculum, its complicity in power. Thus the conservatives held the line against all curriculum reforms designed to increase retention, or better prepare students for living, or adapt to students' circumstances (Barcan 1978; Chipman 1978; Partington 1982; Partington 1985; Sheridan 1985c). Like Hayek, they had little interest in broadening the reach of citizenship through education. 'Schools are in danger of becoming leisure centres, adolescent custodial institutions, achieving little more than keeping kids off the street and teachers employed' (Sheridan 1983a). 'Social issues of a transitory kind . . . do not provide a sound intellectual training' (Kramer in IPA 1987).

The best solution to relevance and student motivation was hard work, and more of it, of a traditional academic kind. Learning was about 'the arduous and difficult' (Kramer 1989). Difficulty *itself* was important, it strengthened the mind, as if the mind was a kind of muscle and school was military or physical training. Rigour was enforced directly by classroom discipline, and indirectly by competition and selection. Chipman opposed the abolition of the concept of failure, because he believed that the fear of failure was the source of student motivation (Chipman 1978, 1980, 1982). The conservatives also opposed any reduction in the role of competitive public examinations in tertiary entrance, and favoured the use of 'hard' subjects (especially mathematics and the physical sciences) as principal selectors. The leading private schools were particularly successful in these subjects: ironically, Chipman argued that reforms in secondary examinations, increasing the use of school-based assessment, denied gifted poorer students the opportunity 'to transcend their historic circumstances' (Chipman 1982).

Discipline and rigour were also synonyms for order and control. These were constant themes in the conservatives literature. The early stages of the debate established the myth of a government schooling system out of control, anarchic and violent, rife with illicit sex and drugs (SRG 1979). In conservative critiques of progressivism, the relaxation of traditional requirements relating to uniforms and modes of address, and the individualisation of pedagogies and assessment, were used to build a picture of 'softness' rather than 'hardness' or 'toughness'; of schools that had emptied out their moral standards along with their academic content; of indulgence and permissiveness; an end to child safety and moral security (Chipman 1984; Conway 1985). The nostalgia for a 'visible pedagogy', with more rigid curriculum and assessment requirements, was a desire for classrooms in which the teachers exercised explicit control over students and reflective cognition was not encouraged. 'Rather the teacher, primarily in reformulating, does the work of generalisation, specification, increasing precision, testing hypotheses and the like' (Young 1983).

The question of order posed a dilemma for conservatives, especially in government, because social order was better served by containing youth within a high retention education system than by facilitating unemployment outside education. But they also feared what they saw as the organised disorder created by a radicalised teaching profession committed to Deweyan self-realisation. It was feared that discussion of moral and social issues in the classroom would allow teachers to politicise their charges, that students were exercising value judgements, and engaging in critical thinking before 'morally defensible beliefs and actions' had been inculcated; that is, before a conservative subjectivity, based on self-regulation as subjugation, had been secured (Partington 1982; 1983). Sheridan declared that students should not be expected 'to have opinions about issues on which they are almost entirely ignorant' (Sheridan 1985a).

The cultural conservatives were especially critical of teachers. They were unprofessional, they were incompetent *in loco parentis*, they were 'anti-Christian', they were 'anti-Australian' (Partington 1983; 1985). Their dress, grooming, manners, deportment, language and personal habits left much to be desired. For *The Age* columnist Peter Ryan the 'average schoolteacher' was 'slack-twisted, idle, greedy, feeble, disaffected, subversive, dogmatic and disturbed' (Ryan 1986). Chipman referred to a 'foul-mouthed rabble', 'sloppily dressed and grubbily obese', from 'the bottom of the graduate barrel' (Chipman 1980; Maslen 1985). The deepest aversion was to left-wing teachers. The claims that teachers were of low quality were linked to claims about their politicisation, as if the two were symbiotic. Thus Partington juxtaposed the support of the World Confederation of Organisations of the Teaching Profession for human rights issues, to the alleged indifference of teachers to Shakespeare's *Hamlet* (Partington 1985).

The teacher unions were the main target (for example Chipman 1978; Carlton 1985; Conway 1985; Partington 1985; Sheridan 1985b). One editorial in the *Australian Financial Review* stated that it was in the interests of the whole of Australian education 'that the power of the NSW Teachers' Federation be broken, before it totally ruins the public school system with great harm to Australia generally' (AFR 1984). It became a truism that teachers had undue influence on educational policy through the links between unions and Labor governments. Contrarily, it was also argued that teachers were a law unto themselves. 'The main function of teachers' unions today is to resist external accountability, both at the educational and the management levels' (Chipman 1980). Teachers were 'accountable to no-one' (AFR 1987). To Gottliebsen (1985), teachers wanting to reduce external examinations were like 'business leaders preferring not to produce an audited profit statement which might show up their faulty performance'. Opposition to standardised testing was seen as 'proof' of the refusal of accountability and standards.

The approach was polemical in the extreme, the claims were sweeping and apocalyptic. 'Education in Australia is nothing short of a disaster and the most radical and urgent action is needed' stated *The Australian* (1988a). Such claims were often hard to reconcile with evidence and experience. During the 1980s, as positional competition became tougher and parental involvement in school decision making increased, secondary schools were bound more tightly to competitive assessment requirements, with little scope for even modest egalitarian experiments. At the time when the standards debate was reaching its climax, government schools were already conservatising. Yet the objective of the Right was not to make balanced judgements or to isolate 'bad' behaviours in order to improve the government school system. Rather, it created a negative myth based on a small number of real or imagined cases, and widened the critical arc so as to apply that myth to government schooling as a whole, splitting the education communities, weakening the consensus about equality of opportunity, strengthening private schooling and pressuring governments to reconstitute government schooling.

The strategy was successful. Those programs of government designed to secure higher retention and greater vocationalism departed from cultural conservative vision, but the authority of traditional academic standards was maintained. It is doubtful if the conservatives, always mindful of the true scarcity of 'excellence', ever wanted it practised in every government school. Because conservative standards – exclusive and excluding – were *not* universal in practice, they remained hegemonic.

Competitive individualism

Cultural conservatism in education did not always sit easily with market liberalism or the needs of employers. Market reforms had the potential to weaken academic authority. For example tertiary fees were 'an alternative method of rationing entry' in which 'willingness to pay' replaced 'exceeding the cut-off scores as the eligibility criterion' (Parish 1987).[4] Employers wanting vocationalism had little commitment to education for its own sake. Nevertheless, the conservatives spoke for the whole New Right when they attacked government education and teachers and demanded accountability and control, and especially when they asserted the role of competition. For the whole New Right, untroubled by the desire for solidarity, 'competitive individualism' was at the core of its normative expectations of education.

Here competition played a multiple and sometimes contradictory role. Economically competition was used to drive institutional efficiency and responsiveness (Friedman 1962: 91–94; Friedman & Friedman 1984: 152, 162–163). At the same time it was used to shape student behaviours, being the common ingredient in discipline, control, self-regulation and motivation. Fair and open competition was seen as the surest way to raise standards. 'A market not only provides rational use of resources, it encourages academic rigour. No one wants to pay good money for a second-rate education' (Sheridan 1983b). It was also used to naturalise 'talent' and the identification of success and leadership *via* education. It underpinned the authority of professional educators. Competition was used to sort students and graduates, rank institutions against each other, and measure the performance of teachers, schools and systems of education. It mediated and naturalised relations between schools and further education, and schools and the labour markets.

The New Right developed a synthesised narrative in which the conservatively defined 'problems' of standards and discipline were resolved by the liberal 'solution' of marketisation. These heterogeneous elements were bound together by the notion of competition, in its dual role as a system of economic production and distribution, and a system of pedagogical control.

In 1988 Sheridan prepared a series of articles for *The Australian* which described education in Japan and Taiwan as models for Australia. The Japanese system was highly competitive. Students worked very hard to qualify for often high fee and private institutions. There were few options in the curriculum and rote learning was used. Teachers were respected. Class sizes were large because 'the teacher tends to relate to the class as a group rather than to individual students'. Sheridan concluded 'the achievements of Japanese education are staggering. It is the most successful education system in the world today. But in truth there is little mystery to the Japanese success . . . the heart of the system is simply a commitment to excellence and a sustained, hard slog of work, work and more work' (Sheridan 1988a). Education in Taiwan was described in much the same terms, as 'ultra-competitive' and 'more hard-working even than the hard-working Japanese system. It runs longer hours with larger class sizes.' Sheridan implied that the near absence of 'social pathologies' such as drugs, teenage pregnancy and street crime in Taiwan was linked to the educational workloads and traditional teaching (Sheridan 1988b). He contrasted Japan and Taiwan with 'the appalling complacency' of 'educational authorities' in Australia 'who are effectively insulated from the forces of the market' (Sheridan 1988c).

Sheridan's argument rested on the assumption that the educational achievements of Japan and Taiwan were freely transferable across cultural contexts. It was an enormous leap of faith, and hardly a feasible policy. But it was also a clever blend of liberal and conservative ideas, equating market competition with scholastic competition and joining cultural standards, student discipline and social order to the national interest.

III. Standardisation and choice

Parental choice

The Karmel report of 1973 was careful to blur the distinction between two models of choice in schooling: 'freedom of choice' based on individuation, negative freedom and markets, supported by the New Right; and choice as collective self-determination within the framework of site based planning, supported in some government systems (see chapter 3). Under the Fraser Government from 1975 to 1983, the balance of policy favoured the market model (SC 1978: 6–11; CSC 1981: 35–37) and the New Right drew support for choice in education in an anti-statist and pro-market direction.

The market model of choice was propounded in Australia by the Australian Parents Council (APC), using an individualist reading of Article 26 (3) of the United Nations Declaration of Human Rights which referred to the 'prior right' of parents to choose their children's education. The United Nations Declaration had carefully referred to the rights of all, acknowledging the broader effects of the unfettered exercise of market choices. Nevertheless, the APC conceived the rights of individual parents in abstract and absolute terms *vis-à-vis* other parents, the child and the state; and all parents were seen as equivalent, without regard to differing material or cultural circumstances.

Linked to arguments about equal treatment before government, the demand for freedom of choice in schooling tapped an 'egalitarian individualism' (Kapferer 1989) typical of Australian practices, although the defence of wealthy private schools was perhaps less consistent with the tradition. In this manner the choice debate was used to decouple self-determination and autonomy from egalitarian and collective forms of education. Like equality of opportunity before it, the appeal of the freedom of choice argument was that it situated economic and social self-interest on the high moral ground. Unlike the earlier policy, freedom of choice was centred on private schools, and stigmatised direct government intervention, seen to interfere with the market rights of parents. Eventually government education was pressed into conformity with the market model in order to survive.

The exercise of choice was one question, the nature of the choices was another. In a choice-based system, parents might choose between schools that were self-determining and diverse, or schools that conformed to imposed norms and offered a narrower range. The New Right supported self-determination as the operating condition of private schools, but was wary of extending self-determination to the government sector. In *Children, education and schooling* the APC argued that school communities should control their own curricula and enrolment policies (APC 1983). Conway (1985) acknowledged that in such systems, instances of low standards were inevitable. 'There are a number of independent schools on the fringes of society which are even more down-at-heel and anti-intellectual in outlook than their worst government counterparts'. These fostered 'some of the most disagreeably xenophobic forms of child indoctrination. Yet such is the price we pay for freedom of choice in education.' To Sheridan, devolution and diversified curricula were features of private schooling that parents valued. Yet he also argued that school-based curricula were a prime source of dissatisfaction with government schools, and closer control was needed.

The Parliament, the Ministers, the Education Ministers, need to regain central control over education. Authority within education, the principles of authority, need to be reasserted ... to reassert control over the education system and take it away from the minority groups that Geoffrey has described, and also the activist teacher unions, who are ideologically motivated and who should have no role at all in curriculum formation (Sheridan 1985c).

The political message was that governments were accountable for government schools and should intervene to impose order. Thus open ended choice was used to deconstruct government education from outside, but inside that sector, even if reformed along market lines, the ambit of choice was to be severely constrained. All strands of the New Right agreed on the need to strengthen systemwide examinations and introduce standardised testing in government schooling, to facilitate competition, accountability and control; to measure standards, and to create pressures for their improvement. The 1986 BCA survey showed that employers supported uniform national exams, credentials and standards of curricula (BCA 1986).

Here the main policy issue was standardised testing. In the United States, student testing was used to measure outputs; to monitor the performance of schools, school districts and state systems; to distribute tertiary places; to determine budgetary allocations and sometimes teachers' pay; and to settle questions of educational quality. Standardised tests also enabled greater State government control over schools, weakening the power of local school boards and educational professionals. In the United States there was a market in standardised testing, and the commercial publishers of tests lobbied for their extension (Parkin 1984; Madaus 1985; Salganik 1985).

Among professionals in America, Australia and many other countries there was considerable disquiet about standardised testing, especially minimum competency tests, on the grounds that it reduced higher level achievement, and the range of achievement, and did not necessarily improve teaching (OECD 1985: 71). Nevertheless, if tests were rigid, narrowing and pejorative in pedagogical terms, in economic and managerial terms they were flexible and powerful instruments, offering a means of standardising curricula and regulating educational choices without using direct intervention. Standardised testing also offered the prospect of 'league tables' in which every institution and every teacher could be ranked competitively against every other, judged by a common set of norms that bound them all. So much for diversity.

Standards and market reform

The standards debate played the role in education policy that monetarism played a little earlier in economic policy. The myth of decline, and the images of chaos and collapse, constituted the break with the past. The claims about standards generated a formidable sense of crisis. Educational decline was joined to the narrative of national decline, undermining the egalitarian and progressivist strands which had grown out of the late Keynesian period. Space was cleared for new educational policies and new systems of control.

As in economic policy, it was market reform that was poised to fill the vacuum. In 1975 the editor of the *Black Papers* and later minister of education under Thatcher, Rhodes Boyson, wrote that 'the two pillars of a sound educational system' were market principles and central control. Schooling should become a parent-based market within a standardised national curriculum (Jones 1989: 16, 42). In the 1988 Education Reform Act these 'twin pillars' became the basis of Thatcher's schooling programs. The way through the dilemma of choice and self-determination *versus* authority and control, was to establish a governed market where curricula and standards, and the other forms and terms of competition, could be regulated. Market competition, devolution and parent choice, and standardised testing, together promised to answer the needs for standards, autonomy, comparative information, accountability, hierarchy and control. At the same time, the standards and choice debates shaped the future educational markets: weakening government schooling, confirming the positional advantages of the leading private schools, ensuring that *their* cultural practices would remain the criterion by which all other schools were judged. The future educational markets would be vertically segmented. Movement into the top echelon would continue to be very difficult, elite education and its clients would be protected, and the highest positional outcomes would retain their value.

Thus market reform could be made consistent with the conservation of the existing social elite; and education's role in producing and reproducing social hierarchy would increasingly overshadow its role in the constitution of universal citizenship.

Notes

[1] Friedman was interested in the externalities generated by an additional government dollar, i.e. marginal not average externalities. If parents would cover the full costs of externalities, the marginal value of the additional dollar was

zero. This implied the targeting of families unable to pay themselves, rather than universal government funding (Friedman 1976: 92).

[2] West (1967) claimed that nineteenth century government education suppressed a vigorous private school market. Subsequently Friedman changed his position, arguing that the public systems should not have been established. 'In Britain, as in the United States, schooling was almost universal before the government took it over . . . [this] reduced the quality and diversity of schooling' (Friedman & Friedman 1980: 154; Friedman & Friedman 1984: 143–144).

[3] Friedman made little comment on the constitutional barrier against aid to private schools in the United States, which blocked a universal voucher scheme extending across both private and government schools (see West 1976, 1ff; Friedman & Friedman 1980: 171; Friedman & Friedman 1984: 156–158).

[4] When arguing for market reform in universities as the solution to the student revolt, Buchanan and Devetolgou acknowledged economics would govern entry, but argued that 'academic criteria for university admissions reflect the personal preferences and prejudices of faculties . . . How, then, can such criteria be held sacrosanct?' (1970: 32–49).

PART III

THE ECONOMIC CITIZEN
1985–1995

'Indeed, we are reduced almost to infinity.'

Patrick White, Voss,
Penguin, Harmondsworth, 1960, p. 216.

Market liberalism transformed government, but did not guarantee an inclusive social order and something more was needed. With youth labour market collapsing; and with higher education, training and research, in conjunction with technological change, at the cutting edge of international economic competition, it again became necessary to use education as the vehicle for social formation. The old goal of full employment was replaced with 'full education' in a high participation system. But this educational expansion was different to the 1960s, being part financed by the 'user', in government controlled markets, and dominated by vocational concerns. The objective of the strategies of government was now to produce *economic* citizens.

CHAPTER 7

Education and national economic reconstruction

'The labour market challenges that call for long-term adjustment of the educational systems stem from the pressures of international competition, technological change and, more generally, the need for flexibility. Though individual member countries all have their own economic, cultural and educational legacies, they now face largely the same market conditions and use more or less the same technologies and sources of information. In this situation, each country's prosperity hinges to a great extent . . . on its ability to enhance its competitiveness under what are inherently unpredictable market conditions. . . . a fact which inevitably raises serious concerns for countries whose education systems perform poorly by international standards – be it in terms of quantity, quality or flexibility.'

Structural adjustment and economic performance,
*Organisation for Economic Cooperation and Development, OECD,
Paris 1987, pp. 69–70.*

Prelude: Education responsive to industry (1963)

In 1963 the International Economic Association held a conference at Menthon St. Bernard on the economics of education. While many speakers explored the aggregate relations between education and economic growth, in 'Resource requirements and educational obsolescence', Selma J. Mushkin, a consultant to the OECD in Paris, focused on the micro-economic relations between education and industry. Policy makers saw education as the selection and preparation of future leaders, but to Mushkin it was a universal system, with a recurrent role in the workforce. She saw the services occupations becoming dominant in the economy; the requirements for knowledge and skill were rising, increasing the role of education. 'Technological displacement' and unemployment were likely to become serious problems, but education could be used to reduce unemployment and provide retraining. However, to do this education would need to become more flexible and responsive in the face of technological change:

> It is one of the most striking failings of our educational system that it seems to be unable to readjust its way of doing things to meet changing requirements. Scientific progress and technological advances have altered the educational requirements of society. More trained people – people trained in the skills required by scientific and technological innovation – and a deepened capacity for scientific research, are widely recognised as prime requisites for economic progress ... While we have historically regarded our working force and its skills as a concern separate from the structure and organisation of education, more and more there is acceptance of the fact that the skills of the working force are a resource to be explored and developed through education (Mushkin 1966: 463).

Mushkin argued that educational institutions should move closer to industry. She called for research exchange between the universities and industry in order to disseminate scientific advances and to guide the development of research according to business needs. In many occupations training would need continuous upgrading. 'Womanpower' should be used more effectively, and women returning to the workforce after child rearing would also need retraining. An expanded recurrent education system should be jointly financed by governments, employers and employees, and the need for training should be talked up by governments, using the rhetoric of national needs. 'Motivation rests on more than personal advantage. It can be generated through imaginative national publicity which identifies re-education with national objectives and the purposes of fuller development of human resources as an integral component of technological advances and economic growth' (Mushkin 1966: 477).

In her focus on the convergence of education and work, and the 'responsiveness' of education, Mushkin had moved beyond the 1960s policies in which the economic contribution of education was simply taken for granted. Her vision of client-oriented and self-managing education institutions, regulating their own adjustment to external pressures, foreshadowed corporate devolution and market reform. The discussion following her paper showed that it was not well understood by her peers (Robinson & Vaizey 1966: 708–725). But it was a remarkable anticipation of the policy themes of the 1980s, when the OECD was orchestrating a renewed interest in the role of education in national economic reconstruction, and was linking this to reform in the government of education itself. Rather than the nationalisation of programs and funding as in the 1960s, the governments of the 1980s used globalisation and micro-economic reform to open education to business, to vocationalise curricula, and to create market-based systems of accountability and control.

I. Policies for reconstruction

Economic rationalism and education

At the 1981 OECD inter-governmental conference on higher education, the chair, Australia's Peter Karmel, referred to the 'exaggerated' expectations built into higher education 'during the heyday of its expansion'. The conference noted 'the belief that higher education contains the key to social equality or to economic growth is now widely disputed' (OECD 1983). In Australia educational professionals remained committed to the twin objectives of investment in human capital, and equality of opportunity through education, that set the framework of educational expansion in the 1960s and early 1970s. Yet in the key economic departments of government, faith in these policies had largely collapsed. While opinion polls showed continued support for increased spending on education, neither the Coalition parties nor Labor saw education as a major priority.

But this was only marking time, a hiatus between policies rather than a policy in its own right. Over the next half-decade new strategies and methods of government were developed in education, first of all at the national level, by the coordinating departments of government, Prime Minister and Cabinet, Treasury, Finance. This was parallel to – albeit slightly behind – developments in Britain, America and the OECD.

Everywhere, education was seen as crucial to economic competitiveness, mobilised for economic reconstruction, and embedded in micro-economic reform, corporatisation and marketisation. The formation of citizens in education was subordinated to its new economic mission. There was another expansion in educational provision and popular participation, almost on the scale of the growth of the 1960s and early 1970s. However, this time the objective was not so much the broad development of the skills and talents of the nation, as in the late Keynesian period, but the development of those specific aspects of education and research that assisted national economic competitiveness.

The new policies in education were above all economic policies, and shaped by the market liberal reading of neoclassical economics. They were a symptom of the rise of 'economic rationalism' in national

government in Australia (Pusey 1991; Marginson 1993a). Pusey analyses
the outcome of the mid-1980s reforms in the Commonwealth public
service, led by the then Minister for Finance, John Dawkins. There was
a radical break from the tradition of a lifelong and neutral civil service
that drew its authority from an abstracted 'public interest'. In the
contract-based senior executive service, managers were moved freely
between departments, and subject to ministerial patronage and control.
In the key coordinating departments, 70 per cent of the senior executive service were trained in economics or business, compared to 54
per cent in the whole sample. Economists were promoted more quickly
than non-economists. Senior managers were mostly conservative and
market liberal in outlook, and espoused key policy positions popularised by the New Right, for example that 'individual initiative' should
be encouraged at the expense of government intervention. Only one-
fifth were social democrats. 'National policy . . . is held in the compass
of the restrictive, technically-oriented, neoclassical economics curriculum that swept through the economics departments of Australian universities from about 1947 onwards' (Pusey 1991: 78, 80, 171-172).

The primacy of economics was a feature of all modernising government (Beilharz 1994), and not an invention of the specifically New
Right brand of modernisation. Nevertheless, market liberalism carried
it to a new level and made it market oriented. Not only the purposes
of education programs, but the way of thinking about education, and
the new systems and behaviours emerging from reform, were neoclassical and market liberal. More so than in the 1960s, the education
citizen imagined in government was an *economic* citizen. All other objectives, in education, including social equity, were joined to and subordinated to the primary goal of economic competitiveness.

Anglo-America 'at risk'

The changes in the government of education in Australia were signified
and constituted in a succession of national reports. The forerunners
were the Reagan Government-instigated *A nation at risk* (1983), the
Thatcher Government's papers on schooling and higher education in
Britain, and the policy documents of the OECD. In Australia the key
policy documents on schools, higher education and training were produced in the 1987 to 1991 period while John Dawkins was the Minister
for Employment, Education and Training (Dawkins 1987a; 1987b;
1988; Dawkins & Holding 1987a; 1987b; Deveson 1990; Finn 1991).

Apple (1986) notes the polemical nature of the Reagan era reports
in America. The same comment could be made about the Dawkins
reports. These documents functioned in the manner of a declaration,

a call to arms. They were statements of policy as truth that were designed to secure authority over education and its professionals, to demonstrate that authority to an outside public in business and the media, and to open education to external intervention. They were not descriptions, or analyses, and were not subject to testing or verification. They were declarations true by the force of their declaration (Lyotard 1984). The policy statements created binary oppositions and exclusions. People critical of one or another aspect found themselves positioned against the broader goals to which the reports were directed, such as international competitiveness, access to education or economic progress. Such essential virtues could hardly be refuted, helping the new policies to secure hegemony.

President Reagan's Secretary of Education, Terence Bell, created the United States National Commission on Excellence in Education in August 1981 in response to 'the widespread public perception that something is seriously remiss in our educational system'. A *nation at risk* (1983) argued that technology was transforming work. 'Knowledge, learning, information and skilled intelligence are the new raw materials of international commerce . . . If only to keep and improve on the slim competitive edge we still retain in world markets, we must dedicate ourselves to the reform of our educational system.' Yet student achievement in science and mathematics, and average scores in high school standardised tests and the Scholastic Aptitude Test used for entrance to higher education, were in decline. The incidence of superior SAT scores had fallen (Gardner 1983: 5–8). The arguments were interpolated with familiar cold war overtones.

> Our nation is at risk. Our once unchallenged preeminence in commerce, industry, science, and technological innovation is being overtaken by competitors throughout the world. . . . the educational foundations of our society are presently being eroded by a rising tide of mediocrity that threatens our very future as a nation and a people. If an unfriendly foreign power had attempted to impose on America the mediocre educational performance that exists today, we might well have viewed it as an act of war. As it stands, we have allowed this to happen to ourselves . . . We have, in effect, been committing an act of unthinking, unilateral educational disarmament (Gardner 1983: 5).

In *Investing in our children* (1985) the business based Committee for Economic Development (CED) urged business to 'face up to the challenge of restoring the nation's public schools'. The CED declared that the corporate reform of schooling, market pressures, entrepreneurial leadership and the management of performance would lead to improved school effectiveness and teacher quality. Business was urged to enter local school policy making, to lead school reform and encourage managerial efficiency. 'Schools cannot improve very much unless their fundamental practices conform more with what we know to be the principles of effective organisation and management' (CED 1985: xii, 5, 54, 79, 86, 98).

Drawing on the psychology of national decline that sustained both Reaganism and Thatcherism, in *The development of higher education into the 1990s* (1985) the British Government argued 'it is vital for our higher education to contribute more effectively to the improvement of the performance of the economy' (UK 1985: 3). The report argued there was a shortage of scientists, engineers, technologists and technicians in relation to economic needs and that this indicated that higher education needed to be more flexible and responsive to national needs, particularly the universities. Institutions should focus on the needs of external agents, become more client aware, modernise their management and develop private income. They were urged to develop links with industry and commerce, including industrial contracts, consultancies, 'businessmen' on governing bodies, joint academic appointments with business and other employers, updating and sandwich courses, sponsorship of students; Industrial Liaison Officers, science parks, business clubs and industrial professorships.

Educational institutions needed to produce a different kind of graduate, an economic citizen that was better attuned to the requirements of an enterprise culture.

> Our higher education establishments need to . . . beware of 'anti-business' snobbery. The entrepreneurial spirit is essential for the maintenance and improvement of employment, prosperity and public services. Higher education should be alert to the hazard of blunting it and should seek opportunities to encourage it. More generally, higher education needs to foster positive attitudes to work. Most students will have to work cooperatively in groups as well as individually; they will need to be able to show leadership and to respond to it (UK 1985: 4).

Higher education: meeting the challenge (1987) encouraged work experience: 'the Government wishes to see all higher education students made aware of the challenges and opportunities of enterprise' (UK 1987: iv, 2, 7, 21).

OECD education policies

In *Education in modern society* (1985) the OECD focused on 'the alarming scale of current unemployment'. It resisted the fashionable

claim that deficiencies in education were responsible for these problems, but saw education as the medium for their relief. 'In making a
full contribution to help the many who risk being left aside in the
labour market, a substantial program of preparation for work as part
of a widely developed set of opportunities for continuing or recurrent
education is essential.' The report mentioned programs in adult literacy, 'second chance' entry into formal education, and above all, the
need for 'education that is directly relevant to work'. The OECD
declared its disillusionment with labour power planning approaches to
relations between work and education. Instead it emphasised the need
for flexible, adaptable and self-managing workers. It suggested training
that was more general, couched in terms of attributes common to a
number of occupations, and 'endowing people' with the capacity to
'recognise opportunities to change their jobs or to seek new ones,
develop their skills and improve their incomes'.

There was a hidden message here for OECD governments, about the
need to shift responsibility for the seemingly intractable employment
outcomes, from government to individuals. Formal education could be
used to develop in students the capacity to manage their own work and
career paths, thus relocating the self-managing subjects of modern government within a new policy context in which government no longer
provided job creation (OECD 1985: 29–31).

Over the next three years the OECD developed a full set of policies
on education in national economic reconstruction. It argued for a
fusion of education and economic policy: 'that which is "education"
is becoming less clearly distinct from that which is "the economy"'.
Yet this was not a fusion of equal partners. The OECD acknowledged
in passing that education served more than economic objectives, but it
was on the economic plane that the 'interdependency' of education
and the economy had been increased (OECD 1989: 18–20). 'A long-
term strategy of continuing innovation, both technical and social'
would enable member nations to answer the challenge of the newly
industrialising countries. 'International competition, technological
change and, more generally, the need for flexibility' had resulted in
'labour market challenges that call for long-term adjustment of the
educational systems'. This would require a major expansion of participation, the development of relations between industry and all forms
of post-compulsory education and research, and changes to the governance, financing and delivery of education.

In 1986 the OECD prepared a major policy statement on micro-
economic reform, *Structural adjustment and economic performance*

(OECD 1987a). The report opened with chapters on 'Education and human capital' and 'Long term research'. 'Human capital has become even more important in recent years' it stated, because of the requirements generated by 'technical progress, continual change in productive structures and the growing complexity and internationalisation of markets'. In all countries a 'basic policy goal' in education was 'to increase the productivity of human resources' (OECD 1987a: 42, 69).

It was believed that the spread of advanced education would enhance both the capacity for technological innovations and the capacity to respond to technological innovations, as was argued by the 'second wave' human capital theorists (Marginson 1993a: 45–50). 'The crucial role of the human factor in economic performance is today most clearly perceived in those enterprises which operate at the frontier of technological innovation.' It was also seen to enhance flexibility and 'the ability to perceive and exploit emerging opportunities' in the face of exogenous economic shocks, and the requirements of global markets (OECD 1986; 1987a; 1989).

As in the 1960s, the OECD assumed that investment in education would yield direct economic benefits. Unlike the 1960s, the relationship between education and economic production was understood in more nuanced micro-economic terms. The OECD suggested that the strength of the links between higher education and industry was one explanation for relative national performance in technological innovation (Maglen 1990). Further, because of the strategic economic role attributed to technological change, research and development was seen as increasingly important in economic calculations. At its conference on education and the economy in 1988, the OECD announced 'a new phase of science and technology policy: an age of "strategic science"' in which governments sought more explicit links between research and its economic applications (OECD 1989; 56). These were to be achieved by identifying areas of national priority, such as artificial intelligence, materials chemistry and bio-medicine; and by changes in funding systems and incentives, so the production of research would become more responsive to industrial requirements, and in adopting some features of market production, would install within itself a self-regulating dynamic of commercial creativity. In most OECD countries there was partial shift from basic to applied research.

One of the OECD's policy agendas was the marketisation of education, and a partial shift from public to private costs. Between the early 1970s and the late 1980s, in most OECD countries the number of students grew faster than government expenditure on education. *Structural adjustment and economic performance* argued that while governments would need to fund a part of the expansion of education, 'it may prove more feasible to seek alternatives involving more private funding'.

It was suggested that marketisation would make educational institutions more responsive by establishing links between institutions and the labour markets. These links would be mediated by self-investing, choice making students. In systems with a strong market sector 'it would seem that the financial stakes for individuals, in common with the often considerable independence of institutions, contribute to educational flexibility'. The OECD argued that universities 'have the potential capacity to operate as service enterprises, and under some conditions to cover a big part of their expenditure from the sale of their services'. Greater reliance on markets and private funding could reduce the fiscal burden, improve allocative efficiency in funding, create incentives for internal efficiency and consumer responsiveness, and enable a more 'equitable' sharing between public and private costs. The North American and Japanese experience showed that a high participation could be combined with relatively high levels of private costs (OECD 1981b: 53, 60; OECD 1987a: 87–89; OECD 1990a: 9–13; OECD 1993).

> An increase in the private financing of education may appear to conflict with the equity goals of education policies. It must be kept in mind, however, that failure to make a desirable increase in a country's educational effort is hardly a more equitable alternative; nor is it economically sound (OECD 1987a: 89).

In relation to schooling the OECD argued that market competition between institutions, based on 'decentralised management' and competition for enrolments, would lead to responsiveness to the 'customer'. In training, the OECD secured member government agreement to the conception of a national training market, based on 'a diversity of suppliers', with the role of government to provide certain programs that markets would not, to provide information and the framework of accreditation, and 'to set up, or encourage industries to set up, nation-wide standards for vocational training and qualifications' as in Austria, Germany and Switzerland (OECD 1987a: 79–89; OECD 1989: 48–49, 89, 105, 114).

The OECD's proposals for marketisation became part of the accepted international wisdom about the government of education. They offered something for nothing: an expanded education system that could modernise industry and soak up unemployment, while remaining confined within the settings of a restrictive fiscal policy.

II. National government in education

Preparing the ground

British policies and programs shaped Australian education, but the Australian Government was increasingly influenced by American practices, particularly in higher education, and by OECD positions that were themselves affected by North American, Japanese and German models. However, it was not that Australia had substituted American policies for British policies. British education was also moving in the same direction. In *Financing higher education* (1990a) the OECD noted that in the 1980s there was 'a convergence of funding methods and procedures'. In countries with strong private sectors, the private institutions were being subjected to greater accountability and regulation; while in countries with predominantly public institutions those institutions were becoming more autonomous and raising more funds from private sources than before. There was 'a growing interest by many governments in the introduction of a larger element of market types of organisation and incentives' (OECD 1990a: 55). In higher education, TAFE and industry training, although less so in schooling, there was a close resemblance between the policies of Labor policies in Australia and those of Thatcher's Conservative Party governments in Britain. The timing of the initiatives varied; Australia was first to dissolve its binary system of higher education and reintroduce university fees, Britain was first to introduce overseas marketing and competency-based training; but the substance was the same.

In Australia it was the business organisations that first began to develop policies on the role of education in national economic reconstruction. In 1985 a report by the business-based Committee for the Economic Development of Australia (CEDA) argued that an 'information society' was emerging in which 'flexibility and adaptability' would be essential and universal skilling would be required, making education central to the future; though government was too dominant and 'we suggest that the market mechanism be given greater play in the education sector' (CEDA 1985).

In 1984 and 1985 the coordinating departments of Prime Minister and Cabinet, Finance and Treasury began to develop policies on the economic role of education. In February 1986 the Business Council and the Australian Vice-Chancellors' Committee called for greater cooperation between the private sector and universities, and a week later the joint State and Commonwealth education Ministers recommended closer links between business and tertiary institutions through collaborative programs, joint business/government funding of research, personal exchanges, industry use of university research facilities, shared research equipment, and encouraging high technology industries to contract out training courses for their personnel to tertiary education institutions.

At the same time, EPAC released *Human capital and productivity growth*, which argued that compared with countries such as Japan and West Germany, Australia's labour force exhibited 'significant skill width and depth deficiencies'. The education system had failed 'to recognise the emerging needs of the economy'. School retention rates were 'poor', there were inadequacies in curricula; and insufficient university enrolments in 'technology and business related disciplines' (enrolments in advanced education and TAFE were ignored). EPAC urged that business become involved in the evaluation of these courses, and argued for standardised testing in schools. It favoured 'a shift away from comprehensive state secondary schools', with market competition between schools, more streaming within them, and centres of excellence; and the re-introduction of tertiary fees (EPAC 1986: iii, 1–3, 17, 33–35). The Australian Science and Technology Council (ASTEC 1987) confirmed EPAC's position.

In 1986 the Government sponsored a joint Australian Council of Trade Unions and Trade Development Council mission to Western Europe. Its report, *Australia reconstructed* (1987), argued that 'one of Australia's overriding concerns must be its deficient skill base', evidenced by 'the very low levels of exports of technology-based products'. The report appeared to assume that training determined export performance. It declared that tertiary education had to 'lift its game' and 'the most effective way of doing this is through forging closer links between education authorities and industry'. ACTU Secretary Bill Kelty stated in the foreword to *Australia reconstructed* that 'structural change and the promotion of a productive culture are necessary to enhance our international competitiveness ... employers and unions need to recognise their obligation to tackle the problem of skill formation' (ACTU/TDC 1987: v, 118–119).

In the next half-decade, through the restructuring of industrial awards, and government-instigated reform of industry training standards, the unions established more broadly based descriptions of skill, enabling greater flexibility and mobility of labour. Their objective was to tie work classifications to competency based standards, and wage levels, so as to install the chain of causation imagined by human capital theory (education-productivity-wages),[1] and install a training culture that would be sustained by the individual desire for career progression. The ACTU couched its argument for reform in terms of a normative 'post-Fordist' vision in which the truly competitive enterprise was committed to multi-skilling, devolution, on-site initiative, and shop floor quality control and product innovations (Carmichael 1989; Marginson 1993a: 155–167).

The Dawkins era

In mid-1987 the Commonwealth established a new 'super-department' integrating programs in employment, training, education and research on the basis of national economic goals, and Dawkins was appointed as the 'super-Minister' of Employment, Education and Training. In his first statement on higher education Dawkins declared the Government's commitment to the OECD program of micro-economic reform:

> The Government has made clear its determination that our education and training system should play a central role in responding to the major economic challenges which still confront us. The ongoing adjustments required in the structure of our economy will place a much greater premium on technical knowledge and labour force skills, and likewise on quality, innovation and technology. These attributes will also be a vital factor in our productivity performance and in the speed of our adaptation to future changes in economic circumstances (Dawkins 1987a: 1).

In his 1987 Green Paper, *Higher education: a policy discussion paper*, Dawkins foreshadowed the Government's policies in that sector. The Green Paper floated the expansion of participation; the abolition of segmentation between university and non-university institutions; the modernisation of institutions through mergers, the professionalisation of management and corporate reform; marketisation and the introduction of user payments; and the development of business–education links. In the White Paper *Higher education: a policy statement* (1988a), published seven months later, Dawkins confirmed these suggestions as policies. He noted that institutional management was being modernised, and the interaction between industry and higher education institutions had already improved. He added that 'the Government will continue to encourage the development of close links between higher education institutions and employers in all sectors of the Australian economy', emphasising research and technology transfer, the negotiation of work experience during courses, and the need for graduates to acquire the 'conceptual, analytical and communication skills which are increasingly demanded by industry' (Dawkins 1988a: 66–68). The rationale for these new policies was that of the OECD. A more highly skilled population would 'deal more effectively with change'. Education facilitated 'adaptability', learning how to learn during working life, and responses to technological change. In the future economy there would be a greater use of 'flexible production systems', and broadly skilled workers 'at all stages of the design, production, management and marketing processes'. An educated workforce was better equipped to deal with globalisation and the pressures of a more open economy.

> ... What is important is the flexibility to capitalise on new opportunities as they arise and to accept the need for continuing change and adjustment, largely determined by international forces. A well-educated workforce is a key source of such flexibility. The more responsive the workforce, the greater the speed of adjustment to external shocks and the less the impact on Australia's standard of living (Dawkins 1987b: 1–2).

The Green Paper suggested that the number of higher education graduates should be increased from 80 000 to 125 000 per annum by the year 2001. Labor defined equity in education principally in terms of access, the right to participate. Thus equity was advanced by growth in the number of places, together with targeted assistance to groups under-represented in higher education, such as indigenous people, and marketing techniques that encouraged female enrolments in non-traditional areas such as engineering.

The issue of 'talent wastage' enabled national economic interest and equity goals to intersect, provided that enrolments continued to grow (Williams et al 1993). As EPAC and *Australia reconstructed* had argued, Dawkins believed that 'deficiencies' in the supply and the type of graduates had resulted in supply side 'bottle-necks' in the labour markets. Increasing the supply of the right kind of graduate would lead to higher production, employment, exports and economic growth. In this manner the Government supported a relative expansion in the number of graduates in business, sciences, the technologies, engineering and computing; and consistent with this, in April 1988 it announced an increase in immigration intakes in the skilled and business classes.

Policy had returned to a strong human capital line. This in turn created certain policy tensions. First, there were limits to the extent to which the labour markets could absorb advanced skills and additional career professionals. Second, Dawkins emphasised the need for institutions to become more responsive to market pressures and interests, and the Government was *prima facie* committed to deregulation in all economic policies. Yet enrolment growth was being determined by government 'guestimates' of labour market needs as much as by labour market signals.

The Green Paper noted that if higher education was to grow as planned, and this growth was to be funded by the Commonwealth, 'a substantial increase in outlays' would be required. 'The Government will therefore explore the possibility of broadening the resource base to fund increases in the number of graduates'. The Green Paper also declared that 'institutions will have to take full advantage of additional sources of funding'. Success would partly depend on 'the profile of institutions' activities and on the enthusiasm and the entrepreneurial flair that they bring to the task'. New sources of private income had been opened by the commencement of full fee overseas marketing, tax concessions for industry research and development conducted in higher education, and the 1987 budget decision to relax the prohibition on the charging of fees for post-graduate courses. Institutions could also provide non-award courses and hire out their facilities for commercial purposes, and conduct courses on a joint basis with industry. The minister also stated that 'graduates of higher education experience, on average, highly favourable labour market outcomes compared with those without tertiary qualifications', and that the Government would give consideration to possible contributions from students, former students and/or their parents (Dawkins 1987b: 3, 81–87). He set up the Wran committee to develop options for user payments (chapter 9).

These same themes and directions were confirmed in the Minister's pronouncements on schooling, for example *Strengthening Australia's schools* (Dawkins & Holding 1988b), and in the development of training reform and the national training market (Deveson 1990a, 1990b; Finn 1991).

In research, in the formation of the new Australian Research Council (ARC), the Government joined the knowledge-related objectives traditional to academic research, to strategic economic objectives. The decision to set up the ARC was announced under the ALP's 1987 election policy on industry, not education. In Australia basic research in most fields of natural science was well developed, and the funding of research in higher education was around the OECD average, but the level of research financed by the business sector, especially in business itself, was low by OECD standards. In 1986–87 business expenditure on research and development in Australia was only 0.46 per cent of GDP, compared to 1.91 per cent in Japan in 1986 and 1.32 per cent in the United States in 1988 (DITC 1989). This was principally due to the 'branch office' character of the global companies operating in Australia. The Green Paper stated that 'a greater proportion' of basic research 'should be in fields that have the potential to improve the nation's competitive position', and efforts should be made 'to increase the interaction between research agencies and with industry, and by application of research findings to improve Australia's productive capacity' (Dawkins 1987b: 65).

It was hoped that by pushing more university research towards the applied end, concentrating a greater proportion of research activities in research centres, making universities more dependent on commercial clients and more aware of the commercial potential of intellectual property, higher education would drive the economic utilisation of research from the supply side. The Government allocated some postgraduate scholarships (155 in 1993) to research students working on collaborative projects with industry; and provided tax concessions to stimulate industry demand for research. Later it established a program of Cooperative Research Centres jointly funded, managed and staffed by the universities, business and the Commonwealth Scientific and Industrial Research Organisation (CSIRO).

Strategic centralisation

The preparation of the new policy framework was accompanied by the construction of new systems of government in all sectors of education. The role of the Commonwealth was strengthened and modernised; the business sector was drawn into education policy making and programs; and corporate forms of organisation were introduced. The Government strengthened its hand by drawing the BCA, the ACTU, and the major media groups into its purposes; and engaged in its own strategic centralisation, whereby all Commonwealth education agencies were brought under direct Ministerial control and turned into carriers of economic policy. This 'ministerialisation' of education was common to Commonwealth and State government. 'Ministerialisation' was associated with the imposition of economic agendas and the displacement of the role of the directors-general of education by generic managers without the same interest in policy or professional matters. 'The directors-general were supportive of a broader liberal conception of schooling, whereas ministers of all political persuasions tended to be supportive of a more vocationally oriented schooling' (Lingard et al 1995: 41, 53).

The key change in Commonwealth machinery was Dawkins' abolition of the Commonwealth's Tertiary Education Commission (CTEC) and Schools Commission (CSC), which he had inherited from the Whitlam and Fraser years. This eliminated the main source of potential opposition in the bureaucracy, freed the Government to reset the policy agenda, and weakened the capacity of education institutions and interest groups (which had invested in the commissions) to retard government initiatives.

The CTEC and the CSC had operated at 'arm's length' from the government, with a separate legal identity and the responsibility to report to Parliament; and were closer to the institutions and authorities in education than a department could have been. They were governed by Government policy while interpreting it more or less as they saw fit; and they had developed distinctive policy discourses that at times were very influential. In tertiary education the then separate sectoral commissions operated without any clear mandate from the Government until 1976. They were *de facto* policy makers, to a large degree determining the growth of institutions and their pattern of development. However, by the mid-1980s the commissions were under unprecedented pressure to bring their policy positions more in line with the dominant economic doctrines of the day.

The CTEC and the CSC responded differently to these pressures. The CTEC resisted the imposition of tuition charges and the commencement of overseas marketing of courses, and in the mid-1980s it made a trenchant criticism of the decline in per capita government funding of higher education. The CSC decided to accommodate the new pressures, partly moving from its traditional focus on equality of opportunity to the advocacy of a 'productive culture'. Commission chairperson Garth Boomer said that 'at the upper end of the secondary school we have been too "pure" for our own good', and schools should focus on economic outcomes, including the inculcation of attitudes and capacities such as enterprise and efficiency (Boomer 1986).

Being cooperative made no difference to the ultimate outcome. With the Government making less use of statutory authorities, the next year both commissions were abolished and their functions of recommendation, program administration, and the compilation and publication of information were mostly absorbed by DEET. A new National Board of Employment, Education and Training was created, but its role was largely advisory, except in research where the ARC directly administered the Commonwealth programs.

National systems

The Labor Government achieved an unprecedented national control over educational policies and programs; but in contrast to the Whitlam period, this was obtained less by the expansion of Commonwealth funding and provision, and more through the role of the Government in the global economy, and its discursive authority, and by cooperation and negotiated consent, whereby the States worked within a common national framework.

Canberra's total share of government funding in education fell from 42.2 per cent in 1975–76 to 37.2 per cent in 1989–90, rising to 43.3 per cent in 1992–93 (see Table 7.1). Only in student assistance, which was the main means of national population management, was the level and

Table 7.1 Commonwealth share of total funding* of education, by sector of education, selected years, 1975–76 to 1992–93

	Higher education %	TAFE %	Schools %	Pre-schools and special %	School transport %	All sectors** %
1975–76	88.3	37.5	23.4	55.6	1.9	42.2
1982–83	98.3	31.7	24.4	20.2	1.4	39.5
1992–93***	93.7	28.9	28.9	12.5	0.0	43.1

* *Includes* student assistance.
** Includes other tertiary institutions and minor items nei.
*** State funding of higher education *via* payment of the HECS for nurses and teachers.
Source: ABS 5510.0.

share of Commonwealth funding markedly increased. In the 1980s the selective liberalisation of student assistance helped to induce a major increase in demand for education. Commonwealth spending on student assistance rose from $388 million to $1109 million between 1982–83 and in 1993–94, while State teaching scholarships were phased out.

Under Dawkins, facilitated by the presence of Labor governments in most States, a new strategy of cooperative federalism or 'corporate federalism' was developed (Lingard 1993), first in the Australian Education Council (AEC), from 1990 also in the Ministers of Vocational Education, Employment and Training (MOVEET), and from 1993 the combined Ministerial Council on Education, Employment, Training and Youth Affairs (MCEETYA), joined also by the Business Council of Australia (BCA) and the ACTU. The Commonwealth was responsible for national priorities, including micro-economic reform in education, allowing it to shape State agendas. This negotiated cooperation in education was confirmed on a broader scale at the Special Premiers' Conferences of 1990 and 1991, where the Commonwealth and States agreed on national systems in transport, power and finance, and 'the establishment of a national market for goods and occupations'. In 1992 the Council of Australian Government (COAG) was established 'so as to achieve a more efficient national economy and a single national market' (Lingard et al 1995: 42–45).

The emergence of corporate federalism enabled policy makers to conceive of all education sectors in terms of national systems – whether they were subject to single governments or not – and facilitated the development of national markets across the State boundaries and sectors of education. At the end of the 1980s all governments agreed to develop TAFE and training as a 'national training market'. After 1988 higher education was reorganised as a 'Unified National System' conceived as a national market of competing institutions. Private schooling was already organised to an extent on a national basis, through Commonwealth funding. There were also inter-governmental negotiations to facilitate the transfer of teachers and students between the State systems of government schooling, and establish common conditions of labour and common cost structures, foreshadowing the possible emergence of a national system-market in schooling as well.

Business in education

Throughout the OECD, education was moving from 'an operating principle of exclusion to one of inclusion'. Business and the media played an increasing role in policy debates, and business became more involved in program delivery (Papadopoulos 1988; 1991; Kennedy 1988). After release of the EPAC paper *Human capital and productivity growth* (1986) one leading economic journalist declared 'the development of Australia's human capital is far too important to our economic future to be left in the hands of patch-preserving educationalists' (Gittins 1986). It was a view widely shared in government. This 'opening up' of education was a kind of 'market democratisation', where education was meant to become transparent to all its users, but some of these 'stakeholders' had larger citizen's rights than others. Accountability to government and business took precedence over other links. Just as 'responsiveness' was now signified not by political democracy but by markets, 'accountability' in education was now signified by education–business links and producer–consumer relations mediated by corporate management, rather than popular participation in decisions.

The business organisations strongly encouraged business involvement (CEDA 1985). In 1987 *Business Review Weekly* noted that business involvement was becoming more focused, concerted and effective, working partly through the government's education-industry liaison committees (Duncan 1987). The concerns of business leaders were different to those that motivated the public policy makers of the 1960s and 1970s. Business was little concerned about equality of opportunity and 'fair' educational competition, though these were continuing preoccupations of many professional educators. Its objective was to maximise the direct contribution of educated labour to production, firm by firm.

Here business organisations' desire for a more business-oriented education coincided with governments' plans for the micro-economising of education and its management. Governments encouraged and facilitated the involvement of business, working with business to overcome the 'rigidity' of professional educators in the face of reform proposals and the new accountability arrangements (OECD 1986).

Education as business

In a spectacular fashion the standards debate had driven home to governments the need for new forms of regulation that would distance governments from controversy, while more effectively controlling educational professionals. The question was how to do this. On one hand, there was support for the reassertion of direct governance: for example the BCA's 1986 survey of member companies found 91 per cent wanted a return to regular departmental inspections of government schools. However, a return to overt bureaucratic control would tie governments closer to the controversies over sex education and the like. The fashions for parent choice and corporate reform pointed rather towards the location of education in a consumer market under the supervision of the state. Here marketisation, consumer rights and financial accountability allowed the creation of 'operable technical forms for exercising perpetual scrutiny' over professional expertise, while establishing 'new distantiated relations of control' between hired professionals and the state. Audit replaced 'the trust that formulae of government once accorded to professional credentials' (Rose 1993). The key to this was the introduction of corporate management. The demands for global efficiencies and the tightening financial regime within each education institution provided favourable ground for reform.

The notion that education should be run on business lines was not new. What was new was the corporate form of devolution. The development of information and communications technologies made it possible for management to substitute on-line responsiveness and reporting for direct command. Devolved corporate management allowed governments to secure local financial discipline, while facilitating fund raising and the growth of entrepreneurial activity. It was an effective response to the standards debate, establishing local accountability to 'customers' while using forms of operation familiar to business. It weakened the central role of the unions and undermined democratic authority within local institutions. Here governments and individual education institutions were influenced by generic models of business management rather than models specific to education. 'It is assumed that what business knows and does education should know and do.' Rendering as inefficient most of the existing educational activities, this opened a wide ambit for reform (Kenway 1993; Watkins 1992).

To introduce corporate management it was necessary to transform or remove those existing modes of organisation and decision making, and lines of accountability, which conflicted with a corporate approach; including deliberative or consultative processes involving staff, and users of education. Often, the systems of decision making marked down for obsolescence were recent in origin, products of the modernising democratic reforms in education during the preceding two decades. The transition to corporatised devolution was studded with paradoxes. The central powers of reforming governments were used to dissolve the old forms of local control into the systemic interplay of broader market forces. Local democratic forms were replaced by local branches of the corporate system-organisation.

The new forms of managerial organisation in education were linked to a new 'education production function' economics, in which educational institutions and education systems were modelled as input–output systems, and the objective was to optimise the relationship between inputs and outputs (Marginson 1993a). In the Friedmans' version of input–output economics in education (1980: 150–188), institutions were seen as corporations, teachers were understood as 'producers', students were 'consumers', and education systems operated as national or global markets.

At the end of the 1970s governments were primarily concerned with reducing the costs of education without decreasing the number of publicly funded places. Policy was driven by the annual budget cycle, matched by the shortening time horizons of economic analysis: it was hoped that in measuring educational outputs with precision, economics would enable scarce resources to be more effectively targeted. As the 1980s proceeded and a more positive economic role for education returned to the agenda, the first need was to expand outputs without increasing funding, by working the same resources more intensively. Input–output models were used by management in government and institutions for corporate planning and in meeting accountability requirements. By defining education as itself a site of production and subject to the same economic 'laws' as other parts of the economy, input–output modelling laid the ground for micro-economic reforms within education itself. Input–output functions enabled institutions in the public sector, subject to politics, to be reconceived as stand-alone corporations operating within a market, with products, clients or shareholders, and even shadow rates of profit, and their own market share and sources of revenue; as Buchanan and Tullock's public choice theory had imagined (see chapter 5).

Here economics fitted the positivist and linear conceptions of organisational design that dominated mainstream management reforms in the 1980s. Organisations were understood as stable sub-systems with defined boundaries, separable from their external context, while subject to determination from 'outside' or 'above' that is, subject to orthodox hierarchical management and input–output calculation which reduced all local differences to the common formula.[2]

III. The new vocationalism

Education and work

After 1975 there were three important changes in the labour markets that shaped the development of education. First, the end of full employment created a buyer's market for educated labour, a shift in the balance of power that underpinned the 'back to basics' agitation and the growing role of employers in policy matters. Since the mid-1960s the full-time labour market for teenagers had been in decline, although at first this was disguised by the great growth in educational participation at the end of the boom. Despite population growth, between August 1966 and August 1980 the number of full-time jobs held by teenagers fell from 615 000 to 512 900. Full-time work became largely concentrated among 18 and 19-year-olds. The unemployment rate facing teenagers, which was only 3.2 per cent in 1970, shot up to 20 per cent during the mid-1970s recession, and remained high thereafter. Many of the jobs lost in the recessions of the mid-1970s and early 1980s did not return. While part-time work grew significantly, most of it was held by full-time students.

Second, the Commonwealth programs aimed at alleviating the effects of unemployment, and managing labour market behaviour, had grown as large as education programs, and in places the boundaries between education programs and labour market programs were increasingly blurred. Full-time teenage employment dropped further in the 1980s, to 390 000 in August 1990, reaching 260 000 in early 1995 after another recession. Between the 1975–76 and the 1991–92 recession, unemployment benefits rose from $1.7 to $4.9 billion. By then Commonwealth spending on employment related programs was well in excess of outlays on higher education and TAFE. Over the course of three recessions in the mid-1970s, the early 1980s and early

1990s, there was little increase in Commonwealth spending on education provision, but a massive growth in spending on transfer payments – student assistance and unemployment relief – and labour market programs (Table 7.2).

In 1985 the report of the Commonwealth committee of inquiry into labour market programs, the Kirby committee, argued that education programs and labour market programs should both be directed towards ensuring that all Australians could participate in the labour markets. After the creation of the Department of Employment, Education and Training in 1987, the respective policies became more closely integrated. The conditions governing unemployment benefits were partly aligned with those governing student assistance, so as to draw more students out of the labour market and into education, while labour market programs were increasingly focused on skill development in formal education. Education programs were seen as the medium for changes in behaviour, and the means of shifting the responsibility for job creation from government to individual, using techniques of self-management and self-improvement acquired in education. However, if education programs were to work in tandem with unemployment and labour market strategy, they had to be vocationalised.

Third, in the 1970s and 1980s the services industries grew rapidly, and this brought to the fore the attributes used in interpersonal relations and communication ('generic skills' or 'transferable' skills) in services work. In the OECD as a whole, the fastest growing areas of work were the market related services and self-employment (OECD 1994). By 1975 in Australia, the services employed a majority of all workers, and over the next fifteen years employment in services grew much faster than total employment (Table 7.3). Even in public

Table 7.2 Commonwealth outlays on programs in post-compulsory education and training and the labour markets, and assistance to students and the unemployed*, 1975–76, 1982–83 and 1991–92, constant 1984–85 prices

	Higher education $m	TAFE $m	Vocational education nei $m	Labour market $m	Student assistance $m	Unemploy-ment** $m	Total $m
1975–76	2039	177	172	0	290	1694	4373
1982–83	2007	293	142	247	319	2847	5924
1991–92	2382	274	134	464	1084	4800	9137

* Grants for secondary schooling not included, except in the form of student assistance.
** Includes unemployment and sickness benefits.
Sources: ABS 5510.0; CPB.

Table 7.3 Growth in employment by industry, Australia, 1975 to 1990*

Industry	Number of people employed (mill.)		Change in number of people employed 1975 to 1990, 1975 = 100.0			
	1975	1990	1975	1980	1985	1990
Finance/business services	0.431	0.904	100.0	119.5	155.0	209.7
Community services**	0.793	1.423	100.0	130.0	146.3	179.4
Personal services***	0.372	0.561	100.0	104.8	115.9	150.8
Trade	1.157	1.612	100.0	110.1	114.5	139.3
Transport and storage	0.330	0.402	100.0	103.9	114.2	121.8
Public administration/utilities	0.508	0.616	100.0	103.9	120.7	121.3
Construction	0.511	0.585	100.0	95.1	92.2	114.5
Agriculture and mining	0.477	0.521	100.0	102.9	108.4	109.2
Manufacturing	1.263	1.200	100.0	98.2	88.1	95.0
All industries	5.841	7.825	100.0	107.5	114.3	134.0

* Data as at August in the year named; for revisions and qualifications see Foster & Stewart 1991: 164.
** Includes health, welfare, educational, library and museum services.
*** Includes recreational, personal and other services.
Source: Foster & Stewart 1991: 164.

administration and utilities, where growth was slowed by 'small government', employment grew more quickly than in manufacturing.

Work in the services drew on skills in communications, human interaction, social and work organisation, and self-management, to a greater extent than did work in manufacturing or agriculture. Further, these skills were readily seen as common to different sites and occupations, and were the object of similar technologies of classification and measurement. Increasingly, these skills were factored into employee selection and staff development. The notion of generic skills tended to conceal the specific requirements of different sites and occupations, and placed pressure on the individual graduates/employees to manage their own adjustment. In that sense, the use of generic vocational skill descriptors was again consistent with a buyers' labour market, in which the scarcity of work ensured that people were forced to be flexible and responsive in the face of any and every possible opportunity, able and willing to work across a wide range of fields.

This ambiguity of generic skills both strengthened their malleability in the hands of employers, and broadened their potential range in education. Using work-related generic skills it was possible to describe general-academic programs in terms of work-related outputs. Theoretically, it became possible to govern *all* educational programs in terms of vocational objectives. 'Generic skills' were a formula for producing all citizens as economic citizens.

Vocationalism and conservatism

The new vocationalism received broad but not unanimous support. The cultural conservatives in the New Right (see chapter 6) rejected the subordination of schooling and higher education to vocational goals. Here the employer organisations found themselves disagreeing with the academics in the Australian Council for Educational Standards on the other. Modernising reformers in government tended to side with the employers and rejected the notion of education as an end in itself, irreducible to vocational or governmental requirements. They wanted to dignify vocational knowledge, to create freer movement between industry training and university education, and to lift the competence of the whole workforce and not just an elite. As Jones puts it in relation to the similar debate in Britain:

> Thus while no opponent of selection, the modernising tendency has no time for the grammar school tradition. Unlike the cultural right, it considers it to be part of the problem, not the solution. It is thoroughly critical of the anti-industrial values of a liberal education: the state schools of the present century have reproduced many of the failings of the public [i.e. private] schools that some of them have tried to emulate, and have preserved a rigid distinction between high-status academic knowledge and low-status practical training. The modernisers, by contrast, present their program as a means not only of serving industry but – by knocking down the academic/practical barrier – of democratising knowledge, and of enabling students to demonstrate kinds of achievement which the old education neither fostered nor recognised (Jones 1989: 82).

Here the modernisers intersected with the educational progressivists who were the *bêtes noires* of the conservatives. Like the progressivists, the modernisers emphasised the production of self-managing individuals, personal development, non-academic skills, relevance and motivation; though they were no egalitarians, and they gave the modernist project a distinctly vocational twist: 'human development is to be relocated in occupational training' (Jones 1989: 79–116).

This partial adaptation to progressivism was vehemently rejected by the cultural conservatives. In 1987 the IPA bulletin *Facts* published an article by Kramer which argued for the acquisition of general culture and a broad intellectual training in education. Yet on the facing page, the IPA reported a survey of business attitudes to education, which found respondents wanted more emphasis on vocational objectives and skills and less on academic objectives (IPA 1987: 8–9). On the question of whether education should be accountable to vocational purposes, the vocational 'modernisers' prevailed. Here governments were able to secure their objectives by indirect means. By incorporating business into programs and policies, and by introducing corporate reform and marketisation, strategies supported by the cultural conservatives, governments were able to insert vocational imperatives which if imposed more directly, would have been strongly opposed.

Vocational reform in schools and training

The Transition Education program introduced in 1979 set out to provide students with 'options' in education or employment, mostly the former, and it focused on the last stage before entry into the labour market (Fraser & Kennedy 1990). The Transition program focused on those students considered to be most 'at risk'. It was the report of the Quality Education Review Committee (QERC) in 1985 that first developed the new vocational orientation to schooling on a more general scale.

The QERC report specified five 'competences', seen as necessary for participation in adult society: acquiring information, conveying information, applying logical processes, practical tasks and group tasks. 'Competence' was defined as 'the ability to use knowledge and skills effectively to achieve a purpose' in work, further education, community participation and self-management (Karmel 1985: 68–79). These competences were considered to be 'desirable learning outcomes for all students' and were built into the formal objectives of Commonwealth programs in schooling. As Kennedy noted, 'there seems to have been some agreement that the academic curriculum has concentrated too heavily on theoretical aspects of learning and what is needed is a greater concern with practical and work-related issues' (Kennedy 1988: 368). All of the State level reviews of secondary education conducted during the 1980s focused on closer links between school and work.

However, the subsequent vocational reforms had their origins not in schools but in TAFE and training programs, where vocationalism had always been solidly entrenched. The movement for competency based education, which reached its high point between 1990 and 1992, led by the Commonwealth government with the strong support of the 'industry partners' in the BCA and the ACTU, was the most important manifestation of the new vocationalism (Marginson 1993a: 143–171).

Following the British policy making experience, 'competence' and 'competencies' were defined as *work* related attributes, so that competency was 'the ability to perform the activities within an occupation or function to the standard expected in employment'. Work related competence was assessed by identifying the attributes of a person that indicated her or his potential to perform the required tasks or alternately, by directly observing performance of those tasks in real or simulated work situations. This bound education to articulation with work, marginalising those aspects of the curriculum not specific to it.

Through competency based reform in education, aligned to new skill standards in each industry and new training-based work classifications, it was hoped to use the technologies of standards, assessment and reporting to secure closer control over education and its outcomes, establishing accountability to industry through its involvement in standards design, and to define outcomes in product terms. It was also hoped to use competency based standards as the 'currency' of credentials, in the modernisation of articulation, pathways and credit transfer between TAFE, schools and higher education. The orientation to work and economy conferred on the competency movement a broad appeal. It provided education–work links that were simple in design, transparent in form, and commonsensical in purpose (Norris 1991).

The flexible citizen–worker

In 1978 an OECD education conference concluded that 'a convergence should be, and is, taking place' between general education for cognitive and affective attributes, and vocational education for specific skills. In *Education in modern society* (1985) the OECD asserted that notwithstanding the status differentials between vocational and academic-general education, the distinction was 'false'. The OECD repeatedly returned to these claims. Papadopoulos (1988) argued 'the traditional dichotomy' was obsolete: technology was part of 'general culture', vocational specialisation required 'an extended general education', and social skills like communication were essential to all. Governmental reformers set out to achieve a fusion of vocational and general education by converging movements from each side of the old divide. First, vocational education was to be broadened, so that certain work related skills were defined as general and flexible across work sites. Second, the remaining non-vocational strands in education were to be absorbed into the broadened vocational objectives.

The outcome was a new conception of general-vocational education. Claims about the convergence of education and work was grounded in post-Fordist claims about the expanded role of knowledge in production, and the need for continuous transformation, but the 'convergence' was *not* symmetrical. The new vocationalism reduced general education to the purposes of work. It meant a new kind of general education; not the classical liberal education but 'a reconceptualised general education' that valued practical skills and an understanding of work (Kennedy 1988: 371).

The change was not as simple as it seemed. It was difficult to define generic skills so that they were both general to all areas of education and work *and* retained meaningful content in each situation; and to devise a technology enabling those generic skills to be measured in common everywhere. The underlying difficulty here was that skills were acquired in specific contexts and knowledge sets, and were *not* automatically transferable (Perkins & Salomon 1989: 16–25; Golding et al 1996).

In 1991 the Australian Education Council's Finn committee examined the whole of post-compulsory education and training from 'a perspective of employability'. It was principally concerned about education as preparation for work, albeit 'in the broadest possible sense'. The committee argued that a broadened vocational curriculum, based on both occupational and generic competencies, would encompass the whole of education and training, including most of the old functions of general education, and excepting only 'that small part of general education which has no clear vocational character'. It was significant that thereafter this 'small' residue of general education slipped off the Finn agenda (Finn 1991: 6, 10, 55). The committee proposed a system of generic 'key areas of competence', essential to employability and transferable from either work or education to other sites. These 'key areas' were language and communication, mathematics, scientific and technological understanding, cultural understanding, problem solving, 'personal and interpersonal'.

Subsequently, the Mayer committee was established to bring these key competencies to the point where they could be measured, used in teaching and curriculum development, slotted in alongside occupationally specific competencies, and employed in nationally consistent assessment, reporting and management. The Mayer committee redefined the 'key competency strands' as collecting, analysing and organising ideas and information; expressing ideas and information; planning and organising activities; working with others and in teams; using mathematical ideas and techniques; solving problems; and using technology (Mayer 1992). The Mayer committee followed the Finn committee in defining vocational education as the prototype of all post compulsory education, conflating the general and vocational components on the grounds of the vocational, and defining work related 'generic competencies' not merely as generic or transferable, but as universal to all social situations. In a remarkable passage the committee argued that:

Employment-related Key Competencies are competencies which are essential for effective participation in work. They focus on the capacity to apply knowledge and skills in an integrated way in work situations. The Key Competencies are generic in that they apply to work generally rather than being specific to work in particular occupations or industries. This characteristic means that the competencies are not only essential for effective participation in work but are also essential for effective participation in other social settings. The Key Competencies also have use and value for young people entering further vocational education and training and higher education (Mayer 1992: 5).

Thus the Mayer committee inferred that a specifically work based competence, learnt outside work in education institutions, was applicable in any and every other social situation. This was an heroic assumption, but the normative intent was clear. Work was seen as the universal social setting. The 'master discourse' in education was now 'access to education as vocational preparation' (Fitzclarence & Kenway 1993: 92). Vocational education was a zone where economic and social goals met: a means to economic modernisation, a means of managing the unemployed, the provider of hope and equity, and the means of reforming education itself. Anderson comments that a 'utilitarian curriculum' is part of the price that education has paid for greater equality of access (Anderson 1990: 49). The Prime Minister, Paul Keating stated in July 1992 in 'A national employment and training plan for young Australians' that 'Vocational education and training is the key to a competitive and successful economy and, therefore, the key to long term rewarding jobs for young Australians. If a job is to remain a fundamental right of Australians, the right to high quality training must be seen as an equal right' (Keating 1992: 1).

It was not that economic objectives had subsumed cultural objectives. The production of culturally competent individuals remained central to the goals of education programs. What had changed was that cultural competence was now infused with economic content, so the tasks of education included the formation of market economic sensibilities ('flexibility', 'responsiveness'); and outcomes were now defined not only by the judgements of professional educators, but the needs of employers.

Vocationalism in higher education

In higher education the new vocationalism in government policy was expressed as an emphasis on vocationally specific disciplines in engineering, the technologies and computing; on science; and on the generic vocational disciplines in the business and management studies cluster, including administration, accounting and economics (ASTEC 1987; Dawkins 1988). The pattern of enrolments in higher education institutions was also shaped by the interaction between the supply of places and student demand (Table 7.4). For both reasons, the business-related disciplines grew rapidly in the finance and property boom of the second half of the 1980s. Institutions were able to expand business courses quickly to meet demand, because the per capita costs of business training were relatively low. Business studies moved from the fourth largest field of study in 1983 to the second largest by 1987 and in 1994 was pressing hard on the cluster of arts/humanities/social sciences courses for first place. Between 1987 and 1990 the number of students commencing courses in business and related disciplines jumped from 28 337 to 43 200 (DEET 1996a). Business enrolments as a share of total enrolments rose from 18.0 per cent in 1983 to 21.6 per cent by 1990, falling slightly to 20.9 per cent in 1994. There was a marked growth in students in course work higher degree programs in business. Between 1988 and 1994 these students rose from 4332 to 11 992 (176.8 per cent).

The rise of business studies signified a fundamental shift in higher education. Of the classical disciplines only basic economics was provided. Subjects such as marketing, organisational psychology, financial

Table 7.4 Enrolments by field of study, higher education 1983 and 1994

| Field of study | Total student enrolments in: | | Change from |
	1983	1994	1983 to 1994 1983 = 100.0
Health sciences and nursing*	19 626	70 885	361.2
Law and legal studies	10 391	21 236	204.4
Business/administration/ economics	62 821	122 315	194.7
Agriculture/animal husbandry	6127	11 426	186.5
Science	48 520	86 136	177.5
Other (including non-award)	3701	6351	172.7
Engineering and surveying	27 628	47 147	170.6
Architecture and building	7784	12 998	167.0
Arts/humanities/social sciences	86 199	132 935	154.2
Veterinary science	1466	1690	115.3
Education	74 314	72 277	97.3
All fields	348 577	585 396	167.9

* The growth in health sciences and nursing was exceptionally high because of the transfer of nurse education to higher education during the 1980s.
Sources: ABS 4101.0; DEET data.

planning, strategic management and quality control provided a broad, generic training in management; and these were coupled with specific disciplines with broad application such as accounting, computer systems or law. Business studies as a general-vocational cluster of disciplines was a strong competitor with the more traditional generalist courses in social sciences and humanities.

Enrolments in law also grew very rapidly. The Commonwealth did not itemise law as a priority for enrolment growth, but it facilitated the establishment of new law faculties in 12 institutions between 1988 and 1993, doubling the number of law schools, and tolerated rapid growth in some established law courses. Total student numbers in law leapt by 87.2 per cent between 1987 and 1994. Law was used both as a vocationally specific degree and as a generalist-vocational degree applicable to a wide range of public and private sector jobs. New law graduates had the second highest rate of employment, after medicine.

Enrolments in the arts/humanities/social science grouping rose by 54.2 per cent from 1983 to 1994, and 38.9 per cent (37 221 students) after 1987, but the share of student enrolments dropped from 24.7 to 22.7 per cent. This signified the changes taking place in the forms of intellectual training required by government and business. As Lyotard notes in his essay on *The postmodern condition* (1984), the skills now brought to the forefront were those that related to 'world competition', including new technologies and social organisation, and the ordinary functioning of specialist occupations. The old liberal educational mission was less important. 'The transmission of knowledge is no longer designed to train an elite capable of guiding the nation towards its emancipation, but to supply the system with players capable of acceptably fulfilling their roles at the pragmatic posts required by its institutions' (Lyotard 1984: 48). In *Financing higher education* (1990) the OECD argued that in higher education 'the principal social benefit is no longer the preparation of better leaders for the benefit of the whole community. There has been a shift in emphasis away from a general liberal education towards the acquisition of the many specific skills required in a technologically advanced society' (OECD 1990a: 12).

The old liberal mission of elite formation might have been turned towards a broader mission of citizen formation, in which the capacity in languages and knowledges, and awareness of multiplicity and difference, would become highly valued attributes. Some teachers in the humanities cluster (the humanities and the humanistic social sciences such as politics and, in part, sociology) saw their work in those terms. This was not part of the official agenda. In Australia after 1987 the humanities cluster was assigned three possible roles: luxury consumption, niche markets in skills and knowledges, and the production of generic skills. The White Paper argued that the provision of liberal culture was dependent on 'a strong economic base' (Dawkins 1988: 7); though there were some niche opportunities in the growing economic and governmental attention to the East and South East Asian countries, for example in language and historical studies (ASTEC 1987). 'Transferable' generic skills had long been a rationale for the humanities cluster, but the skills had been seen as academic rather than vocational and the definition and measurement of outcomes remained under academic control. Now policy makers saw the humanities cluster as the site of generic *employment* related skills.

> Employers and industry groups have attested . . . to the value they place on graduates with a broad educational foundation and with well-developed conceptual, analytical and communication skills. The general problem solving skills of inquiry, analysis and synthesis are essential to the building of a flexible, versatile workforce able to cope with rapidly changing technology (Dawkins 1988: 9).

Some institutions built the explicit preparation of work related generic skills into humanities and social science courses (Marginson 1993b: 51). The focus on generic skills opened the possibility of a reinvigorated governmental support for the humanities, but one grounded in the new vocationalism.

Notes

1 When the ACTU's Kelty appeared in the 1989 industrial commission hearing on restructuring of the award governing Victorian teachers, his main argument on the role of education was based on Denison (1962) which, as chapter 2 notes, was the classical statement of 1960s human capital theory (Cooper 1989: 3).

2 'If it be the office of comparison to reduce existing differences to identity, the science which most perfectly fulfils that end is mathematics . . . quantitative difference is the only difference which is quite external' (Hegel 1975: 170).

CHAPTER 8

Participation and equity

'As a nation we must be prepared to invest heavily in
human skills. We need a community and workforce that
has the education necessary to cope with and adapt to a
rapidly changing world. We must create a broad base of
skills across the whole workforce. Only if we equip our
people with the capacities and attitudes to compete
effectively, with flexibility and with confidence, can we
make the most of future opportunities. In the present day
world, with its increasingly sophisticated technologies and
the rapid rate of change, people must have the capacity
and skill to move with the times, to be flexible, and to be
innovative and creative. Of particular concern to the
achievement of these objectives is the fact that the
education rate in Australia remains one of the lowest in the
OECD community. . . . far too many young Australians
leave school too early.'

*Bob Hawke, Prime Minister of Australia, speech to Participation
and Equity Program conference, Canberra, 3 September 1984,*
Commonwealth Record, *p. 1707.*

Prelude: Education as virtual employment (1984)

Between August 1981 and August 1983, a period of recession in
Australia, the total number of full-time jobs held by young people aged
15–19 years fell by 100 200, and the rate of teenage unemployment
rose from 15.6 to 23.3 per cent. In late 1983 an OECD team prepared
a *Review of youth policies in Australia* (1984) on the invitation of the
Commonwealth. The report summarised the emerging consensus
about a high participation education system, in which strategies for
unemployment were combined, ironically enough, with visions of economic modernisation based on the full utilisation of labour.

'The current unemployment problem for young people in Australia
is an alarm signalling an economic crisis' stated the OECD team.

180

Educational retention was low, there was insufficient vocational training, industry apprenticeships were biased against women. Disadvantaged young people were forced into marginal jobs or unemployment benefits, rather than education that produced gains over the long term. 'Without substantial changes in the education and training arrangements, and the income support measures to permit participation in education and training, socioeconomic equality will suffer' (OECD 1984). The social costs were youth crime and social disharmony, and the waste of human capital. The full youth population should be incorporated into policy.

> The most important goal of any new youth initiatives in Australia should be to raise educational attainment, increase occupational skills, and assure that education and training opportunities are accessible without regard to sex or socioeconomic status . . . Without substantial changes in the education and training arrangements, and the income support measures to permit participation in education and training, socioeconomic equality will suffer . . . [and] the Australian economy may suffer, lacking the qualified manpower needed to help the Australian economy grow and compete (OECD 1984).

The Australian economy would require 'an increasingly better educated and trained workforce' due to technological change. The report called for a universal 'entitlement' guaranteeing all young people they should reach at least year 12 in school, or pursue an apprenticeship, or receive 'at least a basic preparation for adulthood'. Income incentives should encourage young people to enter education and training, not work or unemployment without training. Nevertheless, the priority should not be income support policy, but reforms in education and training. There, year 11 and 12 curricula should be concerned with not just academic preparation. There should be more 'life skills preparation', and vocational counselling. Educational authorities should 'determine exactly what competencies young people need for employment' and 'how best to measure those competencies'.

These themes were taken up in subsequent government programs. The review also urged that 'as a complement to aggregate job growth and education and training policies' there should be 'selective employment interventions' to 'create jobs quickly for young people' (OECD 1984). This proposal, however, did not enter subsequent programs.

The educational expansion of the 1980s and early 1990s took place in a different policy setting to the 1960s. The education of some people now functioned as a substitute for their employment, and equal economic resources for all citizen–students was replaced by targeting at the margins. Social incorporation was now based on market equity.

I. Towards universal participation

Growth in TAFE

In 1975 the newly elected Fraser Government's first priority was to dampen down demand for the academic stream in secondary school and higher education, whose growth had been such a feature of the previous decade. At the same time, youth unemployment remained high, and the Government refused all strategies of deliberate job creation. The remaining option was TAFE, where costs per student were a third of higher education. This option was pursued with vigour. Between 1975–76 and 1982–83 funding for TAFE, a third of which was Commonwealth money, increased by 78.6 per cent in real terms, albeit from a low base. TAFE enrolments, mostly part-time, increased by a third between 1975 and 1980. At the same time there was a massive 54.2 per cent drop in spending on student assistance in higher education, from $441 million in 1975–76 to $202 million in 1982–83 (ABS 5510.0).

In the late 1970s retention to year 12 in schooling fell slightly, from 34.6 per cent in 1975 to 31.9 per cent in 1980. The increased participation of female students was countered by a decline in male retention, partly due to the growth in male-dominated TAFE. School leaver demand for higher education fell, especially among males. Between 1975 and 1982 the proportion of 19-year-old men enrolled in higher education fell from 15.7 to 13.2 per cent, while among 19-year-old women there was a decline from 15.4 to 13.7 per cent. Growth in higher education slowed in the late 1970s, particularly in the universities, and was largely sustained by mature age students. Conferences on higher education were held under titles such as 'Education in the aftermath of expansion', and 'Academia becalmed'. Policy makers talked about a 'retreat from education' (CTEC 1982; OECD 1983). If so, the 'retreat' had been imagined and abetted in official policies.

Meanwhile TAFE numbers continued to climb. Total TAFE students increased from 1 027 052 in 1982, the last full year of the Fraser Government, rising to 1 316 551 in 1985. Nevertheless, the growth in TAFE, much of it in recurrent education and adult recreation and leisure programs, was not sufficient to absorb the growing levels of unemployment.

Participation in schooling

The sudden jump in youth unemployment between 1981 and 1983 created the political conditions for a new approach. In 1982 the Fraser

Government began to move towards a new strategy, based on increased secondary retention and increased participation in higher education (Karmel 1983), and in the 1982–83 budget secondary student assistance was increased by 16 per cent. Before the March 1983 election Labor promised a modest increase in post-compulsory enrolments, and additional resources for secondary schools with low retention rates. This became the Participation and Equity Program (PEP).

The day after the election, Youth Affairs was transferred from the Department of Employment and Industrial Relations to the Department of Education, and in December 1984 it came under the personal patronage of the Prime Minister and was moved to the Department of Prime Minister and Cabinet. Prime Minister Hawke was photographed in 'youth situations', and the Government launched a public relations campaign assuring teenagers they were 'valued'. On 3 September 1984 Hawke spoke to a national PEP conference in Canberra. 'It is on the quality and reach of our education system that our future rests', he stated. The Government's 'highest priority' was to tackle the linked problems of youth unemployment and inadequate participation in education and training. 'The Government has taken immediate steps to counter young people's flagging interest in participation, and to revitalise an education system suffering from years of neglect.' Direct job creation was not included, but Hawke claimed the new policies would provide young people with 'more effective access to worthwhile job opportunities'. 'We hope to provide a great stimulus to the development of education in this country' (Hawke 1984: 1705–1706).

According to the Minister for Education and Youth Affairs, Senator Susan Ryan, PEP set out to ensure that by the end of the 1980s 'most young people complete the equivalent of a full secondary education, either in school or in a TAFE institution, or in some combination of work and education'. Most PEP funding was allocated to projects designed to lift participation by making school 'more attractive' through changes to curriculum, assessment, credentialling, parent/ teacher relations, teacher development, school organisation, links with the community and with post-school organisations (Fraser & Kennedy 1990). Following reviews of secondary education in each State, all governments became committed to increased retention to year 12. The need for higher retention became a constant theme in newspaper editorials and articles, and government reports. A national consensus had developed. The 1986–87 National Social Science Survey recorded that 68 per cent of Australians thought opportunities to enter tertiary education should be increased, and only 3 per cent wanted them reduced (Bean & Evans 1989).

Along with the PEP, the centrepiece of the new policies was student assistance payments. Financial assistance to secondary students rose by two and a half times during the 1980s, facilitating the transfer of part of the teenage population from the labour markets to education. The number of people receiving secondary allowances rose from 27 960 in 1982 to 171 600 in 1990. By 1992 41 per cent of secondary students and 48 per cent of full time tertiary students were assisted under AUSTUDY, the successor to TEAS and Secondary Allowances (CBP 1991). Between 1982–83 and 1989–90 all government outlays on student assistance in schooling rose from $130 to $329 million, and by 1993–94 total Commonwealth outlays on all forms of student assistance had increased 2.86 times. Policy related studies showed financial factors were significant at the margins of participation; and financial support also signalled to parents the value placed by government on the completion of education, with long-term effects on parental aspirations (Chapman 1992: 160).

In the decade after 1982 there was a growth in the number of senior secondary students of 114.7 per cent at year 11 and 127.7 per cent at year 12 (Table 8.1). This doubled the cohort immediately below higher education, providing the platform for rising demand for higher education and TAFE.

In the 1980s student participation increased at all levels, especially for women. By 1993 retention to year 10 was universal and retention to year 11 had risen from 54.0 per cent to 87.4 per cent since 1980. After 1982 retention to year 12 more than doubled, reaching 77.1 per

Table 8.1 Enrolments in schooling, years 11 and 12, 1982 to 1995

	Year 11	Year 12
1982	139 574	89 645
1983	156 162	98 688
1984	164 220	110 462
1985	175 267	116 316
1986	182 781	128 112
1987	199 095	142 107
1988	210 071	161 469
1989	204 431	167 845
1990	206 973	169 471
1991	214 622	183 257
1992	214 436	192 511
1993	210 672	186 916
1994	203 811	179 863
1995	199 256	172 357

Source: ABS 4221.0.

cent in 1992. At 81.4 per cent in 1993, female retention in schooling remained higher than male retention (71.9 per cent), reflecting the male role in TAFE apprenticeships (Table 8.2).

By the early 1990s year 12 had been completely transformed. It was no longer academically selective, but inclusive. Participation was becoming the norm for the age group and had lost most of its earlier positional value, except in the elite schools. Nonetheless, because the year 12 curriculum remained predominantly academic most young people had thus been brought within the ambit of preparation for higher education. This made competition for entry to higher education even more intense than before.

The speed of the increases in retention moved ahead of government,

Table 8.2 Apparent retention* to year 12 of schooling, 1969 and 1975 to 1995

	Women %	Men %	Persons %
1969	23.7	31.1	27.5
1975	33.6	34.6	34.1
1976	35.3	34.6	34.9
1977	36.6	34.0	35.3
1978	37.3	33.1	35.1
1979	37.2	32.4	34.7
1980	37.3	31.9	34.5
1981	37.8	32.0	34.8
1982	39.9	32.9	36.3
1983	43.9	37.5	40.6
1984	48.0	42.1	45.0
1985	49.5	43.5	46.4
1986	52.1	45.6	48.7
1987	57.0	49.4	53.1
1988	61.8	53.4	57.6
1989	65.2	55.5	60.3
1990	69.9	58.3	64.0
1991	76.7	66.1	71.3
1992	82.0	72.5	77.1
1993	81.4	71.9	76.6
1994	79.9	69.6	74.6
1995	77.1	66.1	72.2

* Refers to the proportion of the student cohort which enrolled in the first year of secondary education that continued to year 12. Note the effects of grade repeating, migration and other net changes to the school population are not taken into account (hence 'apparent' retention).
Sources: ABS 4221.0; Anderson & Vervoorn 1983: 46.

rendering obsolete a succession of official targets. In 1985 the Quality of Education Review Committee stated that by 1992 year 11 retention should reach 79 per cent and year 12 retention should be at 65 per cent (Karmel 1985: 63). The Ministerial Review of Postcompulsory Schooling in Victoria, the Blackburn report, recommended year 12 retention of 70 per cent by 1995. In the outcome the QERC targets were exceeded by 1990 for year 11 and 1991 for year 12, by which time retention was 71.3 per cent. In Victoria retention to year 12 rose to 75.7 per cent in 1991, four years ahead of the Blackburn report schedule. As in the 1960s, the growth in popular demand had developed its own momentum, only partly determined by government.

Growth in higher education

When Labor took office in 1983 it planned a modest growth in higher education of 25 000 additional places by 1990.[1] In the next four years students increased by a slow 13.0 per cent. Nevertheless, with secondary retention increasing sharply, change was in the air. After the 1987 Green Paper set the stage for growth, between 1987 and 1992 total enrolments rose by 165 631 students (42.1 per cent), with the number of women students increasing by 51.5 per cent. The Green Paper's target of 125 000 graduates a year by the year 2001 was exceeded in 1993 (132 860), eight years ahead of schedule.

The strength of demand was such that in higher education growth was achieved without a major liberalisation of student assistance, though total expenditure on student assistance rose along with enrolments. Growth was welcomed by the universities. A comparative international study of Australian academics in 1992 found that 75 per cent believed that higher education should be available to all who met the minimum entrance requirements. Academics were 'comparatively liberal vis-à-vis their colleagues in other countries' in their perception of the percentage of young people capable of completing secondary education (Sheehan & Welch 1994). By the mid-1990s the Australian rate of participation in higher education was in the top quarter of the OECD countries. When TAFE was included in the comparison Australian participation in tertiary education was even higher – having reached North American levels (Table 8.3). This was a sharp change from the situation in the mid-1980s (OECD 1996).

The growth of postgraduate education was even more rapid. From 1987 to 1995 enrolments in research higher degrees increased by 124.1 per cent, and coursework higher degree numbers by a massive 208.7 per cent (Table 8.4). The most rapid growth was in research

Table 8.3 Students in higher education, 1975 to 1996*

Coalition government		Labor government	
1975	273 137	1983	348 577
1976	290 109	1984	357 373
1977	300 835	1985	370 016
1978	312 943	1986	389 968
1979	320 268	1987	393 734
1980	329 523	1988	420 850
1981	336 702	1989	441 076
1982	341 390	1990	485 075
1983	348 577	1991	534 538
		1992	559 365
		1993	575 617
		1994	585 396
		1995	604 177
		1996*	631 025

* 1996 data are preliminary only.
Sources: CTEC statistics; DEET 1996a; 1996b.

higher degrees in business, architecture and engineering; and course work degrees in health sciences, agriculture, science and business.

Building on the relative expansion of female retention at school, there was a striking increase in the participation of women in higher education, signifying the modernising role of education. For the first time, the educational attributes of citizenship were being distributed to women on a more or less equal basis in quantitative terms (Table 8.5). In 1987 the number of women students exceeded that of men for the first time. Between 1981 and 1993 women's share of enrolments in vocational and pre-vocational programs in TAFE rose from 39.2 to 44.9 per cent. Overall, the total participation of men in tertiary education still exceeded that of women, but the gap was closing. Nevertheless, there were still qualitative differences. In higher education women were concentrated in the humanities/social sciences, education and nursing. Much of the growth in women's enrolments resulted from the transfer of pre-registration nurse education programs to higher education. Men heavily outnumbered women in PhD enrolments and the vocationally powerful Masters courses in business. In 1994, 55.0 per cent of bachelor level students were women, but women made up only 46.3 per cent of coursework higher degree students and 40.8 per cent of research students.

Targeted outlays on student assistance to Aboriginal and Torres Strait Islander people rose from $40.2 to $66.7 million from 1982–83 to 1990–91 (CBP), and the number of indigenous students in

Table 8.4 Students in higher education, by level of course, 1987 to 1995

| | Number of all students in higher education, enrolled in: | | | | | |
	Research higher degrees	Course-work higher degrees	Post-graduate diplomas	Bachelor degrees	Other courses*	Total
1987	14 567	13 401	35 745	264 177	65 844	393 734
1988	15 289	14 936	37 803	283 463	69 359	420 850
1989	14 751	15 981	39 263	305 706	65 375	441 076
1990	16 535	19 782	42 445	340 598	65 715	485 075
1991	19 280	24 985	48 638	380 590	61 045	534 538
1992	24 286	29 275	49 894	413 321	42 589	559 365
1993	28 345	33 584	51 714	430 204	31 770	575 617
1994	31 009	37 203	48 560	442 910	25 714	585 396
1995	32 646	41 373	50 106	454 846	25 206	604 177
1987 = 100	*224.1*	*308.7*	*140.2*	*172.2*	*38.3*	*153.4*

Sources: ABS 4218.0; DEET 1995a.

Table 8.5 Women as a proportion of higher education students, 1979 to 1996*

	Higher degrees %	All courses %
1979	26.8	44.7
1980	27.8	45.3
1981	28.8	45.5
1982	30.2	45.9
1983	30.8	46.3
1984	31.8	46.6
1985	33.0	47.6
1986	. . .	48.8
1987	. . .	50.1
1988	37.0	51.1
1989	38.1	52.1
1990	39.6	52.7
1991	41.2	53.3
1992	42.1	53.4
1993	42.7	53.4
1994	43.8	53.4
1995	45.2	53.9
1996*	. . .	54.3

* 1996 data are preliminary.
Sources: Anderson & Vervoorn 1983: 49; ABS 4218.0; ABS 4101.0; DEET 1996a; DEET 1996b.

higher education increased from 1933 in 1987 to 6264 in 1994, of whom 3849 (61.4 per cent) were women (DEET 1993: 217; DEET 1996a). The proportion of students who were indigenous rose from 0.49 to 1.07 per cent. However, 65.0 per cent of indigenous students were enrolled in arts, humanities, social sciences or education courses, compared to 35.1 per cent of all students. Indigenous representation in science and engineering was very low. Only 3.9 per cent of indigenous students were enrolled in higher degrees.

At the same time as the participation of young people in higher education was increasing, participation was also extending within the age structure. The absolute number of students aged over 30 years doubled between 1975 (41 416) and 1981 (85 854) and almost doubled again by 1993 (161 166), and the total proportion of students aged 30 or more increased from 15.3 per cent in 1975 to 27.5 per cent in 1993, notwithstanding the upsurge of school leaver entry in the late 1980s. Similarly, between 1982 and 1993 in TAFE, the proportion of students in vocational and pre-vocational course aged 30 years or more grew from 27.4 to 38.8 per cent. The growing reach of tertiary education was also expressed in the growth of external studies. From 1975 to 1994, externally enrolled students rose from 6.1 to 11.8 per cent, foreshadowing the expansion of learning from a distance via television and telecommunications in the 1990s.

While higher education grew rapidly, there was a dramatic fall in the participation of 16-year-olds in TAFE, from 24.7 per cent of the age group in 1984 to 15.6 per cent in 1988, and the participation of 17-year-olds in TAFE also declined, more slowly. The total number of students in vocational and pre-vocational programs in TAFE fell by 2.0 per cent in 1989, while higher education grew by 4.8 per cent. Academic study was now the focus of aspirations that might once have been centred on TAFE. This did not constitute a preference for less vocationally oriented courses. Rather, it reflected the fact that higher education qualifications were superior vocational credentials. They provided a positional advantage in the labour markets. Nevertheless, with the average cost of a place in TAFE at one-third that of higher education, it was inevitable that the growth of publicly funded places in higher education would slow. The change occurred only half a decade after the Green Paper. In 1992, commencing students in higher education fell by 3.4 per cent and TAFE enrolments rose by 12.2 per cent.

Scale of the expansion

During the 1980s there was a very substantial growth in the educational participation of the 15 to 19-year-old group, the main target of government programs. Between 1982 and 1992 the proportion of the 15 to 19 age group full time in education rose from 44.8 per cent to 62.3 per cent. Taking part-time education into account, the proportion of 15 to 19-year-olds *not* involved in some form of education and training fell from 41.2 per cent to 25.5 per cent between 1975 and 1992 (Table 8.6).

Between 1982 and 1992 the participation of 16-year-olds in schooling advanced from 58.0 to 80.9 per cent, while the participation of 17-year-olds rose from 30.2 to 60.3 per cent. In higher education there was a sharp rise in participation rates among 18 and 19-year-olds; in TAFE, while the participation of 17-year-olds fell (reflecting the decline of traditional apprenticeship intakes), that of 19-year-olds increased. Nevertheless, the full time labour market for teenagers continued to deteriorate, so that youth unemployment remained high. Even in February 1995, during an economic recovery, there were 93 900 teenagers unemployed and looking for full time work, and the unemployment rate among 15 to 19-year-olds was 30.3 per cent (6203.0). Policy makers began to press towards universal teenage enrolment.

In 1991 the Finn committee recommended that by the year 2001, 95 per cent of all 19-year-olds (later modified to 90 per cent) should complete year 12 or an initial post-school qualification, or be enrolled in education and training, a target subsequently endorsed by the Commonwealth and most States. The 1992 Carmichael report on vocational training went further, floating the abolition of full-time work for teenagers who had not reached year 12 or its equivalent in training (Finn 1991; Carmichael 1992: ix, 83). Participation of older students was also rising, constituting a trend to recurrent education, especially

Table 8.6 Participation in education, 15 to 19-year-olds, 1975, 1982 and 1992

	Schooling %	TAFE full-time %	TAFE part-time %	Higher education full-time %	Higher education part-time %	Not enrolled %	All sectors* %
			Proportion of all 15 to 19-year-olds (women and men) who were enrolled in:				
1975	36.3	2.0	13.2	6.0	0.5	41.2	100.0
1982	35.6	3.4	17.8	5.4	0.6	36.5	100.0
1992	48.8	4.2	14.5	9.3	0.5	25.5	100.0

* Includes participation in a small number of other institutions. Note also that there are instances of multiple sector enrolment. For both reasons, the 'all sectors' total is not the sum of the other columns.
Source: DEET 1994a.

in TAFE. The proportion of 20 to 24-year-olds enrolled in some form of education and training rose from 19.8 per cent in 1982 to 27.8 per cent in 1991.

In quantitative terms, the expansion of educational enrolments from the early 1980s to the early 1990s was scarcely less impressive than the growth of the 1960s and 1970s (Table 8.7).

The postwar boom had seen schooling become universal to age fifteen, and the development of mass senior secondary education and then mass higher education. In the expansion of the 1980s and after, education and training became universal to age sixteen and were becoming universal for the whole of the post-compulsory teenage group. Young people's participation in higher education almost doubled. The participation of adults was expanding and perhaps half

Table 8.7 Students in education, by sector, 1975 to 1995

| | Total number of students (full-time and part-time) in: | | | | |
	Primary schooling*	Secondary schooling	Higher education	TAFE and technical**	All sectors of education
1975	1 819 358	1 099 922	273 137	521 312	3 713 729
1976	1 842 128	1 118 122	290 109	555 867	3 806 226
1977	1 874 631	1 120 161	300 835	588 230	3 883 857
1978	1 894 654	1 115 378	312 943	620 514	3 943 489
1979	1 884 753	1 102 178	320 268	654 460	3 961 659
1980	1 884 094	1 100 468	329 523	701 820	4 015 905
1981	1 871 063	1 115 528	336 702	692 014	4 015 307
1982	1 849 016	1 145 676	341 390	759 888	4 095 970
1983	1 809 035	1 206 771	348 577	793 470	4 157 853
1984	1 764 165	1 253 438	357 373	832 105	4 207 081
1985	1 727 897	1 278 272	370 016	859 194	4 235 379
1986	1 711 932	1 289 457	389 968	886 679	4 278 036
1987	1 709 546	1 295 337	393 734	937 175	4 335 792
1988	1 725 688	1 296 641	420 850	951 598	4 394 777
1989	1 754 418	1 276 969	441 076	932 331	4 404 794
1990	1 763 494	1 278 163	485 075	966 846	4 493 578
1991	1 786 529	1 288 608	534 538	985 942	4 595 617
1992	1 804 370	1 294 596	559 365	1 042 547	4 700 878
1993	1 816 066	1 282 309	585 386	1 121 399	4 805 160
1994	1 825 740	1 273 640	585 396	1 131 509	4 816 285
1995	1 833 681	1 275 656	604 177	1 272 748	4 986 262

* Special education enrolments in schools not allocated to sector are included in primary.
** Number of enrolments, not number of students between 1975 and 1980. TAFE/Technical does not include Adult Education before 1981, or the Recreation, Leisure and Personal Enrichment stream after 1980.
Sources: CTEC data; Anderson & Vervoorn 1983: 20–33; ABS 4221.0.

of the school leaver age group was destined to enter higher education, or both TAFE and higher education, at some point in the life cycle. A further group could be expected to enrol only in TAFE. Coupled with the rising participation of mature age students in TAFE, this signified a longer term tendency towards universal tertiary education. Further, credentialism had triggered the beginnings of mass postgraduate education. There were more postgraduate students in higher education in 1992 than students in the whole of Australian higher education in 1967 (Table 8.8).

The trend was towards the closure of the gaps in participation. There had been a major change in Australian education, a movement from a mass post-compulsory system to a near universal system, and the beginnings of lifelong learning on a wide scale. At the same time this was a highly differentiated system, in which some forms of participation were more powerful and more desirable than others. This vertical hierarchy

Table 8.8 The two waves of postwar expansion in education in Australia 1960s/mid-1970s, and 1980s/early 1990s

	Following the expansion of education between the early 1960s and the mid-1970s:	Following the expansion of education between the early 1980s and the early 1990s:
Policy framework	Keynesian economic and social policies, full employment, meritocratic selection of social leaders in education	New Right economic and fiscal policies, universal population management, substitution of education for work
Schooling	85% retention to year 10 and 34% retention to year 12 by 1975; retention slightly higher for men than women	Universal retention to year 10 and 75% retention to year 12 by 1992; retention much higher for women (c. 8–10%)
Post-compulsory years (15–19)	By mid-1970s, three in five 15 to 19-year-olds participating in some form of formal education, including training programs	By early 1990s, four in five 15 to 19-year-olds participating in some form of formal education, including training programs; policy goal is universal participation of age group

Table 8.8 Cont.

	Following the expansion of education between the early 1960s and the mid-1970s:	Following the expansion of education between the early 1980s and the early 1990s:
School leaver participation in higher education	15.5% of 19-year-olds enrolled in higher education in 1975	23.6% of 19-year-olds enrolled in higher education in 1992
	School–higher education transfer rate above 50%	School–higher education transfer rate below 40%
Enrolment in higher education	237 173 students in 1975; women 40.1% of all students	585 396 students in 1993; women 53.5% of all students
Students aged over 30 years in higher education and TAFE*	In 1975, 3.5% participation: TAFE 143 000 (est.); higher education 41 416	In 1992, 7% participation: TAFE 313 219; higher education 150 624
Industry training	Incidence unknown [TAFE related data are inadequate; no data available in relation to on-the-job provision outside TAFE programs]	More than two million workers in industry training *before* the expansion of training in the early 1990s through the training levy, award restructuring and competency-based training
Postgraduate education	36 827 total students 1975 26 142 in coursework Masters and Graduate Diplomas Women 21.8% of all higher degree students	116 772 total students 1993 79 226 in coursework Masters and Graduate Diplomas Women 43.8% of all higher degree students

* Vocational and pre-vocational courses only (excludes recreation and leisure stream).

of participation was hidden by the official policies, in which the objective was participation as an end in itself, and all forms of participation were treated as equivalent, mitigating the sharp effects of inequality with a normative 'parity of esteem', although no one believed that all institutions had equivalent status. But it was easier for governments to increase total participation than redistribute participation on a socially representative basis, or render the different forms of participation more equal to each other.

II. From equality to 'participation and equity'

Equality of opportunity after 1975

The policies of equality of opportunity in education that emerged during the long postwar boom carried the seeds of their own destruction. Compelling as they were in their own time, these policies and the systems of funding and the special programs associated with them were also transitional: in bringing education to the mass of the population, they undermined the outer limits conferred on them by the systems of an earlier era. The specific technologies used to identify, select and nurture 'ability', designed for the selection of a social elite, were already imploding in a system where year 12 retention had reached almost one in three by the mid-1970s. While equality of opportunity policies long postponed their own demise by expanding the boundaries of 'fairness', there were limits to this. Once participation increased to mass levels, then it was clear that more than high 'ability' was determining the distribution of opportunities.

Among the middle-class families that were habitual users of higher education – whose social distinctions had been naturalised, in part, by their educational distinctions – there was some resentment when education's own tinkering with itself revealed for all to see that 'ability', achievement and distinction in education were not simply natural, but were constructed and could be reconstructed. As for the other end of the social scale, in *Poverty and education in Australia*, for the Commonwealth Government's commission of inquiry into poverty, Fitzgerald (1976: 231) commented that 'people who are poor and disadvantaged are victims of a societal confidence trick. They have been encouraged to believe that a major goal of schooling is to increase equality.' The fact that academic achievement of school students continued to be correlated to prior levels of social advantage, and even those poor students who did well at school were less likely to complete year 12, limited the degree of faith in equality of opportunity policies and programs.

After 1975, with the rise of youth unemployment, and the emergence of high participation policies ('full education' policies) in place of those designed to create full employment, the basis for the old collusion between equality and merit disappeared. On the one hand, the definition of equal rights was reduced to universal access, and being identified with the rise of mass education it was readily counterpoised to 'excellence'. On the other hand, the classical equality of opportunity approaches that were based on scarcity and exclusion now became increasingly antagonistic to governmental and popular demands for expanded participation. The notion of limited ability was the antithesis of policies designed to increase participation for its own sake. 'Equality of opportunity is inescapably tied to the machinery of social training, differentiation and selection of which it is in fact a by-product' (Hunter 1993: 276). Blackburn argues that:

> Equality of opportunity itself is essentially a culling notion, content to jettison the unsuccessful by product of a continuous competition from which those worthy of further education will emerge. It has always operated against the possibility of developing an *educated population*, as against trying to make selection into levels of education not universally open apparently fair (Blackburn 1987, cited in Ashenden 1987b).

Policies of equality of opportunity as equal starting points had ceased to be 'fair' or economic, or technically defensible, and had lost much of the popular appeal that had made them effective as a tool of government. In the second half of the 1970s there was a worldwide shift, not only from equality of opportunity policies but from equality more generally (CCCS 1981: 225–226; Apple 1986; Crittenden 1988). An internal OECD secretariat paper on *Educational equality and social justice* reflected that 'looking at the current scene compared with ten or fifteen years ago, one is struck by the comparative absence of the term "equality of educational opportunity" which until so recently was a watchword for innumerable conferences, reports, reforms and policies ... the same rules and issues are not in play today' (OECD 1981b: 1).

In the mid-1980s the OECD turned this movement away from equalising policies – the inevitable accompaniment to the ascendancy of Paretian principles in social policy – into a virtue. The OECD found that equality of opportunity policies had failed to more than marginally shift the socio-economic distribution of higher education (the great rise in women's participation was largely ignored). 'The vastly expanded opportunities for higher education have not significantly reduced differences between social classes in their rates of attendance nor have they equalised the life chances of the rich and poor' (Husen 1985: 400). It called for the abandonment of the more far reaching equality objectives of the 1960s. 'The social patterning of success and failure in schools and colleges is universal', it stated. Social redistribution through education was too difficult a project, and should be abandoned. It should be acknowledged that 'education systems always act as selection mechanisms' and 'the existence of selection should be faced and accounted for rather than wished away as much discussion in this field has tended to do'.

Further, 'social hierarchies and income inequalities are extremely resilient to change. It would be wrong to set education the overarching objective of erasing them altogether'. For 'one of the "iron laws" of educational development is that privileged groups and social strata constantly seek to maintain that privilege'. When structures and institutions were made more open, the 'better-off' had a knack of establishing new criteria of success and developing strategies that sidestepped equalising policies. The struggle for relative advantage would go on regardless. 'The right of parents to seek what is perceived to be the best education for their children cannot be denied.'

While it was possible for students from poor backgrounds to gain access to further education in greater numbers than before, it was extremely difficult to improve their relative position. Indeed, since the early or mid-1970s there had been a decline in the social representivity of the higher education systems in many OECD countries. Fair selection was important, but given the scarcity of good jobs 'it becomes more necessary to focus on the other end of the socio-economic spectrum' (OECD 1985: 38–47).

In Australia the successive election platforms of the Labor Party were an indicator of the policy drift. Equality of educational opportunity dominated the 1972 policy speech. In 1977 the emphasis was not on new programs but on the defence of past achievements. The speech finished with a reference to equality of opportunity, but the tone was unmistakably plaintive and nostalgic. 'There are fundamental changes we made which must never be set aside … above all, the continuing drive towards more equal opportunities, true equality, for all Australians' (ALP 1977: 20–21). With Labor back in government and refurbishing its education policies, the 1984 policy speech noted that 'education contributes to a more equal society', but it linked 'a fairer, more just and more equitable society' to upward mobility and improved material benefit. There was no reference to greater equality of educational outcomes. 'Genuine equality of opportunity for all' was only mentioned at the end of the speech, when the Prime Minister used it to ground his final appeal to the Party faithful (ALP 1984: 2334–2343). In the 1987 policy speech the emphasis was on individual self-realisation – 'Labor's policies on education and training are designed to ensure each individual has satisfying and productive life choices' – and equality of opportunity was again consigned to the concluding rhetoric (ALP 1987).

Equality as equity (access and participation)

The 1959 United Nations *Declaration of the rights of the child* had enshrined equal access as one of the planks of an equality policy in education (R. Connell 1993: 22). In the government of education in Australia, access now became the whole of that equality policy. In the new language the word 'equality' was replaced by 'equity', defined as access and participation for all. The main 'equity' goal of the 1980s and early 1990s was to expand school retention rates and access to TAFE and, for a period, access to higher education. Specific programs were designed to increase the participation of particular groups reckoned marginal to education, such as aboriginal students, rural students, women in the technologies, and students unable to speak English or attending schools reckoned disadvantaged, and disabled students. In the new post-Karmel era the distribution of education to marginal social groups remained on the policy agenda. Their participation was one of the measures of 'equity' at its outer limit (Chapman 1992: 15). But policies on the 'disadvantaged' were no longer based in a framework of equal economic and pedagogical conditions. The right to an equal start now became reduced simply to the right to enter the race.

Labor governments placed a greater importance on equity policies than did their conservative opponents, or the New Right. The Commonwealth Labor Government of 1983 to 1996 saw equity policies in education and other sectors as unifying the nation behind the cause of economic mobilisation. In *Towards a fairer Australia: social justice under Labor* (CA 1988) the Government stated that it was 'committed to making social justice both a primary goal of economic policy and an indispensable element in achieving economic policy objectives' (vi–vii). Labor's social policies were placed at the margins of its economic policies. Efficiency and equity were treated as complementary rather than contradictory, a strategy with some popular appeal. The price was an attenuated reading of equity.

Labor's 'four key elements of a just society' were equality of civil, legal and industrial rights; fairness (equity) in the distribution of economic resources; opportunities for participation in personal development, community life and decision making; and 'fair and equal access' to essential services such as education (Fitzclarence & Kenway 1993; Henry & Taylor 1993). Rather than universal rights to economic resources, there was to be fair distribution of them; and in education, fair distribution boiled down to access. Government was focused on the factors seen to determine individual participation in education, including social group membership, understood as a characteristic of the individual's 'background' that affected performance in education. But it neglected the dynamics of group relations. In reworking his own earlier statements about equality in education, Karmel suggested 'the concept of "equality of opportunity" might be paraphrased "fairness of access of an individual to an opportunity" '. Fairness did not require similar outcomes across socio-economic groups, because there might be differences among them in either 'preferences or abilities' (Karmel 1987: 317–318).

Targeting and the 'disadvantaged'

The retreat from solidarity in equality programs was parallel to the shift away from universality in education financing and provision, and the rise of both targeting in social welfare and later, user payments. In his report for the Commonwealth Government on student loans, Chapman argued that:

> The role of student income support is to decrease financial barriers to educational participation. . . . income support should be targeted to those with the most significant financial barriers and away from those with the least significant financial barriers; and the most appropriate criterion with which to judge policy in this area is whether or not it is effective in diminishing those barriers. . . . if student income support is to work, above and beyond its consequences for income distribution, it should change the educational participation behaviour of financially disadvantaged groups and individuals (Chapman 1992: 18).

Correspondingly, support should be withdrawn from those who would still participate without government assistance (Chapman 1992: ix). Rizvi (1993: 132) argues that the targeting of under-represented groups for increased participation, for example indigenous people, and women in technological courses exemplified a 'deficit view of social justice'. The disadvantaged had to be compensated in the market through its agent the state, which had special responsibility for them.

In education, targeting was made possible by the near universalisation of the positional market. It was no longer necessary to provide universal services on a non-market basis to secure high rates of participation and government resources could be concentrated at the margins. But without a culture of solidarity on which a political strategy of positive discrimination could be built, the extra resources and greater access tended to be counter-balanced by social stigma, and targeted programs had no direct impact on the wealth and power of the socially advantaged, limiting their potential as redistributive instruments. And targeting could be applied in reverse, either by governments or individual institutions, to 'gifted' students seen as able to enhance the competitive position of an institution or a nation (Kenway 1993). Connell suggests the *double entendre* in 'targeting' of the disadvantaged accurately describes the strategy. 'To talk only about poverty is to risk stigmatising the targeted minority.' The most disadvantaged 15 per cent at a given time 'are not culturally distinct, but have a great deal in common with a larger group of working class families' (R. Connell 1993: 105). Jamrozik argues that 'the outcome of residualisation is legitimation of disadvantage, legitimation of inequality, legitimation of exclusion . . . from the mainstream of social life' (Jamrozik 1983: 180).

Nevertheless, targeting was compatible with a universal system in education, provided that it was based on vertical stratification. Targeting *both* helped to secure universal participation *and* underlined the point about stratification. It was also used as an instrument of vocationalism, as when students thought to be at risk of unemployment were targeted for vocational skilling. Through universal participation underpinned by targeting, equity in education became seen as the guarantor for equity in the labour markets, educational equity as vocational equity.

Equity as market equity

Once access for all was secured, and the completion rates of disadvantaged groups were close to the norm, the success or failure of both individuals and groups ceased to be a responsibility of government. Competition and 'natural selection' could be allowed to take their course. Upward social mobility would go to those deserving it. Rizvi argues that in relation to the Labor equity policies:

> The Federal Labor Government's social justice policy . . . suggests that freedoms, prosperity and equality can only be delivered by the market. With such reliance on the market, the Government's main responsibility becomes that of good management of the social and cultural conditions necessary for capital accumulation. Labor's restructuring program . . . has often been justified on the grounds that free association of buyers and sellers in an open market will bring a fair and equitable exchange. . . . 'desert' has thus become well-established as the basis of social policy (Rizvi 1993: 132).

The classical social democratic policy sets out to break the link between market performance and citizen entitlement. During the late Keynesian period, to a degree this approach was adopted by governments from both sides of politics. After 1975, and especially after the mid-1980s, governments from both sides of politics revived that link. Programs such as the Disadvantaged Schools Program in New South Wales, a survival from the Whitlam years, were exceptional in their commitment to the older redistributive objectives (Johnston 1993; R. Connell 1993).

'Equity' meant a government that was modernising in the market sense, one that removed the pre-market barriers to competition and upward mobility – such as the binary segmentation between universities and colleges of advanced education, which was abolished by Dawkins in 1988 – but did not seek to redistribute the places at the top between social groups, let alone flatten the positional hierarchy itself. Thus while Susan Ryan, Labor's Education Minister between 1983 and 1987, exhorted the universities to create a more representative social mix, she took no other steps to secure that end with the means at her disposal, and matters went on as before. The reduction from redistribution and equalisation, to 'participation and equity', was reflected in the official statistics used in framing policy targets. The different forms of participation in higher education were treated as equivalent. In schooling, the dynamics of domination and subordination in the relationship between the private and government schools were officially ignored. All schools were treated as interchangeable. Positional inequality was no longer a public problem. This freed it to remain a private objective.

There was more continuity here than first appears. The characteristic Australian 'egalitarian individualism' had always been open to a shift from collective goals ('mateship') to individualised competitive success, to the rush to be rich. And the equality of opportunity policies of the 1960s and 1970s had augmented the desires for upward mobility, and focused them on education. A fair distribution and opportunities for all were universally attractive notions provided everyone thought that they themselves could benefit. But if a fairer overall distribution was beyond the ambit of governments, people could still pursue their own interests. With equity defined as access, there was no longer a conflict between the privileged self and the general good, between the individual drive for relative advantage, and system government. The individual was free to pursue inequality of opportunity, untroubled by social solidarity and its obligations. However, the people who were disqualified by the redefinition of participation as equity, and the shift to market relation of which it was part, were those who prized a solidaristic system in which competition was reduced rather than enhanced, and everyone in education could win. As Jonathon puts it:

A market in education creates a competitive framework in which parents as consumers are freed to seek advantage for their children, whilst at the same time automatically raising the stakes both for their own children and for others . . . It is immediately evident that a ratcheting of the spiral of social competition is bound to produce a net loss of welfare for some of the young. But it is also of concern, to non-libertarians, that even those children who are most likely to compete effectively and emerge as winners, may be ill-served by the accompanying change in the social ethos. To believe that all, and not simply the current disadvantaged, might benefit from a more even distribution of social goods, is after all a political perspective with a long and enduring tradition. In an education market, however, parents as trustees cannot include these broader matters in considerations of a child's eventual interest. . . . Trustees, far from having free choices, have no responsible option but to make individualistic, competitive moves, even though these *must* entail a worse outcome for some of the young – and *may* arguably entail a worse outcome for all of them – than would have resulted from a less competitive framework for decision (Jonathon 1990: 123–126).

The abandonment of the classical equality of opportunity policies was the end of the fifty-year-old struggle to establish a pure set of conditions for scientific educational selection, in which the 'natural ability' of each child would be revealed, untainted by the effects of economic differences and other social factors. Governments were no longer even nominally required to equalise educational conditions, re-naturalising starting inequalities, inequalities in the kind of participation, and differential private (and public) expenditures. This allowed governments to tolerate, advocate and introduce user charges, despite the differential social effects of those charges. 'It seems equitable to charge the rich for a service they preferentially consume. But it is only dollars they need to find: the poor must find brains' (Teese 1985). It could no longer be argued on official grounds that educational advantage, or social advantage *via* education, constituted a denial of equal rights, or a just sharing of the benefits of education, or a reduction in popular educations.

In this environment, the New Right claim that an attack on educational privileges was an attack on educational 'excellence' was more difficult to reject. Educational privilege now had few critics. But this meant little could be done for the 'disadvantaged', for advantage and disadvantage formed a single system in which the 'advantaged' held control. Unless advantage was modified, disadvantage could not be redressed. In *Schools and social justice* (1993) Connell attacked all programs that favoured certain students ahead of others, including provision for the 'gifted and talented', stricter selection, streaming and tracking, merit awards, 'any of the hundred and one affronts to equal provision in education. Any education that privileges one child over another is giving the privileged child a corrupted education, even as it gives him or her a social or economic advantage' (R. Connell 1993: 15). It was a sign of the times that Connell's statement had nothing like the impact it would have claimed in 1975, when governments were officially committed to the flattening out of pre-given private advantages.

Government in education had a continuing need for norms of justice. In the changes in educational policies after 1975, the old equality objectives in education were not so much abandoned as transformed. They were subordinated to economic objectives, and rendered consistent with the mechanisms of educational competition. Competition was represented as fair as well as efficient. Selectivity and privilege were no longer seen as antagonistic to the growth of participation in education, but were combined with it. Equity as universal participation in education supplied one of the key norms of government, extending beyond education itself to policies on employment and the labour market programs. Equity as participation connected to the solidaristic and egalitarian aspect of the old equality of opportunity policies, and even the radical campaigns for equality of respect, which had emphasised the need for broader access. It also connected to the notion of education as a right of all citizens, one that was necessary for functioning at work and in all other social sites (Finn 1991). It was congruent with the goals of economic policy in education, of vocational modernisation and universal skilling, and eliminating youth unemployment.

At the same time, it was also consistent with the New Right's rejection of engineered equality of opportunity in education, and opened the way to the free development of markets in education and the greater material inequalities that were bound to be the consequence of this.

III. Expectations of education

The government of utopia

The education policies of the late 1980s combined the realistic and the utopian. The need to address youth unemployment and increase international competitiveness were joined to the normative vision of a high skill society, in which optimum levels of human capital, nurtured in education and periodically upgraded at work, would be utilised to the fullest extent. Policy makers claimed that technological advance was displacing uneducated labour, that future economic competition would take place at the high quality and knowledge-intensive end of the product markets, and all labour would need to be educated and skilled to an advanced level.

There was little evidence for these propositions. For example Dawkins claimed that the development of high technology industries was retarded by an insufficient number of science and engineering graduates; yet the number of science graduates in Australia was well above OECD averages, and the number of engineers was average. Similarly, competency based reform and the standardisation of credentials, and the promise that work based learning might become recognised for the purposes of educational credentialling, were presented as the means of opening up the universities and providing equal dignity to all forms of knowledge and skill. This signified the continuing importance of social justice and equity considerations in educational policies, especially under a Labor government. Yet a dignity and a social power was conferred on training reform that was scarcely merited. The 1991 ACTU education and training policy, prepared during consultation with the Commonwealth, stated that:

> The labour market now demands rapidly increasing numbers of people with significantly new and higher levels of knowledge, skill formation and competence, calling for a paradigm shift in and restructuring of education and training systems. It is one thing to recreate a small highly educated and competent elite. It is quite another to meet the requirements of a mass condition which has to be inescapably created from amongst those who previously were ignored and deprived (ACTU 1991: 199).

This glowing vision of a working class whose conditions of life were being lifted *en masse* conferred on what was an economist and corporatist policy a democratic and egalitarian aura that increased its popular appeal, especially on the Labor side of politics. Lyotard comments that 'the State resorts to the narrative of freedom every time it assumes direct control over the "training" of the people under the name of the "nation", in order to point them down the path of progress' (Lyotard 1984: 32). By presenting the reform and expansion of education as egalitarian, modernising and economically rational, educationists and policy makers were able to secure a broad base of support for the new set of policies. The positive sum character of the rhetoric, which implied that all stood to gain from the lifting of their education, underpinned the great growth in popular aspirations.

Popular aspirations

The Commonwealth Government conducted regular surveys of young people, by Australian National Opinion Polls (ANOP), to monitor the effects and effectivity of its policies. Over the course of the 1980s and early 1990s those surveys recorded a major growth in the proportion of the population aspiring to higher education. Increasingly, students accepted that in a more competitive labour market the best single way to improve the prospect of employment was to achieve higher levels of education. Correspondingly, their education ambitions were infused with work-related goals.

In each ANOP survey young people under 25 were asked to identify 'the one thing in particular they would like to do in the next five years'. Between the 1984 and 1990 surveys they showed a declining commitment to travel, from 41 to 28 per cent, and an increased commitment to goals related to work and education, from 25 to 47 per cent. In successive ANOP surveys the overall proportion of 15 to 17-year-olds wanting to go on to post-school education increased from 47 to 70 per cent (Table 8.9), with university attracting much higher support than TAFE. In 1994 there was a small increase in the focus on TAFE, following government promotion of that sector, but university remained much the most popular destination. Young people also evidenced a strongly vocational understanding of education, and of the responsibilities of government in education, and preferred vocationally oriented school subjects (ANOP 1984: 5–25; ANOP 1990: 23, 73–78, 85–88; ANOP 1994a).

The ANOP studies also showed that those official policies designed to transfer students' ambitions from the labour market to further education had achieved significant success. During the 1980s young people's expectations of government were partly shifted from job creation to education and training. Whereas in 1984, 38 per cent of 15 to 24-year-olds identified job creation as a major priority of the Commonwealth, by 1990 that proportion had fallen to 19 per cent (ANOP 1990: 77). At the same time, the structure of the labour market guaranteed that most of the expectations of students would be disappointed. This was the inevitable price of a utopian education policy. The 1994 ANOP survey found that 56 per cent of year 12 students planned to be professionals. But only 13 per cent of the workforce worked as professionals (ANOP 1994a: 1–4).

Table 8.9 Proportion of 15 to 17-year-olds intending to enter tertiary education, 1984, 1988, 1990, 1994

| | Proportion of 15 to 17-year-olds intending to enrol in: | |
	University %	TAFE %
1984	27	20
1988	38	15
1990	41	13
1994	50	20

Source: DEET 1994b.

Even as popular aspirations, enhanced by government policies, were being more specifically centred on education, so that the demand for advanced levels of education was beginning to become universal among young people, the realisation of these aspirations was being undermined by the effects of credentialism. 'Credentialism' refers to an inflation of the level of credentials needed in the labour markets. It is constituted by an increase in the level of education required to 'mark time' in the labour market, to obtain work at a constant level. Credentialism was an outgrowth of the role of education in positional competition, in sorting people for employment. When the number of graduates grew more quickly than opportunities for graduate labour at the same level, credentialism was inevitable. The limiting factor was the scarcity of opportunities for career-based employment, a scarcity which no amount of talking up of education, and student effort, could overcome. The economic 'bottleneck' was on the demand side rather than the supply side. The problem was not inadequacies in educated labour, but the failure of employers to make optimum use of the available skills. Only job creation schemes and full employment could address the problem, and these approaches were off the policy agenda (Hirsch 1976; Marginson 1995a; Marginson 1996a).

Market segmentation and the limits to substitutability of skilled labour between fields meant that the labour market did not operate as a single market. In segmented pockets, the demand for credentials might exceed the supply, running against a general trend to screening and credentialism. At the same time, across much of the labour market there was a partial substitutability of credentials; so that credentialism became a general trend. The expansion in post-compulsory education after 1985, unlike the expansion of the 1960s and early 1970s, occurred in the context of a buyers market in educated labour. Much of the expansion was due to credentialism; the expansion tended to generate further credentialism; and this meant that the hopes associated with educational expansion and vocational reform were bound to be disappointed. The dynamics of credentialism made it inevitable that the rewards associated with educated labour would fall short of expectations. Education was bound to fail in two, familiar respects, and more so than in the earlier period: in itself it was unable to drive the effective utilisation of skilled labour; and as a result it was unable to deliver on the heady promises of social equity and collective advance. The 1960s/ 1970s cycle of expectation of and disillusion with education was bound to be repeated. So it proved: after 1993 retention to year 12 began to fall, and the growth of demand for tertiary education slowed.

The reform program implied that by vocationalising education upward mobility would be enhanced, and that somehow everyone would gain a better access to the labour market rewards seen to be associated with education. Yet an education system more open to the labour markets was one more affected by the inequalities, hierarchies, segmentations and pockets of privilege found there; and by the individualisation of responsibility for individual (and social) outcomes. This was hardly likely to lead to the egalitarian visions called up by the Laborist education reformers. Worse, unemployment persisted. The teenagers who stayed on at school because the alternative was to be unemployed, now found that the problem of finding work had not been evaded, it had merely been postponed.

To the extent that citizenship was determined by labour market participation, and educated citizens was defined in economic terms, the reach of citizenship was fragmented and unequally distributed. Some, the unemployed, were destined to be denied effective citizenship altogether. A citizenship based on the labour markets, like a citizenship differentiated by the dual system of schooling, was a citizenship where some were more equal than others.

Notes

[1] The actual increase in student numbers was 144 000 by 1990.

CHAPTER 9

Economic government in education

'At first glance, it might seem that where a State provides
more staff per unit of service, there is a *prima facie* case for
saying that this reflects a policy decision to provide a
higher quality service. On the other hand, it can be argued
that a State that is providing the same service with fewer
staff per unit of service is operating more efficiently.
Drawing on public choice theory, we have started from the
assumption that, unless there is evidence to the contrary,
high staffing ratios do not provide a better quality service
and are a reflection of other factors, such as vote "buying"
of public sector unions and other similar pressure groups
or attempts to minimise potential vote losses from similar
groups by politicians.'

Institute of Public Affairs, 'Efficiency of States' spending', in
Economic Planning Advisory Council (EPAC), in Background
papers on the public sector, *Background Paper Number 7,*
EPAC, Australian Government Publishing Service, Canberra,
1990, p. 2.

Prelude: Voices in the air (1987 and 1992)

In 1987 the Monash University Centre for Policy Studies published
Spending and taxing, a market liberal blueprint for the reform of gov-
ernment, funded by the business-based National Priorities Project.
Chapter 7, on education, was prepared by economist Ross Parish.

Parish stated that while spending on government education had
risen, its standards and quality were declining and teachers were not
accountable. For this reason many parents were transferring their children to the private schools. Smaller classes and student–teacher ratios
suited teachers, but did not necessarily improve students' education.
Parish cited Hanushek (1986) to show there was 'no strong or systematic relationship between school expenditures and student performance'. He applied Hanushek's findings only to government schooling,

however, arguing that funding to *private* schools should be increased, probably in the form of vouchers that would create 'a predominantly private system of education. In terms of efficiency of production and responsiveness to parents' wishes, such an outcome would be highly desirable.' The money for increased private school funding could be generated by cutting teachers in government schools (Parish 1987: 90–114):

> Whether or not a voucher scheme or similar means of providing equal (or more equal) public funding for private and government schools were implemented, the present extravagant levels of expenditure on government schools should be reduced. *Low student:teacher ratios should no longer be regarded as evidence of high quality education but, rather, as indicative of low teacher productivity.* The aim, therefore, should be to achieve higher ratios. As a provisional aim, it is recommended that a return to the student:teacher ratios of about 1975 would be appropriate. This would involve an increase of about 25 per cent on the current overall ratio in government schools ... 25 per cent cut in the ratio should translate into at least a 20 per cent cut in the number of teachers, which in turn should enable a 15 per cent reduction in expenditure. On the basis of 1986–87 Commonwealth budget estimates and projection of State government expenditures ... about $1000 million (Parish 1987: 113).

The proposed reduction of one teaching position in five, and one billion in spending, attracted much comment but was reckoned too educationally destructive and too politically extreme ever to be implemented. Not so. Five years later, in October 1992, the Liberal and National Parties were elected in Victoria on a platform of reducing public spending. Within two years the Kennett Government had removed 8200 teaching positions in government schools, almost one in every five, and cut spending on government schools by $300 million – the equivalent of $1 billion a year if duplicated in all States. The average primary school student–teacher ratio was increased from 15.8 in 1992 to 18.7 in 1994. Primary and secondary class sizes rose sharply. Special needs staffing was cut by half and those positions tagged to socio-economic disadvantage were abolished. Meanwhile the funding of private schools was increased by $33 million, 15 per cent in real terms. Parish and the Centre for Policy Studies had come into their own. As Keynes put it:

> Practical men, who believe themselves to be quite exempt from any intellectual influences, are usually the slaves of some defunct economist. Madmen in authority, who hear voices in the air, are distilling their frenzy from some academic scribbler of a few years back (Keynes 1936: 383).[1]

In response to these developments the then Commonwealth Treasurer, John Dawkins, called for a reduction of $1.4 billion in State and Territory education spending. In July 1993 EPAC released a paper on *Education and training in the 1990s* stating that the 'application of benchmarking in the cost of service provision in education could result in savings of at least $1.4 billion for State Governments . . . Overseas research shows a remarkable invariance of measured student outcomes to alternative teacher/student ratios, except for extreme high and low levels of provision. Quality rather than quantity of teaching and educational involvement is important' (Clare and Johnston 1993: 5). The figure of $1.4 billion was an 'office estimate' which had been 'used by the Commonwealth in discussions with the States on the potential for reduction in State expenditures and for higher public savings'. It was supported by a reference to Parish's work.

I. Economising education

The efficiency imperative

After 1975 the fiscal imperative was manifest as an efficiency imperative in all sectors of education (except one) that were dependent on government funds. In higher education from 1976, and in the largely State-funded government schools and TAFE sectors from the early 1980s, the politics of resource cuts became ubiquitous, and per capita levels of funding began to decline, especially in higher education. The drive to efficiencies and 'productivity savings' was fed by the annual budget cycle. Regardless of the effects on the range or quality of outputs, savings could always be found. The same or reduced resources were worked more and more intensively, normalising scarcity in place of the Keynesian largesse of the boom period. Only the private schools enjoyed a more permissive regime. For them the period of funding-driven expansion continued right up to 1985, when Labor imposed its new schools policy and slowed the rate of annual increase in per capita grants; and these restrictions were lifted again in 1996.

Efficiency in government is more than a neutral technique. It can only be understood in relation to the purposes it serves (Ball 1990). In the neo-classical definition that became increasingly dominant, efficiency was market rational. It meant that education should be judged by its contribution to value creating activities in the economy, such as the preparation of skilled labour for employers, while its demands on government revenue should be minimised (OECD 1981b: 2).

In this framework it was taken for granted that non-market education programs were characterised by expansionism, feather-bedding, 'producer capture' and waste, so that there was always 'fat' that could be identified by smart management consultants and trimmed by zealous governments. Efficient *non* market production was a contradiction in terms (Buchanan 1976: 119n; Porter 1988: 119). Other perspectives had diminishing weight. In its *Review of efficiency and effectiveness in higher education* (1986) the Commonwealth Tertiary Education Commission (CTEC) defined 'effectiveness' in terms of educational goals and gave it the same weight as cost efficiency. But in challenging the new mainstream the CTEC merely confirmed its isolation from the dominant economic departments. It was unable to retard the advance of economisation.

The economisation of educational government enabled education to be conceived in input–output terms so that system and institutional managers could pare back activities to the minimum needed. Economisation also prepared government education institutions for marketisation: in schools and training, public education provision was partly replaced by private provision; and from the second half of the 1980s, commercial activities were encouraged.

Nevertheless, this politics of efficiency and marketisation required more than a change in definition. As noted in chapter 4, it was necessary to weaken the popular perception that more public spending led to better educational opportunities and educational quality, especially in relation to government schooling where class size reductions were well supported. So it became argued that an 'outcomes orientation' should be adopted *in place of* a focus on inputs, as if the two were mutually exclusive; that the quantity of resources and the quality of teaching and educational management bore no necessary relation to each other; and that economic research showed that the past increases in educational resources had not led to improved educational outputs. Significantly, in the early 1980s these arguments emerged more or less simultaneously in the economics of education, the policy research sponsored by governments, and the New Right think tanks and media commentaries.

The main academic economist cited in support of these claims was Hanushek (1981; 1986). In *Throwing money at schools* (1981), after reviewing 130 input–output studies Hanushek concluded there was no discernible relationship between government spending on schooling, and student achievement. When he removed those studies of input–output relations which showed positive effects but were not considered by him to be statistically significant, the remaining studies showing positive effects were outweighed by those showing negative effects, or no relationship. In *The economics of schooling: production and efficiency in the public schools* (1986) he concluded that 'constantly rising costs and "quantity" of the inputs appear unmatched by the performance of the students' as measured by student scores in standardised tests (Hanushek 1986: 1148, 1154, 1166). The 'raw' relationship between expenditure and outcomes disappeared when student achievement data were discounted for the effects of parental background (Hanushek 1989: 48–50).

Arguably, Hanushek's findings were the product of his limited definition of educational outputs;[2] the statistical method used to 'flatten out' the dynamic effects of social background on achievement; and the meta-analytical method used to eliminate studies unfavourable to his argument. Other research produced very different conclusions (see the discussions in Marginson 1993a: 83–121; Glass et al 1982; Angus et al 1983). In 1994 Hedges and colleagues re-analysed the studies synthesised by Hanushek, using different meta-analytical methods, and found that expenditure *did* matter (Hill & Russell 1994). A large scale study of returns to education for men born in the United States between 1920 and 1949, using 1980 census data, found a strong relationship between student–teacher ratios and the returns to educated individuals. 'Our findings . . . should give pause to those who argue that investments in the public school system have no benefits for students' (Card & Kreuger 1992: 1, 37). But the market liberals campaigning against non-market education, and economic managers searching for justifications for spending restraint and reductions, found Hanushek more than useful. His findings were broadcast throughout the Anglo-American world. The contrary research programs received no publicity and secured little relationship to government.

Government funding after 1975–76

From 1975–76 to 1989–90 total government spending on education increased slowly in real terms and declined as a proportion of GDP from 6.2 to 5.3 per cent (Table 9.1). In this period, in most OECD countries education's share of GDP declined, but Australia's decline was relatively sharp (Maglen et al 1994: 10–11). The recovery to 5.8 per cent of GDP in 1992–93 was partly due to the effects of recession on the GDP.

Between 1975 and 1992 enrolments in years 11 and 12 of secondary school, TAFE and higher education all *doubled* while the GDP share allocated to education declined. Only student assistance payments kept pace. Education spending declined as a proportion of government budgets, from 15.9 per cent in 1975–76 to 13.6 per cent in 1982–83 during the Fraser years, and to 12.6 per cent in 1986–87 under Hawke,

Table 9.1 Public and private expenditure on education, by source, 1975–76 to 1992–93

Year	Expenditure on education in constant 1984–85 prices, from:			Change in spending from the previous year	Expenditure on education as a proportion of GDP:		
	Government sources* $m	Private sources** $m	All sources $m	%	Government sources %	Private sources %	All sources %
1975–76	9847	583	10 430	+ 3.8	5.88	0.35	6.23
1976–77	10 138	554	10 692	+ 2.5	5.89	0.32	6.21
1977–78	10 668	562	11 230	+ 5.0	6.13	0.32	6.46
1978–79	10 540	559	11 099	−1.2	5.77	0.31	6.08
1979–80	10 308	551	10 859	−2.2	5.53	0.30	5.82
1980–81	10 498	565	11 063	+ 1.9	5.44	0.29	5.74
1981–82	10 710	538	11 248	+ 1.7	5.43	0.27	5.70
1982–83	10 922	597	11 519	+ 2.4	5.63	0.31	5.94
1983–84	11 329	671	11 999	+ 4.2	5.51	0.33	5.84
1984–85	11 684	801	12 486	+ 4.1	5.41	0.37	5.78
1985–86	12 083	882	12 965	+ 3.8	5.37	0.39	5.76
1986–87	12 148	947	13 094	+ 1.0	5.27	0.41	5.68
1987–88	11 852	1048	12 900	−1.5	4.90	0.43	5.34
1988–89	11 957	1189	13 146	+ 1.9	4.77	0.47	5.25
1989–90	12 544	1223	13 767	+ 4.7	4.83	0.47	5.30
1990–91	12 791	1430	14 221	+ 3.3	4.95	0.58	5.52
1991–92	13 633	1335	14 968	+ 4.5	5.24	0.51	5.75
1992–93	14 215	1492	15 707	+ 4.9	5.29	0.55	5.84

* Includes student assistance payments.
** Final consumption expenditure and fixed capital expenditure, financed from private sources. Private final consumption expenditure on education services is estimated as fees paid by persons to government schools (including technical and agriculture colleges), fees (other than boarding fees) and gifts to universities, independent schools, business colleges, etc., plus current expenditure of non-profit educational institutions. Current expenditure excludes interest and depreciation and is financed by fees paid by households and current grants from general government. Items not included are school books, uniforms and similar expenses; and fares to and from educational institutions. For private fixed consumption expenditure from private sources, current grants from general government are subtracted; and likewise for fixed capital expenditure from private sources.
Source: ABS 5510.0.

before rising slightly. Spending by the Commonwealth fell from 8.6 per cent of the budget in 1975–76 to 6.7 per cent in 1986–87, before rising to 8.4 per cent in 1995–96. Between 1982–83 and 1992–93 State spending fluctuated between 19 and 21 per cent of budgets.

The trends in spending varied markedly by sector of education. Between 1975–76 and 1992–93 the growth of total government funding of TAFE kept pace with enrolments. Spending on schools increased by 33.2 per cent while total enrolments increased by only 5.4 per cent, but much of the increase was absorbed by student assistance payments, and by private schools, and after 1992–93 the position of government schools deteriorated sharply. In higher education public funding increased by 33.2 per cent, but between 1975 and 1992 student load rose from 222 400 to 440 540 (98.1 per cent). Government funding per student underwent a marked deterioration. Higher education was the first sector to experience the fuller implications of the efficiency imperative (Table 9.2).

The primary responsibility for increases in funding swung from the Commonwealth under Whitlam, to the States under Fraser and the early years of Hawke, to the Commonwealth again from the late 1980s. Under Fraser increased State spending was partly financed by growth in the general purpose payments from the Commonwealth, there was a major growth in Commonwealth allocations to the private schools (see chapter 3), and the Commonwealth held down higher education funding, where it had sole governmental responsibility. This benefited the sectors most dependent on the States, government schools and TAFE. Similarly, in the first seven Labor budgets after 1982–83, total Commonwealth spending increased by only 13.0 per cent. Student assistance rose from $319 to $739 million but there was little change in expenditure on higher education and schools, and funding for TAFE fell (Table 9.3). Overall between 1975–76 and 1989–90 total Commonwealth funding rose by $0.5 billion while State spending increased by $2.2 billion.

From the late 1980s the pattern changed. In the five years after 1988–89 total Commonwealth spending on education jumped by 41.9 per

Table 9.2 Government expenditure on education by sector* 1975–76 to 1992–93, constant 1984–85 prices

	Schools $m	Higher education $m	TAFE $m	Other tertiary $m	Pre-school & special $m	Student transport $m	Other $m	Total $m
1975–76	5900	2557	566	17	369	227	133	9769
1982–83	6623	2255	1061	26	521	325	112	10 922
1992–93	7861	3407	1523	23	775	460	168	14 215
1975–76 = 100								
1992–93	133.2	133.2	269.1	135.3	210.0	202.6	126.3	145.5

* Includes student assistance payments.
Source: ABS 5510.0.

Table 9.3 Commonwealth outlays on education, by sector, 1975–76 to 1995–96, constant 1984–85 prices

	Higher education $m	TAFE & vocational $m	Schools & pre- schools $m	Student assistance $m	Other $m	Total $m
1975–76	2039	177	987	290	568	4061
1982–83	2007	293	1525	319	55	4199
1989–90	2112	237	1495	739	209	4792
1992–93	2534	374	1910	1115	113	6045
1995–96	2765	502	2072	1179	77	6595
1975–76 = 100						
1995–96	*135.6*	*283.7*	*209.9*	*406.4*	*13.5*	*162.4*

Source: CBP.

cent in real terms, particularly in student assistance and tertiary education. However, at the same time the Commonwealth reduced its general purpose grants to the States, cutting into the resources available for government schools and TAFE. From 1989–90 to 1992–93 Commonwealth outlays increased by 31.9 per cent while State outlays increased by only 2.6 per cent.

Efficiencies in government schools

After 1975–76 there were three distinctive phases in school resourcing. In phase one between the mid-1970s and the early 1980s, the States continued to improve their government school staffing ratios and private school funding was massively increased, mostly by the Commonwealth. The overall student–teacher ratio in government schools fell from 18.6 in 1975 to 15.2 in 1984 (ABS 4202.0) and there were significant reductions in class sizes.[3]

In phase two up to the end of the 1980s, real resources in government schools fluctuated, staffing ratios deteriorated slightly in some systems, and private school funding growth slowed. In the four years after 1985–86 the recurrent funding of government schools fell by $352 million, or 8.5 per cent (ABS 5510.0). Enrolments in government schools also fell, but only by 1.6 per cent. The number of teachers in government schools – which had increased every year since the mid-1950s – fell in 1980, 1981 and 1986.

In phase three the States faced more severe budgetary difficulties. Their share of government funding of TAFE increased from 62.5 to 71.1 per cent between 1975–76 and 1992–93, and they carried close to full funding responsibility for government schools. They had a limited political capacity to raise additional revenue, given the absence of income taxing powers, and were unable to run sizeable deficits. After 1986–87 the Commonwealth reduced general purpose grants to the States. Between 1986–87 and 1993–94 these fell from $11.5 to $9.3 billion, from 17.4 to 12.5 per cent of Commonwealth outlays (Table 9.4).

Between 1982–83 and 1992–93 Commonwealth specific purpose grants to the States increased by $3.7 billion (51.5 per cent), and specific purpose payments for education rose by one-third, but these payments went mostly to higher education and private schools. Overall, State governments increased their own education outlays – that is, outlays paid from their own revenues and Commonwealth general purpose grants, but not specific purpose grants – by 22.5 per cent in real terms, while their Commonwealth general purpose grants dropped by 10.4 per cent. This made State revenue raising activities more vital; but income from State taxes on property and financial transactions fell in the 1991 to 1993 recession. The State governments passed the resulting fiscal constraints down to their school and TAFE systems. There were fierce efficiency pressures.

In the early 1990s the effects of this deterioration on the fiscal position were compounded in some States by a change in policy. In December 1990 the Commonwealth's Economic Planning Advisory Council (EPAC) published an Institute of Public Affairs (IPA) study of State Government spending on education, health and transport. The IPA found that the main factor explaining differences in the level of expenditure between States was higher or lower staffing ratios. 'Drawing on public choice theory', it defined these as differences in the level of efficiency. 'Higher expenditures were a reflection of factors such as vote

Table 9.4 Commonwealth general revenue grants to the States and Territories, 1982–83 to 1995–96, constant 1984–85 prices

	$m		$m
1982–83	10 412	1989–90	9256
1983–84	10 933	1990–91	9215
1984–85	10 970	1991–92	9160
1985–86	11 156	1992–93	9329
1986–87	11 528	1993–94	9316
1987–88	11 500	1994–95	9640
1988–89	9560	1995–96	8549

Source: CBP.

"buying" of public sector unions and other similar pressure groups or attempts to minimise potential vote losses from similar groups by politicians.' Lower student–teacher ratios 'did not translate into a higher quality of educational output', and smaller classes were not related to improved test scores. The IPA used references to Hanushek and Parish in support. It concluded that in the three service areas, $6 billion could be saved Australia-wide 'by efficiency improvements rather than cuts to quality or level of services' if all States adopted the same per capita expenditure levels of Queensland (IPA 1990: vii–viii, 2, 6–7, 23–25, 39, 64).

Although the reasoning in the IPA paper was thin, its citations were selective, and there was no empirical investigation of the claims about efficiency or producer capture, 'benchmarking' State service expenditure on the basis of best practice as cheapest practice was attractive to governments. It promised a dynamic of continuous spending reductions. As the States wound their spending back to the national average, the average would fall, creating room for further reductions, and so on.

In 1990 the Tasmanian Government reduced the funding of its schools by $43 million, over 10 per cent and retrenched 1074 staff (Richards 1991). Between 1990 and 1992 the proportion of junior primary classes with over 25 students rose from 19 to 37 per cent, while the proportion of junior secondary classes at this size rose from 35 to 55 per cent (AEU 1994).

In Victoria, following its election in October 1992 the Kennett Coalition Government closed 230 government schools, many against the wishes of their communities; removed 8200 teaching positions – almost one in five – and cut spending on government schools by over $300 million. Expenditure on students in government schools per head of population fell in *current* price terms from $545 in 1992–93 to $511 in 1993–94 (Senate EETRC 1995: 10). Between 1992 and 1994 the average student–teacher ratio rose from 15.8 to 18.7 in primary education and 10.8 to 13.5 in secondary education. The number of English as a Second Language teachers was halved and 568 positions allocated for socio-economic disadvantage were removed. The proportion of classes with more than 25 students rose sharply, as was confirmed by the department of education (Ryan 1994). A Government spokesperson stated that the Government had 'no concern whatsoever' about increased student–staff ratios. 'Our analysis of 60 research findings throughout the OECD economies indicated that there is no discernible difference in student outcomes [with] between 15 and 35 students' (Painter 1994). Nevertheless, private schools obtained a 15 per cent funding increase. In *some* schools more resources were beneficial.

In Australia as a whole the average student–teacher ratio in government schools rose from 14.7 in 1987 to 15.4 in 1995. Between 1988 and 1994 the proportion of primary school classes with over 25 students rose from 60 to 72 per cent, while the proportion of junior secondary classes with over 25 students rose from 40 to 47 per cent. Average class sizes were increasing to early 1980s levels (AEU 1994). The number of teachers in government schools fell from 148 972 in 1987 to 143 787 in 1995. While enrolled students increased by 0.5 per cent, teacher numbers fell by 3.5 per cent (Table 9.5).

Subsequently the IPA's claims about funding for education were challenged directly by Shapiro and Papadakis (1993) in *The Economic Record*. 'One view of public expenditures is that they are determined by the power of special interest groups . . . There is another point of view as well. Namely, the public expenditure decisions are taken to satisfy the preferences of the citizens.' Shapiro and Papadakis investigated the hypothesis that variations in expenditure between States were due to variations in the level of demand for public educational services, as expressed through the electoral process. Using survey data on private demand for public goods, they found that 'the amount spent by States appears to correspond strongly, and is certainly not more than, the amount demanded by the median voter'. In Queensland – the State with the lowest expenditure levels, the one the IPA saw as the 'benchmark' – the strong voter preference for more spending on education had not been met by the State Government. Fifty-nine per cent of Queenslanders supported an increase in education spending, even if it meant more taxation. In Victoria, there had been continued demand for higher spending even in years when per capita education

Table 9.5 Teachers in government schools, 1975 to 1995*

1975	123 441	1985	148 762
1976	129 668	1986	148 334
1977	135 931	1987	148 972
1978	138 360	1988	148 905
1979	141 210	1989	146 957
1980	141 206	1990	146 477
1981**	140 987	1991	145 895
1982	142 157	1992	147 845
1983	145 908	1993	146 637
1984	148 560	1994	143 379
		1995	143 787

* Effective full-time teachers. ** Change in data collection. Using previous methods, 1981 total was 140 052.
Source: ABS 4221.0.

spending was high relative to other States, before the Kennett Government. Further, parent satisfaction with government schools was high (Shapiro & Papadakis 1993: 149–162).

The findings of Shapiro and Papadakis were grounded in a careful reading of the survey data, and were more rigorously argued and evidenced than the alternative claims of the IPA. Nevertheless, the Shapiro and Papadakis argument secured no discernible impact on policy.

Efficiency pressures in higher education

In the thirteen years from 1975–76 to 1988–89 government spending on higher education fell in real terms and declined from 1.53 to 0.99 per cent of GDP. From 1975 to 1988 enrolments in higher education grew slowly, so that funding per student fell, especially after 1984. After 1988 enrolments grew more rapidly. Spending rose, but slower than enrolments, so that per capita resources from government sources deteriorated further (Table 9.6).

Between 1975–76 and 1988–89 fixed consumption expenditure by governments – that part of government funding which was used to finance operating costs, including salaries – rose by 6.1 per cent, but total student load rose by 48.3 per cent, and the unit costs of staffing increased as the 'bulge' of academics recruited between the mid-1960s and mid-1970s moved up the incremental and promotional scales. The spare capacity of higher education institutions was absorbed. Additional enrolments were funded at marginal rather than average cost, forcing

Table 9.6 Commonwealth outlays on higher education,*
1975–76 to 1995–96, constant 1984–85 prices

	$m			$m
1975–76	2039		1986–87	2093
1976–77	2185		1987–88	2097
1977–78	2162		1988–89	2009
1978–79	2086		1989–90	2112
1979–80	2008		1990–91	2276
1980–81	2006		1991–92	2382
1981–82	2027		1992–93	2534
1982–83	2007		1993–94	2670
1983–84	2031		1994–95	2670
1984–85	2071		1995–96	2823
1985–86	2149			

* Excludes student assistance.
Source: CBP.

Table 9.7 Student load in higher education, 1975 to 1996*

1975	222 400	1986	289 945
1976	235 500	1987	303 830
1977	242 800	1988	328 971
1978	248 000	1989	350 137
1979	249 800	1990	383 838
1980	249 900	1991	423 685
1981	253 000	1992	440 540
1982	256 100	1993	449 425
1983	257 412	1994	453 309
1984	264 750	1995	467 748
1985	274 772	1996*	488 957

* 1996 data are preliminary.
Sources: CTEC 1986: 275; DEET 1996a; DEET 1996b.

economies in overheads and infrastructure (Table 9.7). In March 1985 the CTEC adopted an aggressive approach to its annual budget bid. Existing resources could no longer be 'squeezed', it stated. Fees and substantial increases in private funding were impractical and undesirable, and the only option was more government funding. In 1986 the Government's *Review of efficiency and effectiveness in higher education*, run from the CTEC office, noted that since 1975 there had been a dramatic fall in operating resources per student. Capital spending was at a fifth of its 1975 level. Mergers and closures of small advanced education institutions had produced some economies of scale, and efficiencies had been achieved, but there had been a decline in educational standards (CTEC 1986: 4–5, 66–67).

CTEC's attempt to draw the line against further per capita reductions was a complete failure. From 1985–86 to 1988–89 government final consumption expenditure per unit of student load, the most accurate measure of the government contribution to operating costs, deteriorated by almost one-quarter. Within a year of making its stand, CTEC had been abolished; and the new expansion was being funded largely by increased private contributions through the Higher Education Contribution Scheme (HECS) and other private sources, and a further decline in per capita resources.

From 1988 to 1992 there was an explosive growth of enrolments, with student load increasing by over one-third (Table 9.7). In the four years after 1988–89 government spending on higher education rose by $0.9 billion (37.4 per cent) and returned to 1.27 per cent of GDP in 1992–93, but much of the funding increase was absorbed by student assistance, or accounted for by student contributions to government spending *via* HECS. Between 1988–89 and 1992–93 government

Table 9.8 Government final consumption expenditure on higher education compared to student load, 1975–76 to 1992–93, 1975–76 = 100.0

	Government final consumption expenditure	Student load (average over financial year)	Ratio of expenditure to student load
1975–76	100.00	100.00	100.0
1979–80	106.24	109.13	97.4
1980–81	108.01	109.83	98.3
1981–82	110.65	111.18	99.5
1982–83	109.10	112.15	97.3
1983–84	109.04	114.13	95.5
1984–85	108.41	117.83	92.0
1985–86	113.97	123.33	92.4
1986–87	112.59	129.67	86.8
1987–88	113.85	138.20	82.4
1988–89	106.07	148.31	71.5
1989–90	119.86	160.29	74.8
1990–91	106.73	176.35	60.5
1991–92	114.48	188.78	60.6
1992–93	122.40	194.36	63.0

Sources: ABS 5510.0; CTEC 1986; DEET 1996a.

consumption expenditure rose by only 15.4 per cent. Government consumption expenditure per unit of student load fell by 11.2 per cent. Overall, between 1975–76 and 1992–93 the ratio of government consumption expenditure to load fell by over one-third, dramatically weakening the public contribution to teaching and research (Table 9.8).

Yet in the context of micro-economic reform and the policy emphases on efficiency and entrepreneurial management, declining government resources per student were no longer seen as a political negative, except in the higher education sector itself. In 1990 the Commonwealth proposed two 'efficiency indicators' for use in higher education – the cost per student place and the average student–staff ratio – without regard to the potential effects of declining expenditure per student and rising staffing ratios on the quality of learning. Data provided by the Government itself highlighted the reduction in public resourcing. Between 1979 and 1991 operating funds per full-time student fell from $11 888 to $9989 (constant December 1991 prices), declining in all but two calendar years. In Australian universities between 1961 and 1983, the average student–staff ratio varied from 11.5 to 12.9; in colleges of advanced education between 1975 and 1980, the average ratio varied between 11.3 and 11.7. The combined higher education student–staff ratio was 11.7 in 1983. It increased during the mid-1980s, reaching 12.9 in 1988, and climbed rapidly to the hitherto unheard of level of 15.3 students per staff member in 1992 as shown in Table 9.9 (data from CTEC and predecessors).

The growth in higher education at the end of the 1980s, with its additional cost pressures, took place in institutions required to improve research, teaching and community service; to address national economic goals and the needs of industry, establish international links; and compete with each other. Most were involved in mergers, and many were upgrading to university status. In the first instance all of these activities required extra resources. It was inevitable that once the Government sanctioned international marketing, commercial training and fee-based postgraduate courses, market activities would become a high priority. The long period of attrition from 1975 to 1988 empowered the marginal dollar and conditioned institutional managers for the more entrepreneurial regime after 1988 that is described in Part III below.

II. Government and private effort

The retreat from public infrastructure

The Whitlam Government policies in education were the high point in the government sector's share of the financing and provision of education in Australia. It was believed that if education was to facilitate equality then government should carry the costs and for the most part, education should be provided in government institutions (chapter 2). The exception was private schooling, but there Labor moved towards the full government funding of costs, and the renovation of those schools took

Table 9.9 Average student–staff ratio in higher education 1975 to 1992

1975	11.7	1984	11.8
1976	11.8	1985	12.0
1977	11.9	1986	12.3
1978	11.8	1987	12.7
1979	11.7	1988	12.9
1980	11.7	1989	13.9
1981	...	1990	14.1
1982	...	1991	14.8
1983	11.7	1992	15.3

Sources: CTEC; DEET 1993: 138, 334.

place alongside not in place of government system building.

After 1975, to an increasing extent governments used non-government institutions and self-managing individuals to secure the objectives of their policies, and there was a retreat from government institution-building. The first trend, beginning in the mid-1970s, saw the running down of financing for government sector capital works, while the growth of private schools was encouraged. The second trend, beginning in the early 1980s, saw a temporary increase in secondary student assistance payments in order to build participation, accompanied by tighter targeting in tertiary student assistance, enabling a partial transfer from government to private support. (This transfer was later extended to secondary assistance as well.) The third trend, beginning in the mid-1980s, was an increase in the total proportion of costs borne by private sources such as tuition fees, donations and corporate payments.

In this manner the growing governmental reliance on non-governmental institutions and private individuals to sustain participation, rather than driving the growth of education through spending on public infrastructure and personnel – as was the case before 1975 – led eventually to the privatisation of funding itself.

Between 1975–76 and 1992–93 total government expenditure on student assistance rose from $0.7 to $1.5 billion (100.6 per cent), while outlays on capital works in education, nearly all of which were spent on public infrastructure, fell from $1.5 to $0.9 billion (Table 9.10). Only in TAFE, which had been in an early phase of development when the change in policy hit in the mid-1970s, was public infrastructure expanded on the pre-1975 scale.

The retreat from investment in infrastructure meant that government institutions were increasingly reliant on rental and leased accommodation, or financing from their own resources. Government capital works had enabled a distinctive public sector space to be constructed.

Table 9.10 Government expenditure on capital works in education, by sector, 1975–76, 1982–83 and 1992–93, constant 1984–85 prices

	Schools $m	Higher education $m	TAFE $m	Pre-school & other* $m	Total $m
1975–76	972	360	94	96	1522
1982–83	373	140	191	34	739
1992–93	381	278	225	66	950
1992–93 (1975–76=100)	*39.2*	*77.2*	*239.4*	*68.9*	*62.4*

* Includes special education.
Source: ABS 5510.0.

The cutting back of capital works signalled not only the desire for fiscal economy and more flexible resource use, but that governments intended to work with identities and institutional forms that were generated from outside the state sector.

The individualisation of student support

In the mid-1970s, governmental financing of the living costs of full-time tertiary students was the norm. State government scholarships for teacher education were non-means tested, and only affluent families were excluded by the means test on the Commonwealth's Tertiary Education Assistance Scheme (TEAS).

After 1975 the quasi-universal system of financial assistance for full-time students in tertiary education was replaced by a more targeted approach. When the State governments withdrew their teacher scholarships amid a surplus of teachers in the second half of the 1970s, if all else had remained equal this would have led to a major increase in the number of students receiving TEAS. However, eligibility for TEAS had been tightened. In 1974 the parental income means test governing TEAS began reducing payments at a family income of 105.0 per cent of Average Weekly Earnings. By 1984 the cut-off point had fallen to 74.0 per cent of Average Weekly Earnings. Data prepared by Chapman (1992: 101) suggest a further decline to 65 per cent by 1990. At the same time the level of TEAS fell in real terms.[4] Despite the expansion of enrolments, the number of students in receipt of some form of student assistance fell from 116 883 in 1976 to 60 650 in 1982, before rising again to 78 144 in 1986. The proportion of full-time undergraduates *not* receiving student assistance rose from 35.1 per cent to 61.9 per cent over the twelve-year period.

By the mid-1980s the norm was not government support but self-support. The stricter targeting of student assistance helped prepare the ground for the later introduction of user payments and the cultivation of private investment behaviours.

For a time in the 1980s eligibility for secondary student assistance expanded, and the levels increased. However this trend was determined not by citizen rights, but by the governmental objective of lifting school retention to a near universal level (see chapter 8). Once the participation of 16-year-olds in education reached 90.9 per cent in 1992, the Commonwealth announced in the 1993 budget that secondary allowances would not be paid to that age group, transferring the cost of student support back to the family. The structure of incentives and benefits governing payments was employed economically, so as to minimise expenditure while maximising the effects.

Private expenditure on education

In the Fraser years between 1977–78 and 1982–93, the proportion of education expenditure that was both government financed and took place in public sector institutions, the statist 'core' of education activity, fell from 88.3 to 85.3 per cent. Under Hawke it fell further to 80.3 per cent. Overall, between 1977–78 and 1992–93 the statist core increased from $9.8 to $12.6 billion but it fell from 5.7 to 4.6 per cent of GDP, while all forms of expenditure outside this core rose from $1.3 to $3.1 billion, from 0.7 to 1.2 per cent of GDP (ABS 5510.0).

The Coalition years saw a relative expansion in the role of private sector institutions, especially schools, with most of the costs paid from government budgets. In the Labor years both the role of private institutions and the role of private financing of education – whether in public or private sector institutions – began to increase.

As noted in chapter 2, in the last year of the Whitlam Government the proportion of total education costs paid by governments reached 94.4 per cent, with only 5.6 per cent from family, private institutional and corporate sources (note however that these data exclude industry outlays on in-house training). Under Fraser this reached 4.8 per cent in 1981–82, only $0.5 billion out of an education outlay of $11.3 billion, 0.27 per cent of GDP. Over the next decade the decline was reversed. From 1982–83 to 1992–93 private spending rose by 149.9 per cent, albeit from a low base, while government spending rose by 30.2 per cent. By 1991–92 private spending was at $1.2 billion, 9.5 per cent of all education spending (Table 9.11).

This relative growth in private funding was affected by commercial research and consulting, sponsorship and corporate training in TAFE and higher education, but primarily due to a partial shift in the responsibility for funding, from government to the individual or family. Later data were expected to show that after 1992–93, the private share of costs had continued to increase, because of the growth of fees in higher education and TAFE.

III. Marketisation

The abolition of free tertiary education

In 1983, when the Hawke Labor Government took power, 91 per cent of the funding of the higher education system was provided by governments and only 3 per cent from all forms of fees and charges, including commercial research. Labor faced a choice between three possible funding regimes in higher education. The first was to fund the

Table 9.11 Expenditure on education from private sources*
as a proportion of total education spending, 1975–76 to
1992–93, 1984–85 prices

	Total spending on education from private sources* (1984–85 prices) $m	Change in spending on education from private sources* from previous year %	Total spending from private sources* as a proportion of all spending %
1975–76	583	−2.7	5.59
1976–77	554	−5.0	5.18
1977–78	562	+ 1.4	5.00
1978–79	559	−0.5	5.04
1979–80	551	−1.4	5.07
1980–81	656	+ 2.5	5.11
1981–82	538	−4.8	4.78
1982–83	597	+11.0	5.18
1983–84	671	+12.4	5.59
1984–85	801	+19.4	6.42
1985–86	882	+10.1	6.80
1986–87	947	+ 7.4	7.23
1987–88	1048	+10.7	8.12
1988–89	1189	+13.5	9.04
1989–90	1223	+ 2.9	8.89
1990–91	1430	+16.9	10.06
1991–92	1335	−6.6	8.92
1992–93	1492	+11.8	9.50

* Excludes employers' training costs, estimated by Maglen et
al (1994) at 0.9 per cent of GDP in 1989–90, and government
advances to students via the Higher Education Contribution
Scheme (HECS). Arguably, HECS advances constituted
deferred private spending. If so, in 1992–93 the total private
share of expenditure on education was 12.03 per cent.
Source: ABS 5510.0.

expansion on an open-ended basis, treating higher education as a
common good, akin to primary education, or the institutions of the
law. This was incompatible with the fiscal imperative and the growing
pressure for market deregulation. The second was to fund a modest
expansion from public resources. But this was incompatible with the
scale of the growth in school retention, and the policy emphasis on
'upskilling' the workforce. The third was to develop a mixed public–
private funding base and use it to fund a higher level of expansion
whose limits would eventually be set by social demand and labour

market requirements. This was the course that was taken.

However, there was a political obstacle: Labor's own abolition of tertiary fees in 1974. The Labor Party's commitment to free education dated from its foundation years. The 1891 platform mentioned 'free, compulsory and technical education, higher as well as elementary' (Evatt 1942: 25, 208). Though the abolition of fees had been more symbolic than economic – in 1973 student fees were less than 5 per cent of higher education income and paid by only one-fifth of full-time students (Wran 1988: 3–4) – it was a powerful symbol, signifying a universal rights-based approach to educational programs, and it retained both the continuing adherence of Labor's rank and file, and popular support.[5] The Fraser Government had tried to re-introduce fees for second and higher degrees in 1976 and 1981, but was defeated by student protests. Opinion polls found that about three-quarters of respondents were opposed to tertiary fees. After Labor took office in 1983, support for fees began to build in the coordinating departments of government, those of Treasury, Finance and Prime Minister and Cabinet. At the same time, business leaders and economic commentators campaigned hard for fees as a 'test' of Labor's commitment to deregulation and micro-economic reform (Walsh 1985; Steketee 1985). Nevertheless, it was five years before the debate inside the Government and the Labor Party was won.

In February 1985 the Minister for Finance, Peter Walsh, circulated a short paper arguing that 'the socio-economic mix of our tertiary institutions had not changed in the decade since fees were abolished'. He proposed annual fees of $1500 per full-time university student. Although Walsh's evidence was thin, and his policy proposal was headed off in the Labor caucus by Education Minister Susan Ryan, the Walsh argument became part of the public mythology (Hywood 1985). The 1986 EPAC report on *Education and human capital* and the 1987 ASTEC report on higher education both supported fees. Within the Government, CTEC was opposed to fees, and developed a general argument against market reforms in education. A competitive market would not necessarily encourage efficiency, CTEC argued. The student consumer lacked information. There were lags between demand signals and the supply of places. 'Lowest cost' bidding between institutions would become a 'lowest common denominator approach' that would threaten standards and inhibit diversity and innovation. (CTEC 1986: 242–254).

Nevertheless, in 1986 the Government announced that a Higher Education Administration Charge (HEAC) of $250 per student would commence in 1987. This established a fee collection mechanism in all institutions, which were allowed to retain 10 per cent of the revenue collection costs. The HEAC raised $105.4 million in 1987, and at $263 per student raised $111.1 million in 1988 (CBP).

In December 1987 Dawkins announced the formation of a committee on higher education funding, chaired by former New South Wales Premier Neville Wran. The committee reported in May 1988. Fee abolition 'was not able to achieve its stated objective of broadening participation'. Between 1974 and 1987 the proportion of students who were women had risen from 38.5 to 50.1 per cent, but the committee dismissed this democratisation of gender on class grounds. 'Despite these overall gains, participation by women in low socio-economic groups has not improved.' It argued that:

> The fundamental inequity in our present system of financing higher education is that small and privileged sections of the community who benefit directly from access to higher education make no direct contribution to their tuition costs. The bulk of the funding burden falls on PAYE taxpayers, the majority of whom are middle to lower income earners and who will only receive in return the valuable but amorphous benefit of living in a well educated society (Wran 1988: 15).

But the Wran committee's real brief was not to universalise higher education or redistribute its benefits, it was to craft a fees system that was supportable inside the Labor Party. The committee proposed a deferred fee, an income contingent 'graduate tax' based on an average 20 per cent of course costs. In Japanese and American higher education, it stated, fees were combined with expanded enrolments *and* 'broader levels of representation from lower socio-economic groups'. Fees would create 'access and equity' by financing growth, enabling more students from poorer backgrounds to enter (Wran 1988).

By dividing the population between 'beneficiaries' and 'payers' Labor fractured the social solidarity necessary to a system of universal financing and provision. In place of equity as equal economic conditions and rights, it substituted equity as participation. It substituted the public choice theory notion of individualised benefits in exchange for individualised taxes, in place of the notion of social programs as common benefits.

Before the Government could adopt the Wran proposals it had to abolish its own policy of free education at the Labor Party's conference in Hobart in June 1988. At the conference ACTU President, Simon Crean, argued government could not provide the full costs of growth in higher education. In contrast Victorian Premier John Cain stated that:

> I rank free education with the policy of social security that was introduced in this country in the 1940s . . . Simon Crean . . . [argued] that we ought not require government to provide all of the funds for tertiary education. I believe we should and I believe government has the capacity to provide those funds for tertiary education. I think it's very difficult to say we can't fund those additional places when we're aiming for a considerable surplus – three, four or five billion dollars – and when we have just reduced the company tax rate from 49c to 39c. I believe that if we were to apply some portion of a slightly increased company tax, we could fund all the tertiary education we require (John Cain, ALP conference, 6 June 1988).

Nevertheless, free education was abolished by 56 votes to 41. The next year the Higher Education Contribution Scheme (HECS) was introduced as a deferred fee of $1800 per full-time student, repayable through the tax system. HECS levels and debts were indexed to inflation. Students could pay 'upfront' at enrolment with a 15 per cent discount, later 25 per cent; about one student in five were to do this. Otherwise repayments were at 1 per cent of taxable income for incomes of $22 000–24 999, 2 per cent for $25 000–34 999, and 3 per cent for $35 000 and above. This structure remained stable for the next six years, except that the rate of repayment was increased to 3–5 per cent of taxable income, and the HECS as a proportion of average course costs rose to 23 per cent (Vanstone 1996: 8). By 1995 repayments began at 3 per cent of incomes of $26 853 and above, rising to 5 per cent at $42 006. All fee-paying international and postgraduate students, trainee nurses (until 1993), many students of post-initial teacher training, most research students and a small number of bachelor honours students were exempt from paying the HECS.

The arguments in favour of tertiary fees were grounded in two claims. First, that because higher education was dominated by students from the more affluent social groups, the public funding of higher education was a regressive tax-spending transfer, from non-student taxpayers to non-paying students. Second, that the abolition of fees had not changed the social composition of higher education. The two claims reinforced each other. The assumption there had been no equalisation of higher education reinforced the assertion that higher education was *ipso facto* exclusive. The assumption that higher education was exclusive pre-empted the possibility that equalisation strategies might change its socio-economic composition.

Both of these claims were ahistoric. The rhetorical contrast between non-paying students and non-student taxpayers ignored the taxes paid later by the same students as graduates. In government services, redistribution takes place within income classes across the life-cycle, not from poor to middle income groups, so that people are recipients as students and pensioners, and payers during their working lives (NSSS 1988). The claim there had been little or no improvement in the social composition of higher education was never comprehensively tested – there was no ongoing longitudinal study of the social composition of the student body conducted by either government or academic researchers – and the available evidence appeared to contradict it. For many people the abolition of fees had brought higher education within reach for the first time. Along with rising participation in secondary schools, and credentialism, free education had helped to normalise enrolment in higher education. The rise in women's participation was dramatic by any measure, and the proportion of students with fathers from trades or manual backgrounds had increased from 14 to 19 per cent (Marginson & McCulloch 1985). Arguably, the abolition of fees modified the regressive impact of the phasing out of teacher scholarships, and the mid-1970s recession.

The socio-economic composition was subject to many factors, and the extent to which particular changes were related to fees was a matter for conjecture. By the same token, there was no good evidence that the abolition of fees had made 'no difference'.[6] It appears that the socio-economic composition of the student body became less representative in the 1980s, but it remained more representative in Australia than in the higher education systems of most other OECD countries (Anderson & Vervoorn 1983: 172; Anderson 1990: 33). The 'failure' of the grand strategy of redistribution concealed the gradual progress towards a system that was becoming broader in its social use.

Nevertheless, the argument for fees rested not on logic or evidence, but on post-Keynesian disillusionment. The case for fees drew strength from the growing competitiveness in education and the labour markets, the sense of scarcity and positionality, and the reassertion of privileged routes through the consolidation of private schooling. Higher education enrolled only 15 per cent of the age cohort. A system based on competitive selection was bound to be dominated by students from those groups best equipped to compete for the prizes of life. Anderson (1990) argues that the progressive redistributive effects of fee abolition were undermined by the growing competitiveness for entry in the 1980s.

The problem also lay in the limits of the Whitlamite strategy itself. The reformers had imagined that the equalisation of economic conditions in education would create 'fair' academic competition by abolishing the effects of social background on educational achievement. But even if the economic conditions of all students *had* been equalised – and it would have taken more than the abolition of tuition to achieve this – such a reform could only have modified the effects of

social origin, not abolished them. Free education was not supported by
the other policies necessary to maximise its effectivity as a reform. The
dual private–public system of schooling limited the potential effects of
more egalitarian financing in higher education. The very mechanisms
of academic competition worked in favour of students from middle-
class families, yet changes to academic selection were not seriously
pursued.

If participation had grown more rapidly in the period 1975 to 1985,
the popular experience of higher education might have been somewhat
different. Ironically if the system had remained much smaller 'ability'
might have continued to signify an automatic right to public financial
support, as in the older public good argument about the training of
leaders. But the growth of mass education undermined this. Free education fell into the gap between the universal financing of elite participation, and universal financing of universal access.

Universal systems are never very effective redistributive instruments.
They do not take from the rich to give to the poor, they give the same
service to both. They are relatively expensive to run, and as the level
of taxation increases it becomes less progressive in character. Universal
systems are egalitarian, but their egalitarianism rests not on income
transfers but on social solidarity and shared citizenship. They block the
possibility of elite services of superior quality, so that good quality education, health and transport and other social services no longer take
the form of scarce goods available only to the rich, but are included
in the sum of citizen entitlements shared by all. It is partly to protect
the value of its private services that the *bourgeoisie* becomes the strongest
opponent of universalism. It was in the interests of the rich to support
the charging of tertiary fees in Australia because fees would protect the
value of their private investment in secondary education, shielding
them from scholastic competition from poorer families. The propo-
nents of fees were little interested in social solidarity and shared citizenship, and mostly opposed to economic redistribution.

In this way the conflict between universalism and redistribution was
exploited in cynical fashion, by people with a commitment to neither
objective, in order to deconstruct the free education system and clear
the way for policies of market reform that were pitched against *both*
social solidarity and tax/spending redistribution. The argument that
'equality has failed' was designed to confirm rather than reverse that
failure, and provide a fake egalitarian pretext for Labor politicians to
abandon their earlier notion of education as universal citizenship in
favour of smaller government, targeting and market reform.

The old egalitarianism had coupled the argument for non-market
provision with expanded opportunity and the need for human capital.

The new dynamic of universalism, competition, private responsibility and differentiated provision now changed the terms of debate. Once participation was normalised, the operations of user payments and commercial education, and the existence of unequally ranked institutions (hierarchies of product) were no longer a barrier to participation *per se.* Non-universal financing meant instead of citizens receiving a shared education of good quality, there would be consumers competing with each other on the basis of capacity to pay, with some forms of participation much more valuable than others. The continuing argument for universal financing lay not in the need to encourage participation, but to equalise the forms of participation, and thus to modify the shattering effects of positional competition on social solidarity.

Labor's 1988 debate on fees was a decisive moment in Australian education, sealing the transition to market liberal policies begun in 1975. The HECS was a user charge rather than a market fee. It was collected by government rather than the producer institution. Because of its deferred character, its effects on the pattern of participation was slight. In itself the HECS did not create a market dynamic of demand and supply. Nevertheless, it universalised user charges as the norm for all students. It sanctioned the new markets for international students and postgraduates, and the introduction of 'upfront' fees in TAFE.

In restoring fees, Labor gambled that the demand for higher education was robust enough to sustain a high participation regime; and it shrewdly softened the blow by introducing HECS as a deferred income-contingent payment so minimising the immediate impact. However, the same safeguards was not applied to the fee-based courses in the wake of the HECS; and once free education was abandoned there was no basis for limiting the extension of user payments. In 1992 it was argued in a Commonwealth report on student loans that in principle governments were obliged only to provide funding for the *externalities* of higher education, and other costs could be assigned to the student (Chapman 1992: 14). The HECS was designed as Labor's alternative to upfront fees because of their regressive effects (Chapman 1996), but when the Coalition Parties were elected in 1996 they found no policy barriers to the introduction of 'upfront' fees for a quarter of the domestic undergraduates, and doubling the level of the HECS.

The market in higher education

In the Dawkins reforms of 1987–1989 higher education was reconstructed as a 'quasi-market' of competing institutions. A quasi-market is a system in which some but not all of the features of an economic market are present. Undergraduate education remained free of direct fees, and non-fee paying student load was determined by negotiation between the Commonwealth and institutions rather than consumer demand, but institutions competed with each other for a range of private and public funds, and a growing part of university activity was commercial in purpose and character.

In 1988 the Government abolished the separate college of adult education (CAE) sector and created a 'Unified National System' in which all institutions were designated universities. The CAES had been funded for teaching but not for research. In the new system, all universities were expected to conduct research and offer doctoral programs. The universities were funded using a common formula designed to create a 'level playing field' for inter-institutional competition. Institutions raising private money were no longer penalised by loss of public funding. The government encouraged institutional mergers in order to engineer a smaller number of larger institutions able to compete nationally and internationally. By 1994 there were 36 universities in place of the 70 institutions of 1987.

It was decided to marketise the public universities rather than create a mixed public–private system. Private institutions were tolerated but except for the Australian Catholic University and two small specialist institutions which were already funded similarly to public institutions, tuition subsidies were not provided, rendering new private institutions uneconomic. Of the many private universities proposed during the late 1980s, only Bond University and Notre Dame Australia took root, and like Buckingham University in the UK they remained small (Marginson 1997b).

The Government deliberately fostered the development of corporate-style institutions. All institutions were autonomous in educational matters and the detailed expenditure of public monies. At the same time, reporting and data collection were standardised and intensified. Central planning gave way to institutional planning, and the annual quasi-contractual negotiations between government and institution over student numbers (the 'profile'). The balance between fields of study was de-regulated, though not the balance between levels of study. The Government encouraged institutional managers with the business skills of entrepreneurship and strategic and financial planning. It funded management reviews and training, urging a reduction in collegial decision making (Dawkins 1988). Growth, mergers and competition, and the reforging of missions and course profiles, encouraged both organisational restructuring and changes in personnel. This favoured the emergence of a new layer of innovators and entrepreneurs.

At the same time the Government used new systems of funding and allocation to stimulate intra-systemic competition. Certain public monies were made subject to competition, including the Evaluations and Investigations Program, the Priority (Reserve) fund, the Committee for the Advancement of University Teaching and the Committee for Quality Assurance. Initiatives such as Open Learning were put out to tender. Through the terms and conditions governing competitive bidding, the government shaped the pattern of activity. Williams (1992: 151) notes that 'relatively small amounts of expenditure can exercise a powerful leverage on the system if they are used strategically'. Further, a growing proportion of research support was distributed *via* submission-based projects rather than open-ended research programs. This strengthened competition and outputs as norms of research, bringing publicly funded research closer to the dynamics of commercial research. The latter was encouraged through the Cooperative Research Centres, jointly funded with industry, which facilitated marketing and trade in intellectual property.

The Government also strengthened a consumer culture by encouraging student evaluation of teaching, and a focus on the employability of graduates (Marginson 1993b). This coincided with the emergence of a 'market in markets', consumer comparisons of institutions such as the *Good universities guide* (Ashenden & Milligan 1994b).

Fee-based courses in higher education

In 1985 the Government decided to develop full fee international marketing of education as an export industry. It provided higher education institutions with strong incentives to enter the new market: there was no upper limit on numbers, institutions retained all revenues apart from a small charge for capital facilities, and minimum fees were set well above marginal costs: 24 per cent in university engineering, 40 per cent in science and 56 per cent in business (CTEC 1987: 36). Once the market was established, fees were deregulated.

The number of full fee paying students grew rapidly, from 1019 in higher education in 1987 to 46 520 in 1995, 7.7 per cent of all enrolled students (Table 9.12). Of the international students 40 per cent were in business courses, and 26 per cent in engineering and science. Hong Kong, Singapore and Malaysia provided over half the international students; with smaller groups from Indonesia, mainland China and Taiwan (DEET 1996b). By 1995 there were 4929 fee paying students at Monash University (12.6 per cent), 4431 at the Royal Melbourne Institute of Technology (RMIT) (17.2 per cent), 3594 at the University of New South Wales and 3123 at Curtin University in Perth.

In 1994 international marketing generated AUD $384.5 million in fees, 5.6 per cent of total university income, including $37.5 million at

234   THE ECONOMIC CITIZEN 1985–1995

Table 9.12. Full fee-paying international students in higher education 1987 to 1995

	Total full fee international students			Change from previous year (%)	Proportion of all overseas students (%)
	Women	Men	Persons		
1987	341	678	1019	. . .	5.9
1988	1411	2184	3595	+ 252.8	19.7
1989	5009	3456	8465	+ 135.5	33.3
1990	9708	7097	16 805	+98.5	58.0
1991	10 155	13 377	23 532	+40.0	68.4
1992	13 285	17 011	30 296	+28.7	76.7
1993	15 302	19 980	35 282	+16.5	82.9
1994*	17 229	22 545	39 774	+12.7	85.6
1995	20 781	25 739	46 520	+17.0	89.6

* More recent information states that in 1994 the number of fee-paying students was under-estimated by 'approximately 774'.
Source: DEET 1996a.

Monash and $36.9 million at the University of NSW (DEET 1996c). Average fees in Australia were lower than the UK, New Zealand and American private universities, though higher than Canada and American public universities, albeit subject to exchange-rate fluctuations (DEET 1995b).

Growth prospects were good but there were concerns that in striving for market share, some institutions neglected educational values. A Murdoch University study found that 'Singaporeans hold widely to the view that we treat overseas students as a "money making racket"; their reverence for education clashes with our treatment of it as a commodity item' (Laurie 1992: 42–44). While the growth in international students suggested that the universities were being 'internationalised', there was little evidence that courses had changed. Globalised education brought different cultural groups into contact on an unprecedented scale, but on the grounds of an Anglo-American-Australian curriculum that Australian universities continued to essentialise as the only possible education. Cultural sharing was mostly by accident.

Universities have not been eager to examine their curriculum for the cultural biases it might contain. Those universities which have looked at these issues have treated cultural difference as a fact to be taken into account but not as constitutive of curricular and pedagogical relations. They have often assumed a position of neutrality in the formation of Asia–Australia relations, as somehow external to the more general processes of cultural articulation . . . At the heart of the export of educational services is a major contradiction. Education is increasingly viewed by both the students from Asia and Australian universities as global, yet we know the Australian curriculum to be ethnocentric. Individual students view their needs in global terms, yet we are witnessing in many Asian countries a new form of nationalism, and a confidence that is an outcome both of their economic progress and their postcolonial aspirations. In such a context, Australia may not be able to enjoy its current advantage unless its higher education takes drastic steps. Not only does it need to examine its marketing practices, but it also needs to express a concern for cultural sensitivities within its curriculum and teaching methods (Alexander & Rizvi 1993: 19).

The second area of fee-based market development was in vocational postgraduate subjects and short courses in occupational training. These markets were proclaimed in 1987, and gradually deregulated. By 1995 35 426 postgraduates paid fees (28.5 per cent), including 23 184 noninternational students. Postgraduate fees generated $54.8 million in 1994, 0.8 per cent of total income (DEET 1996c). More than 70 per cent of the domestic fee-paying postgraduates were in business or law. From 1988 to 1995 enrolments in coursework Masters programs in business grew threefold. There was a wide range of fees, and the relationship between price and quality was not always evident. In 1994 students in the State of Victoria could choose from nine different MBA programs, from $6500 at RMIT to $45 500 at Monash. The largest numbers of fee-paying postgraduates were at Monash (2360), the University of Technology, Sydney (2320), New South Wales, Melbourne and Macquarie University. Only 40 per cent of fee-paying students were women. A 1992 survey found that half of male postgraduate students in fulltime employment were supported by employers, compared to one-third of women. Students from the bottom socio-economic quartile were also under-represented (CAPA 1994; DEET 1995c; Martin 1995).

By 1993 short award and non-award courses in professional and corporate training were raising 1.0 per cent of university income. That year Deakin University created Deakin Australia as a private company within the university and secured franchises for upgrades in accounting, architecture and engineering. Enrolments were projected to grow from 22 000 in 1993 to 100 000 by 2001 (Ashenden & Milligan 1994a). Another area of fee-based development was TV-based learning at a distance. In 1991 open learning was established on a pilot basis, coordinated by Monash University. There were no barriers to entry, except the fee of $300 per unit, equivalent to about one-eighth of a full year's workload. Students could use open learning as the gateway to oncampus study. By 1995 a total of 5779 students were enrolled in degree programs in a range of disciplines.

The growth of international marketing, fee-based postgraduate courses and continuing education, commercial research (Slaughter 1993) and other private income such as university donations, endowments and investments, led to a major increase in the proportion of total institutional income that was derived from private sources. Whereas in 1983, 91 per cent of higher education funding came from governments, by 1994 the public share was only 62 per cent, including 60 per cent from the Commonwealth Government. Student payments for tuition were 20 per cent compared to zero before 1987, including 13 per cent through the HECS and 7 per cent in other fee-based courses (Dawkins, 1987b; NBEET 1995).

Between 1983 and 1994 enrolments expanded by two-thirds, but government funding rose by less than 25 per cent. Three-quarters of the additional income received by institutions came from non-government sources (Table 9.13).

There was variation by institution: in 1993 Macquarie University (45.2 per cent), New South Wales, Newcastle, Queensland, Swinburne, Western Australia, La Trobe, Sydney and Charles Sturt received more than 40 per cent of their income from non-government sources, compared to the Australian National University (ANU) and Flinders University with just over 25 per cent (DEET 1996a).

Following the Coalition's 1996 budget decision to reduce university operating grants by an effective 12–15 per cent in the years 1997 to

Table 9.13 Government and non-government funding of higher education, 1983 and 1990 to 1994

Source of income*	Proportion of total income from this source					
	1983 %	1990 %	1991 %	1992 %	1993 %	1994 %
Governments	91	68	67	65	60	62
HECS	0	12	12	13	13	13
Other fees and charges*	3	8	10	10	12	11
Donations and investments	7	7	6	6	5	3
Other	0	4	5	7	10	11
Total	100	100	100	100	100	100

* Variations in categories and methods mean longitudinal comparisons are imprecise. For example in 1983 'Other fees and charges' includes all charges for commercial research, consultancy and continuing education; while after 1990 some charges for commercial research are included under 'Other'. In the later years some incomes from commercial research, donations and investments are folded into 'Other' while a further group are off-budget and not reported to DEET, so that these data understate the trend to private income.
** Totals not always equal to 100 due to rounding.
Sources: Dawkins 1987b; NBEET 1995; DEET 1996c.

1999, the proportion of income from non-government sources, including income from market-based activities, was expected to again increase markedly.

The national training market

Following the report of the Deveson committee (1990), the Commonwealth Government developed proposals for 'an open national training market, based on a diversity of providers' (Finn 1991: 112–113; Totaro 1990) and these were endorsed by the States on 2 November 1990. The new training market included TAFE and higher education; private training providers including business colleges, correspondence schools and private tertiary institutions; community and voluntary groups, firms offering their own training; professional organisations; and Industry Training Advisory Bodies. TAFE was required to operate on commercial principles and survive on its merits as a supplier. The old prohibition against fees had already collapsed in parts of TAFE. Part cost 'upfront' fees were introduced in all courses in 1989, and fully commercial courses began to grow in importance.

The reforms enhanced the commercial element in TAFE institutions; brought a part of private training within the ambit of regulation, and created areas of direct competition between TAFE and the private sector, such as business studies and computing. The Government formulated a National Framework for the Recognition of Training (NFROT) to facilitate the recognition of private training providers and integrate them into the national training system. All States and Territories established machinery in line with NFROT guidelines. The number of authorised private providers increased. Nevertheless, registration was voluntary, many private providers remained outside the official system and there was a lack of comprehensive data. Anderson (1994) comments that the non-TAFE commercial sector was unready for the role thrust upon it. Quality controls were slow to develop.

These points were illustrated in the fiasco of the English language (ELICOS) colleges, which mushroomed in the late 1980s to service the international market in English language courses. Government policies supporting education export sanctioned a permissive regime at the point of entry – the Government even stopped testing the bona fides of applicants for student visas. The number of ELICOS colleges grew from 19 in 1986 to 91 in 1989. Reports of 'backdoor immigration' and the exploitation of student labour were ignored. In August 1989, in the wake of the crack-down on the democracy movement in China and prospects of a wave of political refugees, the Government established tighter criteria for student visas. The bubble burst. Visas issued in

Beijing dropped from 22 420 in 1989–90 to 1579 in 1990–91. Many applicants denied visas had paid their fees. College after college went bankrupt, and thousands were stranded in Australia.

By October 1992, 11 ELICOS colleges had disappeared, 22 had been suspended or their licences cancelled, and the Government had paid students $60 million in compensation for lost fees. The bankruptcies spread, affecting 14 commercial business colleges in the year to May 1991 (Slattery 1991; Dwyer 1992; Doughney 1992).

Markets in private schooling

Between 1982–83 and 1993–94 Commonwealth funding of private schools increased by 49.2 per cent, while its funding of government schools increased by 13.1 per cent (CBP). In the decade after 1983, government school enrolments fell by 2.3 per cent while private school enrolments rose by 18.4 per cent. Students in schools neither Catholic nor Anglican increased by 66.7 per cent and their teachers rose from 7696 to 13 684 in 1993 (ABS 4221.0). Nevertheless, Labor's policy settings were not as conducive to private school expansion as the Fraser policies of 1975–1983 had been. In 1984 a more restrictive Commonwealth policy on new private schools was introduced. This required that proposals for new schools and extensions of existing schools be weighed against the likely impact on existing schools, and reduced the level of funds available to new schools in their early years. The number of new schools grew slowly until the early 1990s (Table 9.14).

Between 1990 and 1992 the government sector's share of enrolments stabilised at 72.1 per cent, for the first time since the late 1970s (Table 9.14). Nevertheless, the potential demand for private schooling was higher than the level of actual enrolments. In 1986 *The Age* published the results of a national opinion poll on schooling. In response to a question about which school system 'would give children the best start for the future', 38 per cent selected government schools, 20 per cent the Catholic schools and 34 per cent the independent private schools. Among the tertiary educated 51 per cent selected the independent private schools, as did 41 per cent of 18 to 24-year-olds (Mills 1986).

In 1994 another poll published by *The Age* found that 'if money was no object', almost two-thirds of people would prefer to place their children in a private secondary school (including both Catholic and independent schools). Even among government school parents a majority preferred private schooling (Table 9.15). No doubt many of these parents imagined the private schools in terms of elite independent schooling. The desire for elite schooling was becoming near universal, though by definition its realisation could only ever be limited to a few.

Table 9.14 Distribution of school students by sector, 1983 to 1995

	Government %	Catholic %	Anglican %	Other private %	Total %
1983	75.6	18.5	2.1	3.7	100
1984	74.9	18.8	2.2	4.1	100
1985	74.2	19.1	2.3	4.4	100
1986	73.6	19.4	2.4	4.7	100
1987	73.1	19.5	2.5	4.9	100
1988	72.7	19.6	2.5	5.2	100
1989	72.4	19.6	2.6	5.4	100
1990	72.1	19.6	2.7	5.6	100
1991	72.1	19.5	2.7	5.7	100
1992	72.1	19.4	2.7	5.8	100
1993	71.9	19.3	2.7	6.0	100
1994	71.5	19.4	2.8	6.3	100
1995	71.0	19.5	2.9	6.6	100

Sources: ABS 4221.0 and its predecessors.

Table 9.15 Preferred school sector, national opinion poll 1994

Q. 'If you had children, and money was no object, would you prefer them to go to a government secondary school or a non-government secondary school?'

	Government school %	Non-government %	Don't know %	Total* %
Total sample	32	58	10	100
Women	32	61	8	100
Men	33	55	12	100
Children at government school	43	45	12	100

* Totals not always equal to 100 due to rounding.
Source: Richards 1994: 2 (from Saulwick/Age Poll, n=1000, national sample).

When asked which type of school was better at preparing young people for 'finding a job', 49 per cent of people chose private schools and 27 per cent government schools, with 13 per cent saying there was no difference. Private schools rated even higher compared to government schools, on 'developing full potential' and preparing young people to be 'good citizens'. The two kinds of school rated equally only

on preparing young people 'to cope with life' (Richards 1994). The
unrealised desires for private schooling meant that any decline in the
private price of private schooling, any increase in the supply or range
of low fee schools, or any improvement in household disposable
incomes, was liable to lead to an upward surge in private school enrolments at the expense of government schooling.

In the 1996 budget the Liberal–National Party's abolition of the new
schools policy, and its increase in the level of funding of new schools,
provided such a change in policy.

Markets in government schooling

In the early 1990s this near universality of the idea of elite private
schooling facilitated the creation of a quasi-market in the government
school system in Victoria, and an increase in competitiveness in other
States and Territories.

The changes in Victoria were partly modelled on the Thatcher
reforms in Britain (Jones 1989; Edwards & Whitty 1994). In 1993 the
Kennett Government introduced the 'Schools of the Future' program.
The objective was to create corporate-style schools that were autonomous in policy and resources, including some staff selection, though
most teachers remained centrally employed. School councils were in
effect turned into boards of management. The main authority was
centred on the principal, who determined the business of the council
and implemented its decisions. 'The principal will be responsible and
accountable for curriculum leadership, resource and personnel management, and school organisation' (VG 1993). The principal was
accountable to council and department. In the case of conflict the
department took priority, enabling the Government to maintain
unstated but effective control. The department was also able to influence the school through negotiations over the school 'charter', the
quasi-contractual agreement between school council and Government
which was used as the basis for public funding and accountability. By
negotiating separately on a one-to-one basis with each school the Government could shape a division of labour between schools and vary
their resource levels, while evading a public process of planning in
which all schools were considered together.

Caldwell (1993) described it as 'administrative decentralisation
rather than political decentralisation'. The centre was the 'strategic
core', providing the framework of 'mission, strategy, policy, priority and
accountability'. Local units gained 'the capacity for management within
a centrally determined framework' (see also Seddon 1994).

At system level government schools were placed in competition for both government and private resources. Enrolments were dezoned, and funding partly determined by enrolments. Schools were encouraged to charge quasi-compulsory fees, seek donations, and raise funds through fairs, cultural performances and corporate sponsorship (Kenway et al 1993), and to provide commercial services. The capacity to raise non-government income was unevenly distributed between schools. Nevertheless, following the resource reductions of 1992–1994 (chapter 8) it became essential, even for basic teaching and learning facilities. The Schools of the Future program made each individual school responsible for its resource position and educational outcomes, partly de-politicising resource provision and the character of system organisation, thus naturalising the quasi-market.

Government schools were being remoulded as quasi-private schools without the social prestige or the independence from state controls that was associated with the elite independent establishments. The competitive model foreshadowed a system in which some government schools would become powerful attractors of parents while others would become residual schools inhabited by families unable to go elsewhere. This prospect raised doubts about the comprehensive character of government schools, and clouded their future role in citizen formation. It also suggested that market reform might lower the average level of student achievement. The weak schools, continually destabilised by market competition and parental flight, could become educational-social ghettos. The strong schools, with a queue outside the gate, would be largely immune from consumer pressures. There was no evidence to suggest that in a market their educational outcomes would improve.

When education with *social* value ceases to be a citizen right and becomes an economic commodity, it also becomes scarce instead of universal. In the process it gains a *market economic* value for some, but a value that rests on the deprivation of others. The more that people are excluded from a particular kind of education, the higher becomes its value to the privileged few who retain access to it. Thus the dynamics of markets coincide with the maintenance of social hierarchy.[7]

Notes

[1] This was the one passage from Keynes that Hayek admired. It was prominently displayed at the Institute of Economic Affairs, the New Right think tank (Desai 1994: 45).

[2] US-based studies suggest that in the normal class size range of 20–40 students, test scores are relatively weakly correlated to resource inputs. At class sizes

outside the normal range, resource changes induce more dramatic effects on scores (see the meta-analysis by Glass et al 1982). The relationship between resource inputs and test score-outputs is not unit linear. Standardised tests play a central role in American schooling and the essence of teacher professionalism is the capacity to achieve basic student achievement in standardised tests at any class size within the normal range. It can be surmised that within the normal class size range, as class size increases the outputs other than test scores (aspects of the curriculum not covered by testing) tend to deteriorate more rapidly than test scores. This cannot show in studies in which outputs are defined as test scores, such as those relied on by Hanushek.

[3] The resource targets laid down by the 1973 Karmel committee in 1973 were achieved in all government systems by 1977–78, except for secondary schools in NSW and Queensland, the last taking until 1981–82 (Karmel 1985: 11).

[4] In 1977 the TEAS maximum reached $4625 p.a. (constant 1984–85 prices), 23.6 per cent above the 1975 level, following the national student strike of 30 September 1976, proposed by a Macquarie University student meeting and coordinated by the Australian Union of Students. Eligibility was tightened, however. By 1982 TEAS was 18.1 per cent below the 1975 level.

[5] In *The Whitlam government 1972–1975* (1985) Whitlam wrote that 'When I resigned the Party leadership in 1977, among all the hundreds of messages I received, no single reform was as frequently mentioned in terms of personal or parental gratitude as our decision to abolish fees. I still receive letters from those who benefited' (Whitlam 1985: 738).

[6] Bruce Chapman, a consultant to the Wran committee and the policy architect of the HECS, later acknowledged that in the post-1974 period there had been some improvement in the equality of social group representation, stating however that this was unrelated to the abolition of fees (Chapman 1992: 100–109).

[7] These dynamics of education markets are explored more fully in Marginson 1997d.

PART IV

THE MULTI-CITIZEN 1990–

'Since these things have been made, they can be
unmade, as long as we know how it was that they
were made.'

Michel Foucault, Politics, philosophy, culture, *edited by
Lawrence D. Kritzman, Routledge, New York, 1988, p. 37.*

Micro-economic reform and the expansion of education brought not
rising prosperity but the severe recession of the early 1990s. This weakened support for the dominant economic policies, and new issues
began to come on to the agenda: national identity, Asianisation, migration and multiculturalism; native title and reconciliation with indigenous people; citizenship and civics education. The growing recognition
of difference and diversity created tensions, especially after the election
of the Liberal and National parties in 1996, and brought new problems
and possibilities to education.

CHAPTER 10

Civics, citizenship and difference

'It is important that the next generation fully appreciates
what it means to be an Australian and that they understand
our history and our cultural diversity. The report of the
Civics Expert Group released in December 1994 has been
given scant attention by the Labor Government. The
Coalition is committed to ensuring that students leave
school with an understanding of, and pride in, what it
means to be an Australian citizen; with a knowledge of our
system of government and democracy with the knowledge
and skills to enable them to participate as active citizens in
the community.'

Liberal and National Parties, policy on Schools and TAFE,
March 1996 election, p. 9.

Prelude: Education for complete living (1937 and 1994)

In August and September 1937 the Australian Council for Educational
Research (ACER) organised conferences of the New Educational Fel-
lowship in the seven capitals of Australia. The ACER hoped by opening
local education to the global effects of educationists from Britain,
North America and Europe to foster a new spirit of reform and renewal.
Later it published the proceedings as *Education for complete living* (Cunningham 1938). Conference speakers covered almost every subject,
though little was said about the education of girls, and less about indigenous and cultural diversity: it seemed that the task was to extend a
singular system of education to the whole population, not to diversify
it. The guest speakers praised Australian education for its achievement
in bringing equality of opportunity to remote and rural districts,
though it was criticised for excessive centralism, for 'the sentiment' that
'anybody who is anybody sends his children to a private school', and
for an over-emphasis on the vocational aspects of education (Hart
1938b: 664).

F.W. Hart, Professor of Education at the University of California, outlined the results of his research on the preparation of students for citizenship. He reported with regret that American students lacked the knowledge needed by intelligent participating citizens. Schools should organise social studies 'around a critical study of the social, political and economic problems of contemporary life' or they should 'cease claiming to be society's chosen agency for training for citizenship' (Hart 1938a: 195–198). To Dr. William Boyd, Head of the Education Department at Glasgow University, citizenship was more than 'imparting information' about voting or public office. It was helping students to form personal judgements, to deal with the uncertainties of life and to take an active role. We must think of citizenship 'comprehensively', he stated. 'The good citizen is the good member of society in all its aspects: good neighbour, good family man, good worker, good politician' (Boyd 1938: 191).

Six decades later, amid a revived interest in citizenship and national identity, the Australian Government created a review of *Civics and citizenship education* (Macintyre 1994). The same themes returned. Education was failing to prepare good citizens. Students lacked knowledge of the constitution, the parliament, the judiciary and the federal–state system. Submissions lamented the decline of civic knowledge, understanding, attachment, capacity and participation. As in 1937, the citizen was defined in two different ways, as legal-political subject and as broader social being. Like Hart and Boyd the Civics Expert Group took the broad view, arguing that its task was to foster 'measures that would help Australians to become active citizens' in all spheres (Macintyre 1994: 6; Macintyre 1995). But the matter was also more complex than it was in 1937. Gender, ethnic identities, Asianisation, international education, national reconciliation: 'difference' was on the agenda. Questions of plurality in school choice, indigenous studies and Australian history, and multiculturalism remained to be resolved.

Citizenship education was looking for a combination of tolerance and cohesion, unity and difference: a stable legal-political-educational formula in which people could retain their cultural identities, whether born or made, and still remain loyal citizens committed to the common welfare. Then – instead of a sterile debate between mainstream as monoculture and diversity as separateness or exclusion – the elements in the diverse mix could be mingled and mixed together to build a better place in which everyone would live.

I. Beyond the economic citizen?

A new public agenda

In the early 1990s in Australia the public-political agenda began to change. Michael Pusey's *Economic rationalism in Canberra* (1991) and the response to that book tapped an emerging disquiet with the economisation of government and the market liberal program. There was no ready-made alternative, nor any change of stance in the business organisations or the economic profession. The fiscal imperative and smaller taxation retained their power, and corporate and market reform were still working their way through the functions of government, including educational programs. Nevertheless, new issues were emerging, and old questions of national identity and citizenship once again were important, even compelling.

Under Labor's Paul Keating as Prime Minister, in 1992 the Government began to canvass the possibility of Australia becoming a republic, and of changing the national flag to remove British identity. Keating placed a growing emphasis on relations with Asian countries and multiculturalism, and reconciliation with indigenous peoples, the Aboriginal and Torres Strait Islanders dispossessed by European invasion and settlement. In 1992 the High Court recognised a prior right of indigenous people to land, lifting the reconciliation process to a new plane. These issues became important, and controversial; and at times they displaced interest rates, the balance of payments, the foreign debt and the job market. Less clearly, the slippage in civic cooperation and compassion had left a vacuum in public life, and this began to be discussed.

The questions of identity and solidarity coalesced in the revival of interest in citizenship. Being part of even a dynamic economy did not 'by itself provide a strong sense of civic identity' (Salvaris 1995: 25–26). Members of an economy were consumers, or investors, or entrepreneurs, or workers, but for many people this was not enough. Significantly the British Government's attempt to reframe government along the individualised cost–benefit lines of public choice theory, in which a citizen-consumer sought to maximise the individualised value of the tax-spending equation, failed to fire the popular imagination.[1]

Citizenship was on the public agenda in many countries. There were official reports in Britain, the USA, Canada and France, and the UNESCO International Bureau on Education had established a large scale comparative project. In the English-speaking countries the renewed interest in citizenship was a response to economic rationalism, small government and the hyper-individualism and competition fetish-ism of market liberalism. In Europe it arose out from the search for a common social charter and debates about the meaning of European identity.

The definition of citizenship was the subject of much debate. Salvaris argued that 'a 'healthy democracy' required more than periodic voting. He contrasted a 'narrow and technical' sense of citizenship based on national identity with a sense of full membership and active participa-tion, encompassing rights and responsibilities in the legal, social, eco-nomic, cultural and environmental spheres. This conception rested on 'the public and private policies and resources needed to sustain it'. Sal-varis noted the continued relevance of T.H. Marshall's notion of civil, political and social rights, including the right to economic welfare and security, and 'the right to share to the full in the social heritage' (Marshall 1950: 10–11). However, Marshall's notion of citizenship failed to include more advanced kinds of political participation and understandings of relations of power, or to accommodate gender, multiculturalism and indigenous self-determination (Salvaris 1995: 5–10, 37–45).

In August 1994 the parliamentary Joint Standing Committee on Migra-tion (JSCM) delivered a report on *Australians all – enhancing Australian citizenship.* The committee proposed Australia allow dual citizenship, like many other nations, allowing migrants to retain 'a commitment to their country of origin'. The committee also recommended the development of a national curriculum for citizenship education, as 'a national priority' (JSCM 1994: xvii–xviii, 206).

In education, the recession of the early 1990s had undermined the promises of the preceding period. The economic reconstruction of education was not undone (far from it), but the promise of vocational education had been weakened. Vocational competition and the pres-sures of selection retained their potency in the shaping of the choices of individuals, and the courses provided by institutions. Nonetheless, for students who worked hard, passed their courses and graduated into unemployment, economic citizenship was a sham. By tying citizenship to successful participation in the labour markets, throwing the respon-sibility for self-realisation back to the individual within a market she/ he could not control, economic government was excluding many people from .the benefits of citizenship. No doubt this contributed to the falling away in school retention and demand for higher education after 1992. 'The idea that "education is good for you" may prove a fatal legacy of our education policies since the 1980s' (Watts 1995: 96, 100). The Commonwealth Labor Government of 1983–1996 was closely identified with vocationalism. Perhaps Keating was looking for a way out of this policy bind in 1995 when he argued that:

The emphasis we are now placing on vocational education and training must not be seen as antithetical to traditional educational values. In fact we should be strengthening those values as we go. Education is a foundation of the nation's culture and strength. It is where knowledge and an appreciation of our heritage and institutions is passed on; where our sensibilities are broadened; where moral, ethical and aesthetic faculties are shaped. I do not think I am alone in suspecting that some of these things are not the priority they once were. Yet our success as a nation and as a society, as much as our responsibility we have to our children, demands that we do not let these values slip from our education system. Perhaps most of all, our children should know what the privileges and responsibilities of democracy are (Keating 1995: 89–90).

By then civics and citizenship education had already emerged as one of the ways of fostering those neglected attributes.

Civics education

For the half-century after World War I, civics was a core part of the curriculum in the State systems of government schooling. It was often closely linked to the teaching of history, and ranged from the memorisation of legal and political institutions to training in ethics and the management of daily life. However, by the late 1960s civics education was being absorbed into social studies (Thomas 1994).

In the mid-1980s the then Commonwealth Minister for Education, Susan Ryan, canvassed the need to revive civics education in schools. In April 1989 the Commonwealth, State and Territory ministers responsible for education, meeting in Hobart, reached agreement on collaborative goals for improving Australian education. Goal 7 endorsed the teaching of citizenship: 'to develop knowledge, skills, attitudes and values which will enable students to participate as active and informed citizens in our democratic Australian society within an international context'.

In June 1994 Keating established a three-person 'Civics Expert Group', chaired by the historian Stuart Macintyre of the University of Melbourne. It was charged with preparing a non-partisan program of public education on civics issues, to ensure 'that Australians have sufficient information about our system of government to participate fully in decision making processes'. The Civics Expert Group's ambit included schools, TAFE, higher education, and public education through the media and community organisations; the main focus was on schooling. The Group received 180 submissions and conducted consultations in each State and Territory.

Concurrently with the Civics Expert Group, ANOP Research Services conducted a national survey concerning people's knowledge of the legal and political systems, and citizenship. ANOP found that most people were familiar with voting, and the roles of Commonwealth, State and local government, but knew little about the federal system, the Constitution or the High Court. For most respondents citizenship was 'an abstract concept that is never given much thought'. The media was the major source of knowledge about civics and citizenship (Macintyre 1994: 29–31, 159; ANOP 1994b). The results of the ANOP survey were consistent with other studies of civic knowledge, and findings that young people were alienated from the formal political processes (for example Print 1995).

The apparent paucity of knowledge about civics was used to drive acceptance of the Civics Expert Group's report, and was much cited in the discussion that followed. However, the Group also defined citizenship in larger terms. It saw its task as 'encompassing all aspects that would enable Australians to participate as citizens in the operation of our democratic society'. This included the practical operations of government and formal knowledge of it, the global plane – the capacity to be a citizen of the world – and a 'civil' sphere, affected but not wholly controlled by the state. 'In our working lives, in recreational associations, as producers and consumers, we join together in ways that sustain public life. Just as we need to ground citizenship in the daily operations of our schools, so we need to see other institutions as sites of citizenship' (Macintyre 1995: 18–19). Whereas civics education required a formal course, citizenship education should operate as a 'template' across all learning areas.

The Civics Expert Group's report concluded that 'education for citizenship ranks with English and mathematics as a priority' for schooling and was 'an essential component of a liberal education'. A civics and citizenship education program was 'a means of fostering a core of unity in a diverse society'. In the compulsory years, there should be a 'sequential program of civics education' as part of the key learning area of Studies of Society and Environment. 'The curriculum should be inclusive of Aboriginal and Torres Strait Islander, multicultural, gender, regional and international perspectives.' The Group noted that some States, such as New South Wales, were already developing civics and citizenship education in the primary and junior secondary years. In years 11 and 12 there could not be a common unit, because of other pressures, but there should be opportunities to study civics in subjects such as Australian history and studies, politics and legal studies.[2] The report proposed the preparation of comprehensive curriculum materials. In higher education, a civics course should be developed through the television based Open Learning Agency. Curriculum materials should also be prepared for TAFE (Macintyre 1994: 6, 38, 68, 110–113).

The report was publicly well received, and endorsed by education authorities. In the 1995–96 budget the Government allocated $25 million to civics and citizenship education, including $10.6 million to the Curriculum Corporation for materials for schools, $6.3 million for teacher's professional development, $2.3 million for community education initiatives, and $2.4 million for civics and citizenship courses provided on a voluntary basis to applicants for citizenship. The Government took the broad approach. It wanted citizenship education to improve Australians' grasp of their history and systems of government, and the meaning of citizenship 'to encourage practical participation in our nation's civic life'. The aim was 'active and informed citizenship' and agreement around 'a set of core Australian values, rights and responsibilities' (CA 1995; Keating 1995: 102–106).

The Liberal and National Parties supported civic education, provided it was not used for republican propaganda (Pascoe 1996: 21). In the 1996 election the Coalition parties strongly endorsed the Civics Expert Group's report and criticised Labor for neglecting its implementation (LNP 1996: 9). This suggested that there was a strong momentum for an upgrading of civics and citizenship education, one that would outlast a change of government, although curriculum content might alter.

II. Education and difference

The appearance of difference

Citizenship is about identity. The richer politics of identity that emerged in Australia was not so much the product of the Keating Government as the culmination of longer term trends; though by using difference as an aspect of its rule, the Keating Government compressed and magnified those trends. The nation state was weakening and the world was more peripatetic, in that people were more likely than before to cross national boundaries, creating the need for multiple citizenship (Saunders 1996: 32). In Australia cultural and linguistic diversity, the claims of indigenous people, the removal of legal discrimination and aspects of social discrimination against women, the Racial Discrimination Act and the recognition of new family structures, had all made citizen identity a more complex matter.

The 1991 census found more than 7 million people (42 per cent) were born outside Australia or had a parent born outside Australia. 17 per cent of people spoke a language other than English at home. Of second generation migrants, two-thirds married outside their original ethnic groups; and while earlier migration had been British and

European almost half was now from Asia. In the longer term the ethnic mix could only become more diverse. Further, there had been a vast expansion of business and tourist traffic between Australia and East-South East Asian countries. By 1995 Australian exports to East Asia were $43.3 billion, 60.5 per cent of total exports. Australia's prosperity was tied to the mobile middle classes of these countries, and their willingness to travel to, live in and trade with Australia. 'The transformation of the Asia/Pacific from a region of military threat to one of economic progress . . . forced Australia to substitute multiculturalism and regional integration for the original idea of White Australia' (Kelly 1992: 4; SMH 1996).

The roots of this change in orientation lay in the 1970s when government policies began to move away from the old goal of assimilation into a singular Anglo-Australian monoculture. A bipartisan notion of multiculturalism was developed, which permitted a limited kind of dual cultural identity in which people could in some sense retain their original identities without ceasing to be loyal Australian citizens. Harder questions, such as dual citizenship, remained unresolved (Saunders 1996: 32). The multiculturalism policy emerged under the Fraser Government.

> Acquiring Australian citizenship should not require suppression of one's cultural heritage or identity. Rather, the act of becoming a citizen is – symbolically and actually – a process of bringing one's own gift of language, culture and traditions to enrich the already diverse fabric of Australian society. Our vision of our multicultural society shares, with our concept of citizenship, a strong emphasis on building a cohesive and harmonious society which is all the more tolerant and outward looking because of the diversity of its origins. . . . Citizenship is the symbol of a common identity and commitment to the nation. A common national identity should be the tie that binds a multicultural Australia together (Ian Macphee, Minister for Immigration and Ethnic Affairs, in Hansard 1982: 2356).

For indigenous people, formal political-governmental identity was a more recent and precarious achievement. No one classified as an Aboriginal and Torres Strait Islander person, and born before 1967, had been born an Australian citizen. That was the year, 179 years after British colonisation began, when a referendum amended the constitution to admit indigenous people to Australian citizenship. Of the perhaps 600 language groups in 1788, about 30 remained (Woods 1996).

However, in 1982 Eddie Mabo and four others began legal action to secure ownership to the land occupied by their families on the Murray Islands in the Torres Strait; and on 3 June 1992 the High Court recognised the right of the plaintiffs to possession, occupation and use of those lands. This established a new basis for land owning in Australia, that of native title; and abolished the notion of *terra nullius*, the legal fiction that Australia had been unoccupied before the claim of British sovereignty in eastern Australia in 1788. This opened the way to land claims by indigenous people, although it appeared to confine those claims for native title to vacant crown land and those areas where the traditional way of life had survived. Significantly, by establishing land rights that were prior to the dominant legal system, the decision created a fuller notion of difference, of more than one basis for legal personality. The Commonwealth began to prepare legislation for a Native Title Tribunal, a land fund and an Indigenous Land Corporation. Keating argued for 'a new partnership' with indigenous people based on a renovated idea of social justice (1995: 230).

> Isn't it reasonable to say that if we can build a prosperous and remarkably harmonious multicultural society in Australia, surely we can find just solutions to the problems which beset the first Australians – the people to whom the most injustice has been done? And, as I say, the starting point might be to recognise that the problem starts with us non-Aboriginal Australians. It begins, I think, with that act of recognition. Recognition that it was we who did the dispossessing. We took the traditional lands and smashed the traditional way of life. We brought the diseases. The alcohol. We committed the murders. We took the children from their mothers. We practised discrimination and exclusion. It was our ignorance and our prejudice. And our failure to imagine these things being done to us (Keating 1995: 228).

These profound and dramatic changes inevitably had a major impact on education, especially government schooling and TAFE, and the services such as language and literacy teaching which played a key role with newly arrived migrants. From the beginning of the multiculturalism policy in the 1970s, education was at the forefront of official programs. The Fraser Government created a multicultural education program, an ethnic schools program and resources for bilingual teaching. In 1979 the Schools Commission's Committee on Multicultural Education argued that schools should strengthen the founding identities of non-Anglo students. Maintenance of home languages achieved 'the deliberate preservation and encouragement of ethnic identity'. Schools should also offer the opportunity to 'understand and appreciate alternative lifestyles and cultural patterns not their own' (cited in Cope & Kalantzis 1995: 6). This did not lead to the overnight transformation of programs. Nevertheless, it was a crucial shift in approach, breaking with the notion of 'one best' culture and one kind of education.

Aboriginal education programs also moved from assimilation to a partial commitment to the maintenance of identity, though this varied by State and Territory. Research suggested that students who were content with her or his identity as an Aboriginal person were more likely to succeed at school. Indigenous identity was more important in determining achievement than was socio-economic background (Woods 1996). Kennedy argued in 1995 that Australia was no longer 'a country of people claiming some form of Anglo-Celtic heritage'. The 'colonial image of citizenship' was monocultural and monolingual. 'A new image of citizenship is needed for a new age.'

Educators were required to renegotiate the balance between difference and unity. An unbridled notion of difference, without acknowledging its limitations, was insufficient a basis for educational programs. For example claims to a particular difference might be used to suppress other identities within the community concerned. This was one problem with freedom of choice in private schooling: some of its practitioners ran a choice-free curriculum and a monocultural behavioural code within the school. Further, to pursue difference without regard for social harmony would lead to the destruction of the common social capital. This pointed to *diversity within the school*, which was best accomplished in comprehensive settings.

This suggested that in education unity and diversity were not mutually exclusive but closely interwoven. The notions of citizenship based on equal rights, and of equal respect for difference, were both drawn from the same set of rights, and under certain circumstances were mutually dependent. On one hand 'social rights have undoubtedly helped to integrate disadvantaged groups into the political community and strengthened the bonds of community'; that is, the recognition of difference generated unity (Hogan 1996: 16). On the other hand when the common good included the key virtue of tolerance (Kennedy 1995: 17), it could provide space for identity formation; that is, unity generated the capacity for difference. Education had an important social role in producing tolerance. This role was best achieved when students from all groups were educated together; again underlining the role of the comprehensive school. Thus *equality of respect* retained a key role in education, though its practices were contradicted by the emerging market education systems, in which the respect that each person received was correlated to buying power.

The implications of the growing emphasis on difference for civics and citizenship education were noted by the Civics Expert Group:

> It is no longer possible to assume the old values that once bound Australians together as a community. The core value that is most commonly cited now is the acceptance of difference. Australia is frequently extolled as a society

that recognises or even encourages diversity, and we take pride in the way that ethnic, cultural, sexual and other identities can coexist to enrich the whole. During our consultations we frequently encountered the view that diversity is a national strength (Macintyre 1994: 14–15).

Tolerance and the capacity to understand difference were an important part of the broader conception of citizenship referred to by the Group. However, the report missed the opportunity to look more closely at formal education's contribution to the formation of tolerance, and to identify those education practices most conducive to it. The social acceptance of diversity was not something to take for granted, as subsequent events were to show. In a study of year 7 and 11 students in WA, Phillips (1995) asked the students to rate the importance of different kinds of characteristics of a 'good citizen'. Of twenty-six characteristics offered to respondents, being 'well informed about Australia's constitution' and 'well informed about Australia's political system' ranked twenty-fourth and twenty-fifth. Highest support was given to 'respects the rights of others'. Treating people equally regardless of gender (third), disabilities (fourth) and race (sixth) were strongly supported. Given the growing recognition of diversity, it could be argued that the WA students had their priorities right. Living together with respect for each other's rights was more important than formal civic knowledge. However, it was the deficiencies in the latter that exercised the attention of the Government.

Unity, diversity and the future

In 'Racism, anti-racism, and moral progress' Zygmunt Bauman (1993) discusses the way that the nation-state typically deals with strangers. First, strangers are identified *as* strangers, provoking ambivalent sentiments in the population. Bauman calls these sentiments 'protephobia'. Second, the strangers are polarised into two groups: those who are absorbed and those who are expelled: the assimilated and the marginalised. Third, the creation of 'protephobia' provides the nation-state with one of the sources of its power, its capacity to administer 'social space'. The typical nation-state does not eliminate 'protephobia', but 'constantly replenishes its stocks'.

In the election of the Howard Government in 1996, and in the first months of the new Government's term, 'protephobia' became a principal political weapon, weakening the sometimes glib assumptions of the Keating era about plural national identity. The Liberal–National parties' election slogans of 'One Australia' and 'for all of us' were designed so as to emphasise national unity even while cultivating resentment among Anglo-Australians at the Keating Government's commitments to indigenous land rights, multiculturaliusm and Asianisation. They set out to exploit the tensions inherent in the politics of difference. While Coalition candidates were mostly circumspect in their targeting of non-Anglo groups, independent candidates Hanson and Campbell were elected on platforms of open opposition to multiculturalism, Asian immigration and programs for indigenous people. The support given to their stance augmented the support given to the Coalition parties themselves. After the election, the new Government maintained its protephobia. In the first few months it attacked indigenous leaders (the 'aboriginal industry'), made large scale cuts in programs for indigenous people, and developed legislation to restrict the potential of native title. Howard rejected Hanson's claim that indigenous people were not disadvantaged, but he also rejected the notion of an indigenous legal rationale that was conceptually distinct from orthodox Anglo-Australian law. The Government cut welfare benefits to migrants for the first two years after arrival, and Howard refused to endorse the term 'multicultural', except as a term of abuse (the 'multicultural industry') although the word remained part of official programs and ministerial titles. Opinion polls showed majority support for multiculturalism, and strong support for a non-discriminatory immigration policy (SMH 1996), but also that a majority believed immigration was too high. Following an upsurge of attacks on citizens of Asian origin, in the wake of the claims of Hanson and others, Howard moved very slowly to defend Asian people from abuse, and he expressed some sympathy for the arguments against immigration.

To *The Age*'s Gawenda (1996) Howard refused to repudiate Hanson's maiden speech and its claims, for example that Australia was being 'swamped by Asians', because 'in sentiment at least, if not in detail', Howard felt 'closer to the views of Hanson's supporters on what it means to be Australian than to the views of her opponents'. That is, Howard was most comfortable with a singular national identity and an assimilationist policy. In a similar debate on Asian immigration and national identity in 1988, Howard had declared his willingness to 'alter the flow of immigration from any part of the world' if the national interest required it (Ramsey 1996), opening the door to a discriminatory policy. Gawenda commented that:

> Those of us who were sure that reconciliation between black and white Australia was inevitable after Mabo, who thought that there was a community consensus about the contribution of migration and who believed that multiculturalism had become embedded as a key characteristic of our national identity, now have to admit that none of these things can be taken for

granted. Even the belief that Australia would become a republic in the fore-seeable future is now open to doubt (Gawenda 1996).

This placed educational institutions in a more ambiguous position than before. There was now no governmental consensus on the questions of plural identity. Further, in private schooling, the Howard government was creating the basis for a chain of separated monocultures, while also weakening the common government schools which had the chief practical role in producing mixing and tolerance – thus creating difference without unity in private schooling, while seeking unity without difference in government schooling. It was a familiar double standard, akin to the stance taken by conservatives in the choice debate, where they supported freedom of choice in private schooling and opposed it as undiscipline in the government schools (see chapter 6).

At the same time, it was no longer possible for the Commonwealth Government to reimpose an assimilationist monoculture in government schooling. First, government schools were controlled by the States and Territories rather than the Commonwealth. Second, though government schools required all students to conform to a normalising language and curriculum for assessment and student selection, it was no longer educationally or politically feasible to ignore the specific identities of non-Anglo students. If education programs followed the full implications of Howard's preferred position, they were likely to generate strong and disabling resistance.

Educational institutions and educational professionals now had an additional task, that of compensating for and responding strategically to the racist backlash. If the Commonwealth continued to align itself with the anti-modernist reaction to difference, rather than the modernist and multicultural side of the debate, many educators would find themselves moving out beyond the Government. Here the practice of an educational ethic that valued the 'other' as positive and worth supporting had the potential to weaken the nation-state strategy of creating 'protephobia'. It also had the potential to move beyond the Keating years. Woods argues that diversity should be treated as more than variations on the common theme. It can build a different kind of nation. 'Let our diversity and our differences be dialectics from which we spark a better Australia' (Woods 1996: 36).

The Howard Government's handling of education left a number of other issues unresolved. One was the question of Australian history. Any geo-political history permits a diversity of themes and stories, but there is also the question of unifying narratives (Macintyre 1996). The question posed by the Howard attack on what he called the 'black arm-band' version of Australian history was whether it was now possible to tell the nation-building story in Australia without also telling the full story of the indigenous people who had been made into the 'strangers' in a strange land. Their dispossession was the founding act of nation building, and thus an essential condition of 'Australia'.

A second question was the future viability of the comprehensive government school – given that to the Government, the main form of diversity was not within schools but between schools, there was intense competition for individual advantage, and policies were undermining the comprehensive character of the state systems. Given that education should enable people to make their own learning paths for themselves, how could the scope for choice be increased within the common school? And choice of school did not have to be a question of public *versus* private. There was no good reason why community groups wanting to support a school that formed and maintained a distinctive identity of their choosing could not do so *within* government systems, provided that rights of access to families in the immediate vicinity were provided, and curriculum standards were guaranteed.

A third question was the future roles and relationship of media and multi-media on one hand, and formal education on the other. Media, consumption and multi-media had now become the main source of civic identity, and of understandings of difference. At the same time, they encouraged the passive construction of a globalised self and thus a narrowly limited range of possible identities. In contrast, formal education had the potential to provide the technological literacy and critical skills enabling students to retain, enhance and construct their own chosen identities, as they saw fit, *if* the hardware, software and pedagogical frameworks were provided. The question for the future was whether these attributes would become monopolised by some students, or would become available to all.

Notes

[1] Gamble (1995) comments that the strategy of privatisation based on citizen–shareholders also failed to provide the Conservative Party with the new *petit bourgeois* popular base that it had hoped for.

[2] As the Group noted, this fall-back position was less than satisfactory. Recent years had seen 'a dramatic and disturbing decline in the number of students electing to study the humanities in years 11 and 12' because of tertiary entrance requirements, and perceptions that humanities students received lower scores (Macintyre 1994: 44–45).

References

For Australian Bureau of Statistics serials, the catalogue number is used in place of reference date. For Commonwealth Government statistics where a series has been used, such as those prepared by DEET and CTEC, the date refers to the last item used in the series.

Aitkin, Don 1981, 'Australian society of change – a sociological and political perspective', in Peter Karmel (ed.), *Education, change and society*, pp. 36–50. Melbourne: Australian Council for Education Research.

Alexander, Don & Rizvi, Fazal 1993, 'Education, markets and the contradictions of Asia–Australia relations', *The Australian Universities Review* 36, 16–20.

Anderson, Damon 1994, *Private training providers in Australia: charting the terrain*, paper to the conference on training research in university and TAFE, James Cook University of North Queensland, 6–8 July.

Anderson, Don 1990, 'Access to university education in Australia 1852–1990: changes in the undergraduate social mix', *Australian Universities Review* 33, 37–50.

Anderson, Don 1992, 'The interaction of public and private school systems', *Australian Journal of Education* 36, 213–236.

Anderson, Don & Vervoorn, Art 1983, *Access to privilege*, Canberra: Australian National University Press.

Angus, Max, Brown, Sandra, McGaw, Barry & Robson, Greg 1983, *Setting standards for school resources: the contribution of research*, Canberra: Commonwealth Schools Commission.

Apple, Michael 1986, 'National reports and the construction of inequality', *British Journal of Sociology of Education*, 2, 171–190.

Ashenden, Dean 1987a, 'Private or state?', *Time Australia*, 4 May.

Ashenden, Dean 1987b, *Information and inequality: a systematic approach to increasing educational equality*, paper to the Victorian State Board of Education, Melbourne.

Ashenden, Dean & Milligan, Sandra 1994a, 'Unis challenged in rush for corporate dollar', *The Australian*, 25 September.

Ashenden, Dean & Milligan, Sandra 1994b, *The good universities guide*.

Australian Bureau of Statistics (ABS) 2710.0, *Census: characteristics of Australia*, Canberra: ABS.

Australian Bureau of Statistics (ABS) 2722.0, *Basic community profile*, Canberra: ABS.

Australian Bureau of Statistics (ABS) 4101.0, *Social indicators*, Canberra: ABS.

Australian Bureau of Statistics (ABS) 4202.0, *Schools Australia*, Canberra: ABS.

Australian Bureau of Statistics (ABS) 4216.0, *Non-government schools, Australia,*, Canberra: ABS.

Australian Bureau of Statistics (ABS) 4218.0, *Tertiary education, Australia,* Canberra: ABS.

Australian Bureau of Statistics (ABS) 4221.0, *National schools collection, Australia,* Canberra: ABS.

Australian Bureau of Statistics (ABS) 5510.0, *Expenditure on education,* Canberra: ABS.

Australian Bureau of Statistics (ABS) 6203.0, *The labour force,* Canberra: ABS,

Australian Council of Social Service (ACOSS) 1989, *Privatisation and the human services,* ACOSS Paper No. 26, Sydney: ACOSS.

Australian Council of Trade Unions (ACTU) 1991, *Workplace reform, skill development and a high competence, educated workforce,* policy adopted at ACTU Congress, September, Melbourne: ACTU.

Australian Council of Trade Unions and Trade Development Centre (ACTU/ TDC) 1987, *Australia reconstructed,* report of the mission to Western Europe, Canberra: Australian Government Publishing Service (AGPS).

Australian Education Union (AEU) 1994, *National survey of conditions in schools,* Melbourne: AEU.

Australian Financial Review (AFR) 1984, 'Sabotaging the public schools', editorial *Australian Financial Review,* 6 July.

Australian Financial Review (AFR) 1987, 'The three needs: knowledge, skills and character', editorial *Australian Financial Review,* 23 June.

Australian Labor Party (ALP) 1972, election policy speech, 13 November, Canberra: ALP.

Australian Labor Party (ALP) 1977, election policy speech, 17 November, Canberra: ALP.

Australian Labor Party (ALP) 1984, election policy speech, 13 November, Canberra: ALP.

Australian Labor Party (ALP) 1987, election policy speech, 23 June, Canberra: ALP.

Australian National Opinion Polls (ANOP) 1984, *The new traditionalism: a special ANOP study of young people,* Canberra: AGPS.

Australian National Opinion Polls (ANOP) 1990, *Community attitudes to issues affecting young people and to DEET policies and programs,* Canberra: AGPS.

Australian National Opinion Polls (ANOP) 1994a, *Young people's attitudes to post-compulsory education and training,* Canberra: AGPS.

Australian National Opinion Polls (ANOP) 1994b, 'The Australian community and its governments, the constitution, citizenship and civics: community understanding and knowledge', in Macintyre 1994, pp. 128–160.

Australian Parents' Council (APC) 1983, *Children, education and schooling: guiding principles,* Sydney: APC.

Australian Science and Technology Council (ASTEC) 1987, *Education and national needs,* Canberra: AGPS.

Australian, The 1985, 'Concern on education', editorial *The Australian,* 11 February.

Australian, The 1988a, 'The way ahead IV: our education: nothing short of disaster', editorial *The Australian,* 6 January.

Australian, The 1988b 'Testing education', editorial *The Australian,* 3 March.

Bacon, Robert & Eltis, Walter 1978, *Britain's economic problem: too few producers,* London: Macmillan.

Ball, Stephen 1990, 'Management as moral technology', in Stephen Ball (ed.), *Foucault and education,* pp. 153–166, London: Routledge.

Barcan, Alan 1978, 'Four problems of English education', *ACES Review* 5, 3–5.

Barnard, Michael 1982, 'Making a crime of success', *The Age*, 29 June.

Barry, Norman 1990, 'Market politics', *Times Higher Education Supplement*, 23 March.

Bartos, Michael 1993, 'The Schools Commission, citizenship and the national purposes of schooling', in Meredyth & Tyler (eds), pp. 153–180.

Bates, Richard & Kynaston, Edward 1983, *Thinking aloud: interviews with Australian educators*, Geelong: Deakin University Press.

Bauman, Zygmunt 1993, 'Racism, anti-racism and moral progress', *Arena Journal*, 1, 9–21.

Bean, Clive 1989, 'Should government reduce taxes or spend on social services?', *National Social Science Survey Report*, 1(5), 1–2.

Bean, Clive & Evans, Mariah 1989, 'Expanding university education', *National Social Science Survey Report*, 1(5), 12.

Becker, Gary 1964/1975, *Human capital: a theoretical and empirical analysis, with special reference to education*, New York: Columbia University Press.

Beilharz, Peter 1987, 'Reading politics: social theory and social policy', *Australian and New Zealand Journal of Sociology*, 23, 388–406.

Beilharz, Peter 1989, 'Social democracy and social justice', *The Australian and New Zealand Journal of Sociology*, 25, 85–99.

Beilharz, Peter 1993, 'Education and politics', *Meanjin*, 52, 589–592.

Beilharz, Peter 1994, *Transforming Labor: labour tradition and the labour decade in Australia*, Cambridge University Press.

Beilharz, Peter, Considine, Mark & Watts, Rob 1992, *Arguing about the welfare state: the Australian experience*, Sydney: Allen & Unwin.

Bennett, David 1982, 'Education: back to the drawing board', in Gareth Evans & John Reeves (eds), *Labor essays 1982: socialist principles and parliamentary government*, pp. 161–186. Melbourne: Drummond.

Bessant, Bob 1977, 'Robert Gordon Menzies and education in Australia', *Melbourne Studies in Education*, 75–101.

Bessant, Bob & Spaull, Andrew 1976, *Politics of schooling*, Melbourne: Pitman Pacific Books.

Blandy, Richard 1979, 'A liberal strategy for the reform of education and training in Australia', in Williams, Volume 2, Appendix F, pp. 143–173.

Blandy, Richard & Goldsworthy, Tony 1975, *Educational opportunity in South Australia*, Working Paper Series No. 21, Adelaide: National Institute of Labour Studies, Flinders University.

Blaug, Mark 1981, 'Can independent education be suppressed?', *Economic Affairs*, October, 30–37.

Boomer, Garth, 1986, *Towards a productive culture in schools: curriculum and the economy*, address to Federation of Parents and Citizens Associations of NSW, July, Commonwealth Schools Commission (CSC): Canberra.

Bosanquet, Nick 1983, *After the New Right*, London: Heinemann.

Boyd, William 1938, 'Education and citizenship', in Cunningham (ed.), 191–192.

Brennan, Geoffrey 1971, 'Fee abolition: an appraisal', *The Australian University*, 9, 81–149.

Brown, Nicholas 1995, *Governing prosperity*, Cambridge University Press.

Buchanan, James 1975, *The limits of liberty: between anarchy and Leviathan*, University of Chicago Press.

Buchanan, James 1976, 'School user taxes and economic efficiency', in West (ed.), pp. 116–120.

Buchanan, James & Devletoglou, Nicos 1970, *Academia in anarchy*, New York: Basic Books.

Buchanan, James & Tullock, Gordon 1965, *The calculus of consent: logical foundations of constitutional democracy*, Ann Arbor: Michigan Institute of Technology Press.

Buchanan, J.M. & Wagner, R.E. 1977, *Democracy in deficit*, New York: Academic Press.

Burchell, David 1995, 'The attributes of citizens: virtue, manners and the activity of citizenship', *Economy and Society*, 24, 540–558.

Burchell, Graham, Gordon, Colin & Miller, Peter (eds) 1991, *The Foucault effect: studies in governmentality*, London: Harvester Wheatsheaf.

Business Council of Australia (BCA) 1986, *Report on education*, Melbourne: BCA.

Butlin, N.G., Barnard, A. & Pincus, J.J. 1982, *Government and capitalism*, Sydney: George Allen & Unwin.

Button, James 1987, 'Education is about to lose an old guide', *The Age*, 21 October.

Caldwell, Brian 1993, *Decentralising the management of Australia's schools*, seminar paper to National Industry Education Forum, University of Melbourne.

Canberra Times (CT) 1985, 'Mrs Hawke sees the tragedy of children's TV', *Canberra Times*, 7 May.

Card, David & Krueger, Alan 1992, 'Does school quality matter? Returns to education and the characteristics of public schools in the United States', *Journal of Political Economy*, 100, 1–40.

Carey, Alex 1987, 'Conspiracy or groundswell?' in Ken Coghill (ed.), *The New Right's Australian fantasy*, pp. 3–19, Melbourne: Penguin.

Carlton, Jim 1985, 'Blueprint for a dynamic Australia', *The Bulletin*, 7 May.

Carmichael, Laurie 1989, 'Here comes the industrial revolution, again', *The Australian TAFE Teacher*, third quarter, 29–37.

Carmichael, Laurie, 1992, *The Australian Vocational Certificate Training System*, Canberra: National Board of Employment, Education and Training (NBEET).

Castles, Frank 1985, *The working class and welfare: reflections on the development of the welfare state in Australia and New Zealand, 1890–1980*, Wellington: Allen & Unwin.

Centre for Contemporary Cultural Studies (CCCS) 1981, *Unpopular education: schooling and social democracy in England since 1944*, London: Hutchinson.

Chapman, Bruce 1992, *AUSTUDY: towards a more flexible approach – an options paper*, Canberra: AGPS.

Chapman, Bruce 1996, 'The rationale for the Higher Education Contribution Scheme', *Australian Universities Review*, 39(1), 43–50.

Chipman, Lauchlan 1978, *Liberty, equality and unhappiness*, Sydney: The Centre for Independent Studies.

Chipman, Lauchlan 1980, 'Teachers and the tenure trap', *Quadrant*, December, 42–44.

Chipman, Lauchlan 1982, 'Stopping the rot in Australia's schools and colleges', *Quadrant*, October, 52–60.

Chipman, Lauchlan 1984, 'Failing Australia's children', *Quadrant*, January–February, 36–43.

Chipman, Lauchlan 1985, 'A national language(s) policy?', *Quadrant*, March, 16–17.

Clare, Ross & Johnston, Kaye 1993, *Education and training in the 1990s*, Economic

Planning Advisory Council (EPAC) Background Paper No. 31, Canberra: AGPS.

Cohen, David 1977, *Feeling free to learn: progressive education*, Sydney: Curriculum Resources International.

Committee for Economic Development (CED) 1985, *Investing in our children: business and the public schools*, New York: CED.

Committee for Economic Development of Australia (CEDA) 1985, *Education for development: the strategic issues forum report*, Melbourne: CEDA.

Commonwealth of Australia (CA) 1988, *Towards a fairer Australia: social justice under Labor*, Canberra: AGPS.

Commonwealth of Australia (CA) 1995, *Government response to the Civics Expert Group report*, Prime Minister's office, Canberra, 6 June.

Commonwealth Bureau of Census and Statistics (CBCS), undated, *Authorities of the Australian Government 1972–73*, Canberra: Government Printing Office.

Commonwealth of Australia (CBP), Commonwealth budget papers, various years, Canberra: AGPS.

Commonwealth Schools Commission (CSC) 1981, *Report for the triennium 1982–84*, Canberra: CSC.

Commonwealth Schools Commission (CSC) 1984, *Funding policies for Australian schools*, Canberra: CSC.

Commonwealth Tertiary Education Commission (CTEC) 1979, *Report for 1979–81 triennium, Volume 3*, Canberra: AGPS.

Commonwealth Tertiary Education Commission (CTEC) 1981, *Report for the 1982–84 triennium, Volume 1, Part 1*, Canberra: AGPS.

Commonwealth Tertiary Education Commission (CTEC) 1982, *Learning and earning: a study of education and employment opportunities for young people, Volume 1*, Canberra: AGPS.

Commonwealth Tertiary Education Commission (CTEC) 1984, *Report for the 1985–87 triennium, Volume 3, Part 3*, Canberra: AGPS.

Commonwealth Tertiary Education Commission (CTEC) 1986, *Review of efficiency and effectiveness in higher education*, Canberra: AGPS.

Commonwealth Tertiary Education Commission (CTEC) 1987, *Higher education: recommendations for 1988*, Canberra: AGPS.

Connell, R.W. 1993, *Schools and social justice*, Sydney: Pluto Press.

Connell, W.F. 1993, *Reshaping Australian education 1960–1985*, Melbourne: Australian Council of Educational Research.

Considine, Mark 1988, 'The corporate management framework as administrative science: a critique', *Australian Journal of Public Administration*, 47, 4–18.

Considine, Mark 1990, 'Managerialism strikes out', *Australian Journal of Public Administration*, 49, 166–178.

Conway, Ronald 1985, 'The new establishment in education', *ACES Review*, 12, 1–8.

Cooper, Lindsay 1989, 'Kelty speaks for teachers', VSTA *News*, 15 November, p. 3.

Cope, Bill & Kalantzis, Mary 1995, 'Pedagogy after pluralism: how multiculturalism can reconstruct the mainstream', *Education Links*, No. 51, 4–10.

Costello, Ray, 1973, 'Teachers back Karmel report', letter *Sydney Morning Herald*, 5 September.

Costello, Ray 1985, 'The world according to ACES', *The Victorian Teacher*, 2, April, 5–6.

Council of Australian Postgraduate Associations (CAPA) 1994, *Goodbye rhyme and reason*, Melbourne: CAPA.

Cox, Brian 1982, 'Subtle and sinister, this infiltration of our pupil's minds', *Daily Mail*, 21 June.

Crittenden, Brian 1988, 'Policy directions for Australian secondary schools: a critique of some prevalent assumptions', *Australian Journal of Education*, 32, 287–310.

Cunningham, K.S. (ed.) 1938, *Education for complete living*, Melbourne: Australian Council for Educational Research.

Davey, Patricia 1978, 'Financing of education', in Scotton & Ferber (eds), pp. 38–82.

Dawkins, John 1987a, *The challenge for higher education*, Canberra: AGPS.

Dawkins, John 1987b, *Higher education: a discussion paper* (the Green Paper), Canberra: AGPS.

Dawkins, John 1988, *Higher education: a policy statement* (the White Paper), Canberra: AGPS.

Dawkins, John & Holding, Clyde 1987a, *Skills for Australia*, Canberra: AGPS.

Dawkins, John & Holding, Clyde 1987b, *Strengthening Australia's schools*, Canberra: AGPS.

Denison, E.F. 1962, *The sources of economic growth in the United States and the alternatives before us*, New York: Committee for Economic Development.

Department of Education, Commonwealth of Australia (DE) 1986, *Selection for higher education*, Canberra: DE.

Department of Employment, Education and Training (DEET) 1988, *The Tertiary Education Assistance Scheme*, Canberra: AGPS.

Department of Employment, Education and Training (DEET) 1993, *National report on Australia's tertiary education sector*, Canberra: AGPS.

Department of Employment, Education and Training (DEET) 1994a, *Education participation rates*, Canberra: DEET.

Department of Employment, Education and Training (DEET) 1994b, 'Young people's attitudes to post-compulsory education and training, 1994', *Higher Education Series*, No. 11, Canberra: DEET

Department of Employment, Education and Training (DEET) 1995a, 'Comparative analysis of costs of postgraduate courses for overseas students in Australia, New Zealand, the UK, Canada and the US', *Higher Education Series*, No. 12, Canberra: DEET.

Department of Employment, Education and Training (DEET) 1995b, 'Fee-paying postgraduate students, 1993', *Higher Education Series*, No. 23, Canberra: DEET.

Department of Employment, Education and Training (DEET) 1996a, *Selected higher education statistics*, Canberra: DEET.

Department of Employment, Education and Training (DEET) 1996b, *Selected higher education statistics*, Preliminary, Canberra: DEET.

Department of Employment, Education and Training (DEET) 1996c, *Selected higher education finance statistics*, Canberra: DEET.

Department of Industry, Technology and Commerce (DITC) 1989, data on international science and technology indicators, Canberra: DITC.

Desai, Radhika 1994, 'Second-hand dealers in ideas: think-tanks and the Thatcher hegemony', *New Left Review*, 203, 27–62.

Deveson, Ivan, 1990a and 1990b, *Training costs of award restructuring*, Volumes 1 and 2, Canberra: AGPS.

Domberger, Simon & Piggott, John 1986, 'Privatisatioṇ policies and public enterprise: a survey', *The Economic Record*, 62, 145–162.

Doughney, Jamie 1992, 'Private commercial vocational training in Victoria – a case for tighter regulation', *Job Watch Working Papers*, No. 92/1.

Dow, Sheila 1990, 'Beyond dualism', *Cambridge Journal of Economics*, 14, 143–157.

Duncan, Tim 1984, 'New Right crusaders challenge the Labor line', *The Bulletin*, 2 October.

Duncan, Tim 1987, 'Business steps in to help mould the class of '88', *Business Review Weekly*, 15 May.

Dusevic, Tom 1990, 'The ideas factories', *Australian Financial Review*, 25 May.

Dwyer, Michael 1992, 'Call to change approach to Australian educational exports', *Australian Financial Review*, 18 February.

Economic Planning Advisory Council (EPAC) 1986, *Human capital and productivity growth*, EPAC Council Paper No. 15, Canberra: AGPS.

Edwards, T. & Whitty, G. 1994 'Parental choice and school autonomy: the English experience', *Unicorn*, 20, 25–34.

Esping-Andersen, G. 1983, 'The incompatibilities of the welfare state', *Thesis Eleven*, 7, 42–53.

Evans, Gareth 1977, *Labor and the constitution*, Melbourne: Heinemann.

Evatt, H.V. 1942, *Australian Labor leader*, Sydney: Angus & Robertson.

Fane, George 1984, *Education policy in Australia*, EPAC Discussion Paper No. 85/ 08, Canberra: EPAC.

Finn, Brian, 1991, *Young people's participation in post compulsory education and training*, Canberra: AGPS.

Fitzclarence, Lindsay & Kenway, Jane 1993, 'Education and social justice in the postmodern age', in Lingard et al (eds), pp. 90–105.

Fitzgerald, Ron 1976, *Poverty and education in Australia*, fifth main report of the Commission of Inquiry into Poverty, Canberra: AGPS.

Fligstein, Neil 1990, *The transformation of corporate control*, Cambridge: Harvard University Press.

Fomin, Feodora & Teese, Richard 1981, 'Public finance to private schools: the argument of the Karmel report and later policy', *Melbourne Working Papers*, pp. 184–200, Melbourne: University of Melbourne

Foster, R.A. & Stewart, S.E. 1991, *Australian economic statistics, 1949–50 to 1989–90*, Sydney: Reserve Bank.

Foucault, Michel 1988, *Politics, philosophy, culture: interviews and other writings, 1977–1984*, New York: Routledge.

Fraser, Barry & Kennedy, Kerry 1990, 'A retrospective account of the Transition Education Program', *Australian Educational Researcher*, 17, 25–46.

Friedman, Milton 1962, *Capitalism and freedom*, University of Chicago Press.

Friedman, Milton 1976, 'Are externalities relevant?' in E.G. West (ed.), pp. 92–93.

Friedman, Milton & Friedman, Rose 1980, *Free to Choose*, Melbourne: Macmillan.

Friedman, Milton & Friedman, Rose 1984, *The tyranny of the status quo*, San Diego: Harcourt Brace Jovanovic.

Galeotti, Anna Elisabetta 1987, 'Individualism, social rules, tradition: the case of Friedrich A. Hayek', *Political Theory*, 15, 163–181.

Gamble, Andrew 1986, 'The Political Economy of Freedom', in Ruth Levitas (ed.), *The ideology of the New Right*, pp. 25–54, Cambridge: Polity Press.

Gamble, Andrew 1988, *The free economy and the strong state: The politics of Thatcherism*, Houndmills: Macmillan.

Gamble, Andrew 1995, 'The crisis of conservatism', *New Left Review*, 214, 3–25.

Gardner, David 1983, *A nation at risk*, Washington: U.S. Department of Education.

Gawenda, Michael 1996, 'Michael Gawenda', *The Age*, 28 October 1996.

Giddens, Anthony 1994, *Beyond left and right: the future of radical politics*, Stanford University Press.

Gittins, Ross 1986, 'EPAC gives a lesson that educators should heed', *The Sydney Morning Herald*, 19 February.

Glass, G.V. and Cahen, L.S., Smith, M.L. & Filby, N.N. 1982, *School class size: research and policy*, Beverley Hills: Sage.

Golding, Barry, Marginson, Simon & Pascoe, Robert 1996, *Changing context, moving skills*, Canberra: NBEET.

Gottliebsen, Robert 1985, 'Six of the best', *Business Review Weekly*, 25 January.

Gramsci, Antonio 1971, *Selections from the prison notebooks*, Quintin Hoare & Geoffrey Nowell Smith (eds and transl.), New York: International Publishers.

Gray, John 1986, *Liberalism*, Milton Keynes: Open University Press.

Hall, Alan 1965, 'Politics and resources for tertiary education, Part 1', in John Wilkes (ed.), *Tertiary education in Australia*, Sydney: Angus & Robertson, pp. 132–147 and Statistical Appendix.

Hall, Stuart 1984, 'The rise of the representative/interventionist state 1880s–1920s' in Gregor McLennan, David Held and Stuart Hall (eds), *State and society in contemporary Britain*, pp. 7–49, Cambridge: Polity Press.

Hall, Stuart 1988a, 'Thatcher's lessons', *Marxism Today*, March.

Hall, Stuart 1988b, 'The toad in the garden: Thatcherism among the theorists', and 'Discussion', in Gary Nelson & Lawrence Grossberg (eds), *Marxism and the interpretation of culture*, pp. 35–73, University of Illinois.

Hall, Stuart 1991, 'And not a shot fired', *Marxism Today*, December.

Hannan, Bill 1985, *Democratic curriculum*, Sydney: George Allen & Unwin.

Hansen, I.V. 1971, *Not free nor secular*, Oxford University Press.

Hanushek, Eric 1981, 'Throwing money at schools', *Journal of Policy Analysis and Management*, 1, 19–41.

Hanushek, Eric 1986, 'The economics of schooling: production and efficiency in public schools', *Journal of Economic Literature*, 24, 1141–1177.

Hanushek, Eric 1989, 'The impact of differential expenditures on school performance', *Educational Researcher*, 18(4), 45–51 and 62.

Harris, Kevin 1994, 'Economic policy and public education in Australia: a response to Simon Marginson', *Melbourne Studies in Education*, pp. 168–177, Melbourne: LaTrobe University Press.

Hart, F.W. 1938a, 'Education for citizenship', in Cunningham (ed.), pp. 193–198.

Hart, F.W. 1938b, 'Criticisms of education in Australia', in Cunningham (ed.), pp. 661–664.

Hawke, Bob 1984, 'Speech to PEP conference', *Commonwealth Record*, 3–9 September, pp. 1705–1708.

Hayek, Friedrich A. 1944, *The road to serfdom*, London: Routledge and Kegan Paul.

Hayek, Friedrich A. 1948a, ' "Free" enterprise and competitive order', in Hayek 1948c, pp. 107–118.

Hayek, Friedrich A. 1948b, 'Economics and knowledge', in Hayek 1948c, pp. 33–56.

Hayek, Friedrich A. 1948c, *Individualism and economic order*, University of Chicago Press.

Hayek, F.A., 1948d, 'Individualism: true and false', in Hayek 1948c, pp. 1–32.

Hayek, Friedrich A. 1960, *The Constitution of Liberty*, London: Routledge and Kegan Paul.

Hayek, Friedrich A. 1967a, 'What is "social" – what does it mean?' in Hayek 1967e, pp. 237–247.

Hayek, Friedrich A. 1967b, 'The principles of a liberal social order', in Hayek 1967e, pp. 160–177.

Hayek, Friedrich A. 1967c, 'Unions, inflation and profits', in Hayek 1967e, pp. 280–294.

Hayek, Friedrich A. 1967d, 'The results of human action but not of human design', in Hayek 1967e, pp. 96–105.

Hayek, Friedrich A. 1967e, *Studies in philosophy, politics and economics*, London: Routledge and Kegan Paul.

Hayek, Friedrich A. 1976, *Law, legislation and liberty. Volume 2: the mirage of social justice*, London: Routledge and Kegan Paul.

Hayek, Friedrich A. 1978a, 'Competition as a discovery procedure', in Hayek 1978d, pp. 179–190.

Hayek, Friedrich A. 1978b, 'Liberalism', in Hayek 1978d, pp. 119–151.

Hayek, Friedrich A. 1978c, 'The campaign against Keynesian inflation', in Hayek 1978e, pp. 191–231.

Hayek, Friedrich A. 1978d, *New studies in philosophy, politics, economics and the history of ideas*, University of Chicago Press.

Hayek, Friedrich A. 1979a, *Law, legislation and liberty. Volume 3: the political order of a free people*, London: Routledge and Kegan Paul.

Hayek, Friedrich A. 1979b, *Social justice, socialism and democracy*, Sydney: Centre for Independent Studies.

Heald, David 1983, *Public expenditure*, Oxford: Martin Robertson.

Hegel, G.W.F. 1975, *Logic* (part I of the *Encyclopedia of the philosophical sciences*), translated by William Wallace, Oxford University Press [first published 1830, this translation 1873].

Henry, Miriam & Taylor, Sandra 1993, 'Gender equity and economic rationalism: an uneasy alliance' in Lingard et al, pp. 153–175.

Herald, Melbourne 1988, 'What's wrong with education: the bosses spell it out', *The Herald*, 13 September.

Hill, Peter & Russell, Jean 1994, *Resource levels for government primary schools*, Melbourne: University of Melbourne Faculty of Education.

Hindess, Barry 1987, *Freedom, equality and the market*, London: Tavistock Publications.

Hirsch, Fred 1976, *Social limits to growth*, Cambridge, MASS.: Harvard University Press.

Hobbes, Thomas 1651/1968, *Leviathan*, Harmondsworth: Penguin.

Hogan, David 1996, *Framing civics: liberal democratic education and citizenship*, paper commisioned by the Curriculum Corporation, Hobart: University of Tasmania.

Horobin, G.W. & Smyth, R.L. 1960/1972, 'The economics of education: a comment', in Mark Blaug (ed.), *Economics of education 2*, pp. 373–378, Harmondsworth: Penguin.

Howard, Michael 1989, *The big chill? Trends in the level and composition of public expenditure in Australia*, Sydney: University of NSW Public Sector Research Centre.

Hunt, Ian 1991, 'Freedom and its conditions', *Australasian Journal of Philosophy*, 69, 288–301.

Hunter, Ian 1993a, 'Culture, bureaucracy and the history of popular education', in Meredyth & Tyler (eds), pp. 11–34.

Hunter, Ian 1993b, 'The Pastoral Bureaucracy: towards a less principled understanding of state education', in Meredyth & Tyler (eds), pp. 237–239.

Hunter, Ian 1994, *Rethinking the school*, Sydney: Allen & Unwin.

Husen, Torsten 1979, *The school in question*, Oxford University Press.

Husen, Torsten 1985, 'The school in the achievement society: crisis and reform', *Phi Delta Kappan*, February, 398–402.

Hywood, Gregory 1985, 'Fees defeat pointer to ALP debate', *Australian Financial Review*, 27 March.

Institute of Public Affairs (IPA) 1987, *Facts*, December–February, Melbourne: IPA.

Institute of Public Affairs (IPA) 1990, 'Efficiency of States' spending', in *Background papers on the public sector*, EPAC Background Paper No. 7, Canberra: AGPS.

Jackson, Kim 1985, *Commonwealth involvement in education*, Basic Paper No. 2, Canberra: Commonwealth Parliament Legislative Research Service.

Jamrozik, Adam 1983, 'Universality and selectivity: social welfare in a market economy', in Adam Graycar (ed.), *Retreat from the welfare state*, pp. 171–202, Sydney: George Allen & Unwin.

Jay, Christopher 1986a, 'New Right policy moves out of the politicians' hands', *Australian Financial Review*, 11 February.

Jay, Christopher 1986b, 'Economic think tank is growing up', *Australian Financial Review*, 13 February.

Jessop, Bob, Bonnett, Kevin, Bromley, Simon, & Ling, Tom 1984, 'Authoritarian populism: two nations and Thatcherism', *New Left Review*, September–October, 32–60.

Johnston, Ken 1993, 'Inequality and educational reform: lessons from the disadvantaged schools project', in Lingard et al, pp. 106–119.

Joint Standing Committee on Migration (JSCM) 1994, *Australians all: enhancing Australian citizenship*, Canberra: AGPS.

Jonathon, Ruth 1990, 'State education service or prisoner's dilemma: the hidden hand as a source of education policy', *British Journal of Educational Studies*, 38, 116–132.

Jones, Ken 1989, *Right turn: the conservative revolution in education*, London: Hutchinson Radius.

Joseph, Keith & Sumption, Jonathon 1979, *Equality*, London: John Murray.

Kangan, M. 1974, *Technical and Further Education in Australia: First report*, Canberra: AGPS.

Kapferer, Judith 1989, 'Schools for the state: the complementarity of public and private education', in S. Walker and L. Barton (eds), *Politics and the processes of schooling*, pp. 100–125, Milton Keynes: Open University Press.

Karmel, Peter 1962, *Some economic aspects of education*, Melbourne: F.W. Cheshire.

Karmel, Peter 1966, 'Some arithmetic of education', *Melbourne Studies in Education*, 3–34.

Karmel, Peter 1973, *Schools in Australia*, report of the Interim Committee for the Australian Schools Commission, Canberra: AGPS.

Karmel, Peter 1983, 'Learning and earning – education and employment as activities for youth', *Australian Journal of Education*, 27, 260–273.

Karmel, Peter 1985, *Quality of education in Australia*, report of the Quality of Education Review Committee, Canberra: AGPS.

Karmel, Peter 1987, 'Notes on equality of opportunity: a postscript to "Quality and equality in education" ', *Australian Journal of Education*, 31, 317–319.

Keating, Paul 1992, *A national employment and training plan for young Australians*, Canberra: AGPS.

Keating, Paul 1995, *Advancing Australia*, Sydney: Big Picture Publications.

Keeves, J.P., Bourke, S.F., Lewis, R. & Ross, K. 1976, *Australian studies in school performance. Volume 1, literacy and numeracy in Australian schools: a first report*, Canberra: AGPS.

Kelly, Paul 1992, *The end of certainty: the story of the 1980s*, Sydney: Allen & Unwin.

Kennedy, Kerry 1988, 'The policy context of curriculum reform in Australia in the 1980s', *Australian Journal of Education*, 32, 357–374.

Kennedy, Kerry 1995, 'Conflicting conceptions of citizenship and their relvance to the school curriculum', in Print (ed.), pp. 13–18.

Kenway, Jane 1993, 'Marketing education in the post-modern age', in association with Chris Bigum & Lindsay Fitzclarence, in Jane Kenway (ed.), *Marketing education: some critical issues*, pp. 1–62, Geelong: Deakin University.

Kerr, Roger 1992, *Morality, capitalism and democracy*, speech to the Auckland Business Forum, 7 December.

Keynes, John Maynard 1936, *The general theory of employment, interest and money*, London: Macmillan.

Kitson, Jill 1990, 'A conversation with Roger Scruton', *Quadrant*, October, 10–14.

Knight, John, Lingard, Bob & Porter, Paige 1993, 'Restructuring schooling towards the 1990s', in Lingard et al, pp. 2–22.

Kramer, Leonie 1989, 'Principles of education reform for Australia', *Newsweekly*, 15 February.

Kukathas, Chandran 1989, *Hayek and modern liberalism*, Oxford: Clarendon Press.

Langmore, John 1987, *Constructing and restructuring Australia's public infrastructure*, report of the House of Representatives Standing Committee on Transport, Communications and Infrastructure, Canberra: AGPS.

Langmore, John 1992, *Economic policy making from the inside: how policy is decided*, conference of the Economic Society of Australia, Melbourne: University of Melbourne, 9 July.

Laurie, Victoria 1992, 'Learning to export, by degree', *The Bulletin*, 14 April.

Levitas, Ruth 1986, 'Introduction: ideology and the New Right', in Ruth Levitas (ed.), *The ideology of the New Right*, pp. 1–24, Cambridge: Polity Press.

Liberal and National Parties (LNP) 1996, *Schools and TAFE*, election policy, Melbourne: LNP.

Lingard, Bob 1993, 'Corporate federalism: the emerging approach to policy making for Australian schools', in Lingard et al, pp. 24–35.

Lingard, Bob, Knight, John & Porter, Paige (eds) 1993, *Schooling reform in hard times*, London: The Falmer Press.

Lingard, Bob, Porter, Paige, Bartlett, Leo & Knight, John 1995, 'Federal/State mediations in the Australian national education agenda: from the AEC to

MCEETYA 1987–93', *Australian Journal of Education*, 39, 41–66.

Lister, Ruth 1995, 'Dilemmas in engendering citizenship', *Economy and Society*, 24, 1–40.

Little, Graeme 1978, 'Standards', *English in Australia*, 46.

Little, Graeme 1985, unpublished paper on standards and curriculum, Canberra: Curriculum Development Centre.

Lukes, Steven 1973, *Individualism*, Oxford: Basil Blackwell.

Lyotard, Jean-Francois 1984, *The post-modern condition: a report on knowledge*, Geoffrey Bennington & Brian Massumi (transl.), Minneapolis: University of Minnesota Press.

Macintyre, Stuart 1986, *The Oxford History of Australia: Volume 4, 1901–1942*, Melbourne: Oxford University Press.

Macintyre, Stuart 1990, *Exploring the cultural and educational impediments to Australia becoming a "clever country"*, Spring Lecture Series, University of Melbourne: Centre for the Study of Higher Education.

Macintyre, Stuart 1994, *Whereas the people . . . Civics and citizenship education*, report of the Civics Expert Group, Canberra: AGPS.

Macintyre, Stuart 1995, 'Teaching citizenship', in *Melbourne Studies in Education*, 36(2), 7–20.

Macintyre, Stuart 1996, 'Civics and citizenship education and the teaching of history' *Unicorn*, 22, 59–63.

MacMillan, Warwick 1985, 'Think tanks and the New Right offensive', *Tribune*, 23 October.

MacPhee, Ian 1982, in House of Representatives *Hansard*, 6 May.

Macpherson, C.B. 1968, 'Introduction' to Hobbes, pp. 9–64.

Madaus, George 1985, 'Test scores as administrative mechanisms in educational policy', *Phi Delta Kappan*, May, 611–615.

Maglen, Leo 1990, 'Challenging the human capital orthodoxy: the education-productivity link re-examined', *The Economic Record*, 66, 281–294.

Maglen, Leo, McKenzie, Phillip, Burke, Gerald & McGaw, Barry 1994, *Investment in education and training*, prepared for the Business Council of Australia summit on Investing in Australia's future, Sydney, 9–10 March.

Mandel, Ernst 1978, *The second slump*, Jon Rothschild (transl.), London: New Left Books.

Marginson, Simon 1993a, *Education and public policy in Australia*, Melbourne: Cambridge University Press.

Marginson, Simon 1993b, *Arts, science and work: work related skills and the generalist courses in higher education*, Canberra: AGPS.

Marginson, Simon 1995a, 'The decline in the standing of educational credentials in Australia', *Australian Journal of Education*, 39, 67–76.

Marginson, Simon 1995b, 'Markets in education: a theoretical note', *Australian Journal of Education* 39, 294–312.

Marginson, Simon 1996a, 'Markets in education: the formation of markets in Australian education since 1975', PhD thesis, University of Melbourne.

Marginson, Simon 1996b, 'Competition in higher education in the post-Hilmer era', *Australian Quarterly*, 68(4), 23–35.

Marginson, Simon 1996c, 'Competition and control in education', draft book manuscript.

Marginson, Simon 1997a, 'Rethinking Ian Hunter', *Thesis Eleven*, (in press).

Marginson, Simon 1997b, 'Imagining Ivy: Government and private universities in Australia since 1985' *Comparative Education Review*, (in press).

Marginson, Simon 1997c, 'Investment in the self: the reform of student financing in Australia', *Studies in Higher Education,* (in press).

Marginson, Simon 1997d, *Markets in education*, Sydney: Allen & Unwin.

Marginson, Simon & McCulloch, Grahame 1985, *Why would fees increase inequality?* pamphlet, Canberra: Higher Education Round Table.

Marshall, Alfred 1890/1920, *Principles of economics*, London: Macmillan and Company.

Marshall, T.H. 1950, *Citizenship and social class and other essays*, Cambridge University Press.

Martin, Leslie 1964, *Tertiary education in Australia*, Volume 1, report of the Committee on the Future of Tertiary Education in Australia, Melbourne: Australian Universities Commission.

Martin, Lin 1995, *Postgraduate fees*, paper for a conference on the funding of higher education, Sydney, 24–25 July.

Marx, Karl 1973, *Grundrisse: introduction to the critique of political economy*, Martin Nicolaus (transl.), Harmondsworth: Penguin Books.

Maslen, Geoff 1985, 'The reformers and schools must speak out with vigour', *The Age*, 26 February.

Matthews, J.K. & Fitzgerald, R.T. 1975, 'Educational policy and political platform: the Australian Labor Government', *Australian Education Review 7*.

Mayer, Eric 1992, *Employment related key competencies*, Melbourne: Mayer Committee.

McCallum, David 1990, *The social production of merit: education, psychology and politics in Australia 1900–1950*, London: The Falmer Press.

McKinnon, Ken 1981, transcript of discussion between past and present Schools Commissioners and the ALP Education Committee, Canberra.

McKinnon, Ken 1982, 'The Schools Commission: policies and politics in a statutory body', in Grant Harman & Don Smart (eds), *Federal intervention in Australian education*, Melbourne: Georgian House.

Meredyth, Denise 1993, 'Marking the immeasurable: debates on ASAT', in Meredyth & Tyler (eds), pp. 207–236.

Meredyth, Denise & Deborah Tyler (eds) 1993, *Child and citizen: genealogies of schooling and subjectivity*, Brisbane: Griffith University Institute for Cultural Policy Studies.

Miller, Peter & Rose, Nikolas 1990, 'Governing economic life', *Economy and Society 19*, 1–31.

Mills, Steven 1986, 'Most Australians prefer private schools for their children: poll', *The Age*, 9 September.

Moore, Bette & Carpenter, Gary 1987, 'Main players', in Ken Coghill (ed.), *The New Right's Australian fantasy*, pp. 145–160, Melbourne: Penguin.

Murray, Keith 1957, *Report of the Committee on Australian Universities*, Canberra: Commonwealth Government Printer.

Mushkin, Selma 1966, 'Resource requirements and educational obsolescence', in E.A.G. Robinson & J.E. Vaizey (eds), *The economics of education, proceedings of a conference held by the International Economic Association*, pp. 463–478, London: Macmillan.

National Board of Employment, Education and Training (NBEET) 1995, *Efficiency and equity in education policy: a statistical overview of Australian education and training*, Canberra: NBEET.

National Centre for Vocational Education Research (NCVER) 1996, *Selected vocational education and training statistics*, Leabrook: NCVER.

National Social Science Survey (NSSS) 1988, Canberra: Australian National University.

Norris, Nigel 1991, 'The trouble with competence', *Cambridge Journal of Education*, 21, 331–341.

O'Brien, John 1987, *A divided unity! Politics of NSW teacher militancy since 1945*, Sydney: Allen & Unwin.

Organisation for Economic Co-operation and Development (OECD) 1977, *Australia: transition from school to work or further study*, Paris: OECD.

Organisation for Economic Co-operation and Development (OECD) 1981a, *The welfare state in crisis*, Paris: OECD.

Organisation for Economic Co-operation and Development (OECD) 1981b, *Educational equality and social justice: a preliminary statement of issues and suggestions for future work*, Paris: OECD.

Organisation for Economic Co-operation and Development (OECD) 1983, *Policies for Higher Education in the 1980s*, Paris: OECD.

Organisation for Economic Co-operation and Development (OECD) 1984, *Review of youth policies in Australia*, Paris: OECD.

Organisation for Economic Co-operation and Development (OECD) 1985, *Education in modern society*, Paris: OECD.

Organisation for Economic Co-operation and Development (OECD) 1986, *Education and structural adjustment*, note by the OECD Secretariat, Paris: OECD.

Organisation for Economic Co-operation and Development (OECD) 1987a, *Structural adjustment and economic performance*, Paris: OECD.

Organisation for Economic Co-operation and Development (OECD) 1987b, *The control and management of government expenditure*, Paris: OECD.

Organisation for Economic Co-operation and Development (OECD) 1989, *Education and the economy in a changing society*, Paris: OECD.

Organisation for Economic Co-operation and Development (OECD) 1990a, *Financing higher education*, Paris: OECD.

Organisation for Economic Co-operation and Development (OECD) 1990b, *Public management developments: survey*, Paris: OECD.

Organisation for Economic Co-operation and Development (OECD) 1991, *OECD Economic Outlook*, 50.

Organisation for Economic Co-operation and Development (OECD) 1993, *OECD contribution: background report*, OECD conference on 'The transition from elite to mass higher education', Sydney, Paris: OECD.

Organisation for Economic Co-operation and Development (OECD) 1994, *Employment outlook*, July.

Organisation for Economic Cooperation and Development (OECD) 1996, *Education at a glance*, Paris: OECD.

Painter, Joanne 1994, 'Government rejects claim on big classes', *The Age*, 26 July.

Papadakis, Elim 1990a, 'Attitudes to state and private welfare: analysis of results from a national survey, *SPRC Reports and Proceedings 88*, Sydney: University of NSW Social Policy Research Centre.

Papadakis, Elim 1990b, 'Privatisation and the welfare state', in Barry Hindess (ed.), *Reactions to the Right*, pp. 99–124, London, Routledge.

Papadopoulos, George 1988, 'Education: the search for a new consensus', *OECD Observer* 154, 4–8.

Papadopoulos, George 1991, 'An educational agenda for the 1990s', *OECD Observer* 168, 36–38.

Parish, Ross 1987, 'Education', in Centre for Policy Studies, *Spending and taxing*, pp. 90–118, Sydney: Allen & Unwin.

Parkin, Andrew 1984, ' "Back to basics" and the politics of education: minimum competency testing in Australia and the United States', *Politics*, 19(2), November, 54–70.

Partington, Geoffrey 1982, 'Our ailing schools', *Quadrant*, August, 32–36.

Partington, Geoffrey 1983, '(Im)moral education in Australia', *Quadrant*, June, 18–24.

Partington, Geoffrey 1984, 'Opportunities more equal than others', *The Bulletin*, 30 October.

Partington, Geoffrey 1985, 'After the Sheridan affair: Australian education in 1985', *Quadrant*, June, 48–54.

Partridge, P.H. 1965, 'Tertiary education – society and the future', in John Wilkes (ed.), *Tertiary education in Australia*, pp. 3–30, Sydney: Angus and Robertson.

Partridge, P.H. 1979, 'The universities and the democratisation of higher education', *The defence of excellence in Australian universities*, University of Adelaide, pp. 10–19.

Pascoe, Susan 1996, 'Civics and citizenship education: the Australian context', *Unicorn* 22, 18–29.

Perkins, D. & Salomon, G. 1989, 'Are cognitive skills context-bound?', *Educational Researcher* 18, 16–25.

Phillips, Harry 1995, 'The ideals of citizenship: perceptions of Western Australian youth', in Print (ed.), pp. 19–24.

Pope, David 1989, 'The relevance of human capital', in David Pope & Lee Alston (eds), *Australia's greatest asset: human resources in the nineteenth and twentieth centuries*, pp. 2–35, Sydney: The Federation Press.

Porter, Michael 1988, 'Tertiary education', in Centre for Policy Studies, *Spending and taxing II: taking stock* pp. 119–137, Sydney: Allen & Unwin.

Praetz, Helen 1983, 'The non-government sector in Australian education' in Ron Browne & Lois Foster (eds), *Sociology of Education*, pp. 34–46, Melbourne: Macmillan.

Print, Murray (ed.) 1995, *Civics and citizenship education: issues from practice and research*, Canberra: Australian Curriculum Studies Association.

Print, Murray 1995, 'Research on political literacy as a basis for civics education in schools', in Print (ed.), pp. 25–38.

Priorities Review Staff (PRS) 1973, *Interim report on goals and strategies*, Canberra: Commonwealth Parliament.

Pusey, Michael 1991, *Economic Rationalism in Canberra*, Melbourne: Cambridge University Press.

Ramsey, Alan 1996, 'Replay of '88 to haunt Howard', *Sydney Morning Herald*, 2 November.

Reisman, David 1990, *The political economy of James Buchanan*, Houndmills: Macmillan.

Richards, Christopher 1994, 'Government schools fail confidence test', *The Age*, 2 August.

Richards, Mike 1991, 'Cutting costs without cutting quality: restructuring Tasmanian education', *Education Monitor* 2(2), 5–8.

Rizvi, Fazal 1993, 'Multiculturalism, social justice and the restructuring of the Australian state', in Lingard et al, pp. 120–138.

Robbins, Lord 1963, *Higher education*, report of the Committee on Higher Education, London: Her Majesty's Stationery Office.

Robinson, E.A.G. & Vaizey, J.E. 1966, *The economics of education*, London: Macmillan.

Roper, Tom 1970, *The myth of equality*, Melbourne: National Union of Australian University Students.

Rorty, Richard 1983, 'Post-modernist bourgeois liberalism', *The Journal of Philosophy* 80, 583–589.

Rose, Nikolas 1990, *Governing the soul*, London: Routledge.

Rose, Nikolas 1993, 'Government, authority and expertise in advanced liberalism', *Economy and Society* 22, 283–300.

Rose, Nikolas & Miller, Peter 1992, 'Political power beyond the state: problematics of government', *British Journal of Sociology* 43, 173–205.

Ryan, Denise 1994, 'Class sizes over 25 on the rise', *The Sunday Age*, 16 October.

Ryan, Peter 1986, 'Teaching now and then', *The Age*, 6 September.

Salganik, Laura Hersh 1985, 'Why testing reforms are so popular and how they are changing education', *Phi Delta Kappan*, May, 607–610.

Salvaris, Michael 1995, *Discussion paper on a system of national citizenship indicators*, Senate Legal and Constitutional References Committee, Canberra: Commonwealth Parliament.

Saunders, Cheryl 1996, 'Challenges for citizenship', *Unicorn* 22, 30–34.

Sawer, Marian 1982, *Australia and the new right*, Sydney: George Allen & Unwin.

Schools Commission (SC) 1975, *Report for the triennium 1976–78*, Canberra: AGPS.

Schools Commission (SC) 1978, *Report for the triennium 1979–81*, Canberra: AGPS.

Schultz, Theodore 1960, 'Capital formation by education', *Journal of Political Economy* 68, 571–583.

Schultz, Theodore 1961, 'Investment in human capital', *American Economic Review* 51, 1–17.

Scotton, R.B. 1978, 'Public expenditures and social policy', in Scotton & Ferber (eds), pp. 1–34.

Scotton, R.B. & Ferber, Helen (eds) 1978, *Public expenditures and social policy in Australia: Volume 1, the Whitlam years 1972–5*, Melbourne: Longman Cheshire.

Scruton, Roger 1984, *The meaning of conservatism*, London: Macmillan.

Seddon, Terri 1994, *Schools of the future and schools of the past: assessing the institutional context of decentralised school management*, unpublished paper, Melbourne: Monash University Faculty of Education.

Selleck, R.J.W. 1982, *Frank Tate: a biography*, Melbourne University Press.

Senate Employment, Education and Training References Committee (SEETRC) 1995, *Report of the inquiry into accountability in Commonwealth-State funding arrangements in education*, Canberra: Senate Printing Unit.

Shapiro, Perry & Papadakis, Elim 1993, 'Citizen preference and public education in Australia: an analysis of interstate differences', *The Economic Record* 69, 149–162.

Sheehan, Paul 1985, 'The Right strikes back', *The Sydney Morning Herald*, 2 March.

..

Sheehan, Barry & Welch, Tony 1994, *International survey of the academic profession: Australia*, unpublished paper, University of Melbourne.

Sheridan, Greg 1983a, 'Buck-passing on campus: the new realities', *The Bulletin*, 22 February.

Sheridan, Greg 1983b, 'Education in chaos: your kids are losing', *The Bulletin*, 8 February.

Sheridan, Greg 1985a, 'The lies they tell our children', *The Australian*, 2 February.

Sheridan, Greg 1985b, 'Bread and circuses just not enough', *The Australian*, 9 February.

Sheridan, Greg 1985c, comments during the Australian Broadcasting Corporation program *Education Now*, 21 February.

Sheridan, Greg 1986, 'Just who are the New Right?', *The Australian*, 6 September.

Sheridan, Greg 1988a, 'The Samurai of Yoyogi', *The Australian*, 27 February.

Sheridan, Greg 1988b, 'The Taiwan secret', *The Australian*, 5 March.

Sheridan, Greg 1988c, 'Why our system is the worst in the world', *The Australian*, 26 March.

Slattery, Luke 1991, 'Government acts on malpractices in private colleges', *The Age*, 9 March.

Slaughter, Sheila 1993, *Professionals in a global economy: differentiation, market relations and reward structures – Australian cases*, draft paper, Tucson: University of Arizona.

Smart, Don 1978, *Federal aid to Australian schools*, Brisbane: University of Queensland Press.

Smith, Adam 1776/1979, *The wealth of nations*, Harmondsworth: Penguin.

Smith, Bruce 1991, 'Crime and the classics: the humanities and government in the nineteenth century Australian University', in Ian Hunter, Denise Meredyth, Bruce Smith & Geoff Stokes (eds), *Accounting for the humanities: the language of culture and the logic of government*, pp. 67–115, Brisbane: Griffith University Institute for Cultural Policy Studies.

Sociology Research Group, (SRG) 1979, 'Literacy and the schools: a political critique of the educational standards debate', *Melbourne Working Papers*, pp. 3–25.

Start, Brian 1989, 'Education – who runs the state system?', *Newsweekly*, 24 June.

Steering Committee NSW Labor Party (StC) 1987, *The New Right: a threat to democracy*, Sydney: Olde Caveman Reds.

Steketee, Mike 1985, 'The bovver boy now a tough time crusader', *Sydney Morning Herald*, 29 March.

Sweet, Richard 1979, *A labour market perspective on the basic standards debate*, Sydney: NSW Department of TAFE.

Sydney Morning Herald 1996, 'Why we must not lose our way on race', editorial *Sydney Morning Herald*, 2 November.

Tawney, R.H. 1938, *Equality*, London: George Allen & Unwin.

Teese, Richard 1981, 'The social function of private schools', *Melbourne Working Papers*, 2, pp. 94–141.

Teese, Richard 1984, 'The evolution of the Victorian secondary school system', in *Cultural politics: Melbourne Working Papers Series* 5, 95–167.

Teese, Richard 1985, 'Scholarships do not help create education equality', letter in *The Age*, 9 July.

Teese, Richard 1986, *Academic standards and Australian private schools*, unpublished paper, University of Melbourne Faculty of Education.

Teese, Richard 1989, 'Australian private schools, specialisation and curriculum conservation', *British Journal of Educational Studies* 37, 235–252.

Thomas, Julian 1994, 'The history of civics education in Australia', in Macintyre 1994, pp. 161–171.

Thompson, Graham 1984, ' "Rolling back" the state? Economic intervention 1975–82', in Gregor McLennan, David Held & Stuart Hall (eds), *State and society in contemporary Britain*, pp. 77–118, Cambridge: Polity Press.

Totaro, Paolo 1990, 'States say yes to national TAFE plan', *The Sydney Morning Herald*, 3 November.

Townley, Barbara 1993, 'Performance appraisal and the emergence of management', *Journal of Management Studies* 30, 221–238.

Transnational Cooperative (TNC) 1985, *The New Right: who? what? why?*, TNC Workers' Research Brief No. 13, Sydney: TNC.

United Kingdom, Government of (UK) 1985, *The development of higher education into the 1990s*, London: Her Majesty's Stationery Office (the Green Paper).

United Kingdom, Government of (UK) 1987, *Higher education: meeting the challenge*, London: Her Majesty's Stationery Office (the White Paper).

United Nations Educational, Scientific and Cultural Organisation (UNESCO) 1968, *Readings in the economics of education*, Paris: UNESCO.

Vaizey, John 1962, *The economics of education*, London: Faber & Faber.

Vanstone, Amanda 1996, *Higher education budget statement 1996*, Canberra: AGPS.

Vernon, James 1966, *Report of the committee of economic enquiry*, Volume 1, Canberra: Commonwealth Government Printer.

Victoria, Government of (VG) 1993, *Schools of the future, preliminary paper*, Melbourne: Directorate of School Education.

Walsh, Maximilian 1985, 'Assessing the benefits of Whitlam's educational whim', *The Sydney Morning Herald*, 18 March.

Wapshott, Nicholas & Brock, George 1983, *Thatcher*, London: Futura.

Watkins, Peter 1992, 'The transformation of educational administration: the hegemony of consent and the hegemony of coercion', *Australian Journal of Education* 36, 237–259.

Watts, Rob 1995, 'Educating for citizenship and employment in Australia', *Melbourne Studies in Education* 36(2), 83–106.

West, E.G. (ed.) 1976, *Non-public school aid: the law, economics and politics of American education*, Lexington: Lexington Books.

West, E.G. 1965, *Education and the state*, London: Institute of Economic Affairs.

West, E.G. 1967, 'The political economy of American public school legislation', *Journal of Law and Economics*, October, 101–128.

West, E.G. 1976, 'An economic analysis of the law and politics of non-public school "aid" ', in E.G. West (ed.), pp. 1–27.

Wheelwright, Ted (1962/1974, 'Costs, returns and investment in education', in E.L. Wheelwright (ed.), *Radical Political Economy*, pp. 161–71, Melbourne: Australian and New Zealand Book Company.

White, Doug 1972, 'Education and capitalism', in John Playford & Douglas Kirsner (eds), *Australian capitalism: towards a socialist critique*, pp. 219–247, Harmondsworth: Penguin.

White, Doug 1973, 'Create your own compliance: the Karmel prospect', *Arena*, 32–33, 35–48.

White, Doug 1987, 'Introduction', in Doug White (ed.), *Education and the state:*

Federal involvement in educational policy development, pp. 3–37, Geelong: Deakin University.

Whitlam, Gough 1975, *The road to reform: Labor in government*, University of Melbourne ALP Club.

Whitlam, Gough 1985, *The Whitlam Government 1972–1975*, Melbourne: Penguin.

Whitwell, Greg 1990, 'The triumph of economic rationalism: Treasury and the market economy', *Journal of Australian Public Administration* 49, 124–140.

Wilenski, Peter 1983, 'Reform and its implementation: the Whitlam years in retrospect', in *Labor essays 1983: policies and programs for the Labor Government*, pp. 40–63, Melbourne: Drummond.

Wilenski, Peter 1982, 'Small government and social equity', *Politics* 18, 7–25. In Glen Withers (ed). *Bigger or smaller government?* Canberra: Australian National University.

Wilenski, Peter 1986, *Public power and public administration*, Sydney: Hale and Iremonger.

Williams, Bruce 1979, *Education, training and employment*, report of the Committee of Inquiry into Education and Training, Canberra: AGPS.

Williams, Gareth 1992, *Changing patterns of finance in higher education*, Buckingham: Open University Press.

Williams, Pamela 1987, 'New Right exerts its power on liberals', *Australian Financial Review*, 17 December.

Williams, Ross 1983, *Interaction between government and private outlays: education in Australia, 1949–50 to 1981–82*, Discussion Paper No. 79, Canberra: Australian National University Centre for Economic Policy Research.

Williams, Ross 1984, *The economic determinants of private schooling in Australia*, Discussion Paper No. 94, Canberra: Australian National University Centre for Economic Policy Research.

Williams, Trevor, Long, Michael, Carpenter, Peter & Hayden, Martin 1993, *Entering higher education in the 1980s*, Melbourne: Australian Council for Educational Research.

Wiseman, J. 1959/1972, 'Vouchers for education', in Mark Blaug (ed.), *Economics of education 2*, pp. 360–372, Harmondsworth: Penguin.

Woods, Davina 1996, 'Aboriginality, citizenship and the curriculum: a response to Stuart Macintyre's "Diversity, citizenship and the curriculum" ', in Kerry Kennedy (ed.), *New challenges for civics and citizenship education*, pp. 32–36, Canberra: Australian Curriculum Studies Association.

Wran, Neville 1988, *Report of the Committee on higher education funding*, Canberra: DEET.

Yates, Lyn 1993, *The education of girls*, Hawthorn: Australian Council of Educational Research.

Young, R.E. 1983, 'The controlling curriculum and the practical ideology of teachers', in Ron Browne & Lois Foster (eds), *Sociology of education*, pp. 161–174, Melbourne: Macmillan.

Index

Lyotard, Jean–Francois 5–6, 153, 178, 203

Mabo, Eddie 252–3
Macintyre report 246, 249–51, 254–5, 258n
Macintyre, Stuart 6, 249, 250, 257
Macphee, Ian 252
Macquarie University 235, 236, 242n
Malaysia 233
management, *see* corporate management
market failure 13–14, 18, 112
  see also economic externalities in education
market liberalism (neo–liberalism) 7, 38, 71, 77–81, 81–2, 83–5, 98n, 101, 102–13, 114–15, 118n, 121, 122–8, 140–1, 147, 152, 247, 248
market–state dualism 111–13, 114
marketisation 82, 86–7, 91–2, 98, 106, 107–9, 110, 112–13, 115, 151
markets and marketisation in education xiv, 1–3, 122–8, 140, 144, 147, 150–1, 151, 156–7, 158–9, 167–9, 173, 199–202, 210, 224–41
  in schooling 50, 125–8, 159, 166, 208
  in higher education 126–8, 158, 160–2, 166, 224–31
  see also vocational education and training, training reform
Marshall, Alfred 37
Martin report 11–13, 27, 35–6
Marx, Karl xiv, 5, 71, 118n
mass media 116, 119–21, 129–30, 133, 153, 163, 166, 249, 250, 258
Mayer report 175–6
McCallum, David 39
McKinnon, Ken 67
Menzies, Robert 41, 50
methodological individualism, *see* individualism
micro–economic reform, *see* economic policies
migrants and migrant education, *see* immigration
Mill, John Stuart 15, 104
Ministerial Council on Education, Employment and Training (MOVEET) 165
ministerial control 90, 163–6
modernisation 7, 13, 18–20, 25, 32, 52, 69, 81, 83, 99n, 152, 157, 160, 172–3, 174, 176, 200, 202, 203
Monash University 233, 235
monetarism 74, 75, 78, 101, 144
monoculturalism, *see* multiculturalism
Morgan, Hugh 79, 132

multiculturalism 3–4, 129, 243, 246, 250, 252–8
Murdoch University 234
Murray report 27
Mushkin, Selma 149–50

National Board of Employment, Education and Training (NBEET) 164
National Framework for the Recognition of Training (NFROT) 237
national reconciliation 243, 246, 247, 252–4, 256
native title 3, 243, 247, 252–3, 256
neoclassical economics, *see* economics
neo-liberalism, *see* market liberalism
New Right 44, 71, 72, 75, 76, 78–81, 81–3, 85, 87–8, 92–3, 95–6, 98–99n, 103, 114–17, 172–3, 197, 201, 241n
  in Australia 79, 82, 98–99n, 152
  in education 119–45
  and nationalism 117
New South Wales (NSW) 23–4, 130, 200, 242n, 250
New Zealand 82, 99n, 234
non–government schooling, *see* private schooling
Notre Dame Australia 232
NSW Teachers' Federation 47, 139

one hundred flowers 58
open learning (technologically–based delivery of education at a distance) 18, 74, 189, 235, 250
Organisation for Economic Cooperation and Development (OECD), and OECD region 11, 12, 26, 35, 42, 47, 49, 69, 73, 81–5, 86–7, 92, 93, 100, 132, 143, 149–52, 154–7, 158, 160, 162, 166, 174, 178, 180–1, 182, 186, 195–6, 203, 211, 229
output definition and measurement *see* production function in education

parents and parenting in education 58, 125, 126, 129, 132, 139, 141–2, 144–145n, 183, 184, 200–1, 238–40, 241
Pareto and Paretian welfare 87, 195
Parish, Ross 128, 207–9, 216
Participation and Equity program (PEP) 180, 183–4
participation, enrolments and retention in education 4, 20–3, 32, 46, 123, 134, 147, 151, 155, 190–4, 197, 198–9, 248
  levels of educability 39–40, 44, 186